The Gnostic Papers

'The Undiscovered Mystery of Christ'

by

John V. Panella

P.O. Box 754
Huntsville, AR. 72740
WWW.OZARKMT.COM

For permission, or serialization, condensation, adaptions, or for our catalog of other publications, write to: Ozark Mountain Publishing, Inc., P.O. Box 754, Huntsville, AR 72740, Attn: Permissions Department.

Library of Congress Cataloging-in-Publication Data
Panella, John V., 1959 -

"The Gnostic Papers" by John V. Panella
A gnostic examination and explanation of the Bible and the teachings of Jesus.
   1. Religion   2. Gnosticism   3. Jesus' teachings   4. Bible
   5. Metaphysics   6. Spirituality
   I. Panella, John V., 1959 -   II. Title

Library of Congress Catalog Card Number: 2001-135280
ISBN: 1-886940-81-9

Cover Design: Jeff Ward
Book Set in: Abadi, Arial, Times New Roman, EngrvrsOldEng
Book Design: Nancy Garrison
Published By

P.O. Box 754
Huntsville, AR 72740

P.O. Box 754
Huntsville, AR 72740
WWW.OZARKMT.COM
Printed in the United States of America

TABLE OF CONTENTS

Introduction

Mystery One 1
Mystery Two 51
Mystery Three 89
Mystery Four 132
Mystery Five 171
Mystery Six 255
Mystery Seven 314

Author 359

INTRODUCTION

The Gnostic Papers are a unique blend of the metaphysical and paranormal as they combine with ancient manuscripts like the Sumerian Cuneiform tablets, Dead Sea Scrolls, Nag Hammadi Library and of course, the Christian Bible. For 2000 years mankind has been led into error by self-seeking individuals who desired glory and honor for personal aspirations and not the enlightenment of their fellow man. Changes were made in portions of what is now called the Bible, a book of many books, that literally dismantled entire segments of thought. Hundreds of years after Jesus walked this Earth the message he was trying to teach mankind was changed into a religion that taught of a vengeful God. Jesus the man was then placed on a pedestal and made to appear before mankind as some special deity directly impregnated into a woman named Mary from a Supreme Being.

What the Gnostic Papers will attempt to do is delve deeply within you and bring out unknown truths that have lain dormant for ages. YES, deeply within each of you there resides the truth of the Father, the Great I AM in the proverbial heavens. The Gnosis of your personal enlightenment will open your eyes to hidden wisdom and secrets that have been sealed away from before the foundations of this world. What you are about to read has been mystically formatted to bring this truth from within. The words you see will mean nothing, but the pattern interwoven within the words will begin to spark a vision, and a light will begin to shine, yet you will feel as though you always knew this to be true.

The Gnostic Papers was not written to become a religious decree that one must follow. It was placed together to open up an avenue that you may have never realized existed. This book was not designed to destroy the Bible or its perceived teachings. NO, to the contrary; it was designed to reveal the true meaning within mystery by using what was deceptively placed into the scriptures, and then reorient the individual's perspective to reveal the divine mystery within the Bible. Many are quite offended when they hear that their Bible may not be what they have always believed it to be. But let the truth be known this day, The Father's WORD is spirit; and truth will prevail always!

MYSTERY ONE
𝔗𝔥𝔢 𝔐𝔶𝔰𝔱𝔢𝔯𝔶 𝔬𝔣 𝔱𝔥𝔢 ℭ𝔶𝔠𝔩𝔢𝔰

Many years ago I was approached with the question, "Do you believe in reincarnation?" At the time I gave an unintelligent reply stating, "Don't be ridiculous, who in their right mind would think they're coming back as a tree?" It did not dawn on me at the time that no one had asked me if I thought we were to come back as trees. I automatically assumed based upon my prior education in this matter, that reincarnation meant to come back as some object other than human. This is a classic example of how often we can give ignorant responses on subjects that we clearly know nothing about, but think we do.

As I look back now I have the stunning revelation of how we as human beings react to certain concepts. It unveils our true lack of inner knowledge, when we often end up repeating ideas that we hear, and not what we have diligently checked out. We tend to think only in terms of preprogrammed information, which was placed on our mental computer disk. We respond more out of a subroutine of preprogrammed information than as free-willed individual thinkers. We would sometimes like to believe our views are original, yet the sad fact remains that most of us will only repeat what we have heard, based on no more than incongruent information and hearsay with entirely no research of our own.

The truth really is, when people start thinking outside the norm of accepted thought consciousness, then they are branded a heretic or a nutcase! Personages like Galileo, Da Vinci, Edison, Einstein and Tesla, were individuals who stepped beyond the boundaries of known science. They had the audacity to question the accepted beliefs and introduce their own. People like this usually lived their lives as outcasts within their generation. People were angered and embittered when these high-minded philosophers introduced a new scientific concept within the realm of consciousness of their individual time-periods.

As these individuals questioned the accepted views of science, many have also questioned the accepted views of religion. Throughout the ages many live their entire lives believing a religious ideology that was handed down through their family generation lines. It is nearly impossible to break away from theories that are welded within our minds from birth. It is unthinkable, as a child growing up, to ever question the veracity of our ancestor's beliefs. Let's be honest, these are the people who raised us, and trained us from children onward. How could they have ever been misinformed? Obviously not everyone is raised within a nice neat structured household with two-parent families. However, most people in general, are taught and trained by someone and that is how they develop their ideologies, whether on the streets, or in foster homes, etc. Everyone gains their initial ideas from someone else until they are mature enough to begin to use their own minds. Usually though, after a lengthy indoctrination on one idea or the other, it becomes difficult to change these views.

The majority of our convictions stem from others' belief systems, which we have become associated with throughout our lifetime. It is frightening that most people will live their entire lives without ever conceiving an original thought!

Many in the Christian world are certain their beliefs stem from a book called the Bible. Nevertheless, when you begin to reason with these people, you find they really have very little comprehension of the history of this interesting book. They have been taught to accept this book as a fundamental decree set down by the great God himself. And then when you examine this more closely it becomes apparent that understanding is lacking. Again, many have only responded according to another's ideas. It may be a peer, a Priest, a parent, whoever? But somewhere down the line they processed information that was given them by someone they respected. It never occurred to the recipient that they might have received faulty information from someone whom also had inaccurate beliefs. Throughout this whole process of this thing called life many will continue to believe that their ideas are inceptive, when in fact they are only processing information that they received from others, through their mental computer disk, the human brain!

A good example of this is try to entice someone to read and study information that expounds on ideas that are contrary to the belief of the one in question. In most cases they will refuse to read such material, believing it would corrupt their thinking. They usually use arguments such as, "I already know what that subject deals with and I am not interested." Or they are less subtle and state emphatically, "I don't agree with that particular subject. Leave me alone and don't bother me!" They actually have come to believe that to examine others' views would be wasting their time. One of the greatest flaws in human character is what I call the human gullible capacity. The individual who hasn't even studied a particular area but somehow think they know it all. If the truth were known, rejection of knowledge which leads to enlightenment that doesn't set well with previous mind-sets, is usually directly related to that infamous word called FEAR!

It is those that are fearful that tend to argue, and maliciously discredit by several means; such as gossip, ridicule, and all out attack. They believe that this engagement strengthens one's stance against defective material. To humiliate others before the views can be heard from another's perception. Fear that produces this type of attack against others is the plight that rules when one is not so confident in their beliefs as they had hoped. This is created because their information wasn't their own. It was introduced from someone else. So they have no real internal foundation on which to base their beliefs. They end up having to rely on castigation through their fear to protect them from being recognized as a fraud, and not one who is enlightened. One of the dynamic reasons people will not take heed of possible change is because their foundation will be revealed as faulty if they accept another's view. They believe others would think they are inept for not really understanding their own tradition.

All throughout the existence of the human race, most have been inundated with fear of the unknown. We are fleshly creatures of comfort. If something is brought to our attention that begins to take away from our beliefs, nervousness sets in. This should not be the case; we should become excited to learn new concepts so that we can grow within knowledge, no matter where it might come from. But if people keep allowing others to decipher everything for them, then gnosis is never internally gained. And this, my friends, is the problem, and it is also the first secret. If one continues to allow everyone else to decode key elements for them they will become nothing more than dust blowing in the wind. And many will just perish without ever gaining personal insight.

It is my goal to bring an awareness that lives within everyone, *the true gnosis of reality*, while at the same time blowing the lid off previous beliefs that were passed down from one generation to the next. I will attempt to use the Christian Bible to unveil mysteries that have existed before the world was in existence. But to do this I need to parallel this information with concepts known as the paranormal and metaphysical. For without these two balances no one can ever see the truth from within. They will always access it from without. My desire is to bring a new revelation to Christians as well as anyone who is seeking deeper gnosis. For within oneself lay the keys to all known knowledge. If I can show you how to penetrate an area of your mind that has not been functioning properly, then I have achieved my goal. I will attempt to use the Bible to stage this analysis. To teach that mysteries were embedded within the scriptures to unveil secrets to those that are becoming internally aware, thereby decreeing GNOSTIC! For the Bible truly is laced with mystery. It wasn't because someone figured out how to encode this into the Bible, no not at all. It happened purely by divine law. The Bible in its present form is a complicated, confused thesis brought about by humans who decided on their own how to splice a myriad of earlier works together in their incomplete format. If you were to take the Bible and read it as a classroom schoolbook you would become absolutely mystified trying to ascertain its true meaning. That is why it is easy to take someone else's word for the content of this auspicious book. Based primarily on the fact that it is too complicated to be thoroughly understood by the novice. For the true meaning of this book will never be identified if you read it as it stands, in the letter, or written form. You must be able to decode its information through an internal awareness that exists within you. Again, I repeat, EXISTS WITHIN YOU! For the true definition of gnosis is internal awareness!

LAYING THE FOUNDATION

To begin let us start with the Biblical verse, I Corinthians 15:22 "As in Adam 'ALL' die, even so in Christ 'ALL' shall be made alive." We can begin this research by first ascertaining that the word ALL is used in relation to both concepts. ALL shall die; ALL shall be made alive. We can all relate to this first aspect because truly all die, don't they? But what about the second part, how many have understood that this verse says, "ALL shall be made alive?" How many have inadvertently been guilty of teaching and believing that ALL are not going to be made alive. In fact, many believe within their religious circles that only a certain type of person will be given life. But how many times have we been guilty of accepting a specific dogma that teaches something contrary to what you just read. Why would a God supposedly sacrifice his only Son, under the auspices that this is the greatest love to offer, but then, Lo and behold, we find that many will not be saved? What purpose would any of this serve? Did God send his Son to sacrifice his life for the world, or didn't he? Does God plan to save everyone, or doesn't he? Who is this God who would give his only Son as a sacrifice for the world, when in reality most who believe in this concept don't believe everyone will be saved? And finally if God is an all-powerful, omnipotent Creator, then doesn't he have a better

5

strategy than just saving a few? Furthermore, wouldn't you have a better strategy?

Based on this alone, if this scenario were true then God had obviously designed a potential for everyone to succeed. If not, then our awesome limitless God has flaws, for we can't place our human frailties upon the Creator of the universe to try to understand his inadequacies. Either this being is all that we claim he is, or he is something less than one would hope for. I for one certainly wouldn't want to place my trust in a being that can't even save his own creation from total disaster.

Why are the world's religious communities the first to declare this being in terms of a Judge and avenger, who waits patiently to take his wrath out upon an unknowing world? Are we talking about the same God? Is the God that wants to save the world, by giving his only SON the same God who wants to avenge, judge and punish? I think it is high time to recognize who Jesus the Christ is and what he did 2000 years ago!

INTRODUCTION OF THE FATHER

Nearly two-milleniums ago a man appeared on the world scene who claimed that he was sent to reveal the Father. The mission of this unique individual has fallen upon deaf ears. For as the years have passed most have forgotten Jesus' mission, and have centered primarily upon Jesus himself. For it never dawned upon the masses of humanity that Jesus wanted to bring new information that had never been given to the human race. Part of that information was introducing the Great Spirit known as the Father. Jesus attempted to bring "KNOWLEDGE" that would enlighten truth seekers on their quest for the Holy Grail. But to do this he had to open the doors to bring about a reality that had up until that time not been realized. That reality was "A God existed that the human race was never aware of, at least consciously!"

Now lets take a couple of steps backward. How could the great Father not be recognized? How could this Great God not have been known? We have an entire Old Testament that brings to light a God who declared that there was none like him. And he was to be worshiped before all other Gods. Now we are learning that Jesus was attempting to identify another God, named the Father, which was never known. He was the Great Unknown Spirit. So as I set up this entire scenario I think it prudent that we begin by first identifying the man Jesus, and what his mission really was. And that the Father certainly did not give his only Son so that only a few would be saved. Truthfully in reality, the Father of spirits sent his Only Begotten Son, the Logos, the Word, the Christ so that all who entered into darkness would be awakened to enter into the light, and return to their heritage. What I am about to reveal is a gnosis of personal awareness that will begin to identify a subject that has been terribly misunderstood.

We must begin by addressing the problem that all human beings are in the same family. Whether race, creed, color, it matters not. We are all family and must begin to act as such. Entertaining this knowledge alone will not quell the divisions, but it is certainly a starting point. We need to look deep within our own hearts and ask the all-persuasive question, "Why were we born?" Are we just here to live out our feeble days and then perish? Were we placed on this planet for a purpose? If we are the creation of a God then are new souls being created every time a mother gives birth to a child? If this is the case then why does God allow newborn souls to enter such a sick and dying world, especially in famine-controlled areas? When little babies are raised in darkness how can God ever expect them to understand quality and peace from righteousness, when they have never understood the relation with such examples? The more children are brought up in despair and darkness the more impossible it will become for them to see the light. It will become a land of confusion, a literal Mad Max world... For if mankind is raised with no guidelines, no instruction booklet then how will they ever come to understand a better reality? If we were mere biological entities, mortals of flesh and blood, then why would God keep allowing us to continue to breed more darkness when there is no true opportunity to ever see

7

the light? In effect it would be adding to human's damnation and not their salvation!

What if we really are not mere mortals born of flesh and blood unto biological entities? What if our flesh and blood bodies are just vessels housing something within? What if this entity that is inside has been around for a very long time? What if new beings are not being created every time a mother gives birth, but in reality are just bearing garments for souls to inhabit? What if there were already a set number of entities, soul-spirits that have been in existence since before the creation of this earth? Could it be that soul-spirits that have been here for a long, long time are just occupying vessels to take some sort of training from another awareness? Could we actually be in a type of school to learn lessons from mistakes that were made from previous dimensions? What is the possibility that we are all born spirit children of the Great Spirit presence known as the Father? What if all of us are actually divine beings from the great beyond?

This brings me back to the question of reincarnation! If this theory above is true, then God really is our literal Father, not just some circumspect idea created by religious icons hoping for some aggrandizement by their unknowing followers. Then would a Father ever destroy his children because they failed a test or two? Wouldn't it be more likely that a Father would do everything in his power to help, instruct, and lead for the nourishment of his offspring? Whether one believes in a God or not, let us consider this in principle only. Wouldn't a loving parent who had all power within their capacity, of both heaven and earth, one who is limited by absolutely nothing, do everything in their power to help their children triumph? Remember that we are not talking about a flawed humanity trying or attempting to help one another. We are talking about a God who is omnipotent, omnipresent and omniscient. Could this creator not find a way to do whatever it takes to enlighten their child unto mastery?

Or is it that we want to continue to view this from animalistic terms, "Well, I gave the bum my best, and he just didn't get it, let him burn!" Who really is the great God that religions will fight and die for? What does he truly expect from us? As King David wondered, "What is man that God would be concerned with him?"

RECONSTRUCTING A NEW PARADIGM

This entire thesis that I am bringing forward may sound very absurd and idiotic to a Bible thumping Christian. But if one begins to look within his or her heart, it begins to make total sense. It is only strange to those that have been preprogrammed to believe in a God which is spiteful and vengeful. However, if I am ever able to penetrate this wall that has been built up for many centuries I must approach this subject within the same framework as those that claim they already understand. I must use some of the same rhetoric and theology to enable a gnosis to shine forth from within a previous accepted guideline. For true mysteries are revealed when one is able to relate to them personally. It is an internal awareness, something you will hear me use over again though out this entire book. So in understanding this, it becomes prudent and wise that I use the Bible along with other works to show the parallels that surface within the gnosis of mystery.

Using the topic of reincarnation I must lay the foundation that will bring to light old thought paradigms reconstructed to build a new bridge. Such as, let us suppose that we truly are spiritual beings that were encased within the matter, biological bodies. Would it not then be possible for spirit entities to access many bodies at different times? And if this was possible then could not one conclude that these bodies are actually garments especially chosen for each student in the classroom of life? Thereby decreeing avenues of training or schooling for the spirit notables to literally pursue their degree in the lower matter world called life?

If we begin to compare this idea with a pattern that we see in our lower forms then it is possible to understand that there are

9

those that have advantages over others. Just as in life we see some children born and raised in good homes, and their parents have money. The children of these families view life in an entirely different way than children who are not so fortunate. For we all realize that those who are born in comfort have advantages over those that are raised in tyranny.

As the parallels come to light we can then understand that children are all different based possibly on their environmental setting. Some come from broken homes. Some have ill health, whereas others are strong, healthy and vibrant.

Why is there so much inequality in life? Why is one person born blind and another has 20/20 vision? Why is one crippled and another an athlete? Where is the fairness? Why do some slide through life with ease, yet others wish they had never been born? Why do some live in the ghettos and others on Wall Street?

First let us view this scenario another way, one that is more accepted within the Christian realm. We are only creatures of the flesh, biological entities that have no background other than the birth from our biological parents. Our entire existence began with our earthly birth. We learned that there were two people that God created from the dust of the earth. He named them Adam and Eve. These two earthly people committed a sin by eating of a tree in the Garden that they were not allowed to. So God decided he needed to find a way to save these poor souls and all the children that would ever be born from them. We learned that God existed alone, yet in strange dichotomy, had a Son. He decided to send this Son to earth to allow this new creation that had sinned, and continued to do so, kill his own Son as a type of sacrifice.

So the Son came to this earth and died in a cruel way to take away the penalty of the sin, which had already been committed. But there remained a problem. After the Son died, the world changed not. Everyone still lives like they had prior to this event. Humanity continues to break laws and inequality still exists within the class warfare of mankind.

We are being told that religion is our safety valve, and all we have to do is speak the name of this Son and like magic the sins will be blotted out and we'll be saved. Yet again it is apparent, nothing has changed, just an idea on how to cope with life changed. But it did not bring internal awareness to change mankind. It only gave a pass key to those that think God loves them greater than one who doesn't know to speak the name of this Son. In reality, it only created another class warfare! It did not bring an end to the confusion of inequality. It only created more confusion. As humans we are living in an inconsistent world trying to cope with issues that frankly no one has a clue how to solve. Our lives are predetermined by environmental settings that no one had a choice in. Our status in life is based primarily from those environmental factors that groom each individual accordingly. Our thoughts and attitudes are subjected to those philosophies that were handed down to us from others that were prepared in their environmental setting. Our entire identity is created from a billion or more unseen elements that prance their way into our lives from a myriad of directions making us feel hopeless to ever change our circumstances. And then to top it all off, we are being told that this God who wanted to save us by sacrificing his own Son is about to judge the whole world based upon principles that are obscure at best. And this strong arm of the law is about to take his eternal vengeance out upon a creature that doesn't even understand what they are doing here in the first place. My God, what sort of Father are we evaluating here?

JACOB AND ESAU

When I began my research into the mysteries and gnosis of eternal life I ran across some scriptures that protruded out like a sore thumb. One in particular was the verse that discussed the birth of Jacob and Esau. The Bible elaborated the fact that God, *prior* to these two sons being born actually made a decision about their character. God supposedly said he hated Esau but loved Jacob. Over the years it never really made sense how God would or even could make a decision about

11

someone prior to his or her birth. I had always accepted the Apostle Paul's explanation of this when he stated, God would have mercy upon that which he decides to have mercy upon. Paul asked the question if there was unrighteousness with God for making this decision. I never understood the answer Paul gave, primarily because I never understood the question. Years went by before I began to question whether God, just because he is God, has the right to judge an individual prior to their birth. And furthermore, as Paul reiterated, righteousness cannot be the claim in this picture, if God pronounced someone guilty by fiat. It would make God no better than the flawed creatures he rules. And to make a decision based on no more than a heavenly whim, without any evidence to the contrary would make God sound devious, not righteous.

The very word righteousness comes from the root word "to do right." If Jacob or Esau had yet to be born before this decision was handed out from on high then whose righteousness are we dealing with here? Righteousness is an act, it is not a right. Would God decide to hate one and love another based only on the righteousness of his own being without any regard to the individual he rules? This is not righteousness; this is dictatorship. I am not refuting that the Bible teaches this, I am revealing that the true Father would never declare this.

But was this taught in the Bible and if so why? Why would God ever make a decision so humanly flawed? Remember earlier that I stated that Jesus came to reveal the Father as well as reveal mercy and love. The God of the Old Testament did teach these elements. You are going to learn within the first mystery that there are parallels of the spirit realm within the matter realm. These parallels teach two different discourses to human beings. One is the law that pertains only to the flesh; gods who dwell within the shadow lands administer this law. Simply put, matter is the shadow of spirit. These beings, which I will discuss in more detail later, are not the Father. They are the rulers of the lower matter world. I will prove this as I go forward.

You will begin to envision that matter is like a carbon copy of the spirit except it is not reality; it is only an illusion. But the laws that pertain to matter have to be equivalent to the beings that are subjugated by that law. Laws pertaining to matter have no power over the spirit. Matter in a sense is imprisoned within the walls of law, but spirit can go beyond those walls. It takes spiritual law to deal with spiritual beings. When God stated that he hated Esau but loved Jacob, this is a replica of something much greater. The Father does not hate anyone, for he is love. Love is his energy that creates worlds. However those who rule from the shadow lands approach things on more of a human viewpoint because their laws only pertain to biological entities. What was being implied here was that Jacob and Esau earned their lot in life from previous lifetimes! For the gods (ELOHIM) declared that Jacob was righteous and Esau was not by virtue of their past lives.

Doesn't it make more sense that a ruling that came down from on high was based on our acts of righteousness or our acts of wickedness, not because a God decided to make this decision based on a heavenly whim? This in itself may never convince the opponent of reincarnation, but it plainly shows that something else needs to be understood, and this conclusion at present is as good as any other. However we will begin to see that this truly is the only conclusion.

"My people are destroyed for a lack of knowledge (gnosis)," declares Hosea the prophet. "Where there is no vision thy people perish," cries Solomon.

PERSONAL AWARENESS

As we continue this gnosis we realize that all truth will indeed come from within you. No one need teach you, the church, or a minister or Priest, not even your family. For true gnosis comes from within the recipient.   All shadow forms, including matter and all replica of the spirit are an exterior, including shadow knowledge. But all gnosis is interior through the spirit. I will illuminate how I became aware within myself of these mysteries.   And everyone can do the same!

13

I began asking questions years ago concerning my own family. I have three sisters and although we differed in age, I could never understand why we were so different in personality. This should have been enough to bring our awareness to the forefront. We had a different range of habits and ideas. As I examined my family I wondered why we were all so different yet the same individuals raised us. I took into account the age differences and circumstances that may have changed over the years that might have had some bearing in this. I have also contemplated our environmental settings and weighed them in concerning this topic. Yet when it was all said and done it never answered my questions. I also realized there were families that had many children, but from birth each child was different, and had unique personalities.

Now I know there are those that believe God gives these unique characteristics to us at birth, but this is absurd. God doesn't make one person smart and the other dumb. He doesn't make one pretty and the other ugly. He doesn't make one a virtuoso and the other an illiterate. Again these are concepts brought down by unenlightened people that do not want to see how each of our own responsibility is required. The talents that we have we produced in past lifetimes. God doesn't sit up in the heavens randomly handing out talents to some and weaknesses to others. And just because one may appear illiterate or stupid in one life doesn't mean they have no talent, or are really stupid. They are just not accessing that trait in that particular lifetime. This occurs when individuals are to learn another facet in their training as well as dealing with karmic accountability. People who think God dishes out our talents believe that the Father is playing a game of chess and we are all just pieces on the playing board.

In looking deeper into my family, I realized that our learning ability even differed. Whereas coming by information was easy to some, others had to work very hard to attain the same knowledge level. I became very curious about this. My father was a very brilliant man but he worked very hard to attain his knowledge. It did not come natural to him. Whereas myself, I seem to gain things much easier but I didn't have the drive he had to access it. Then came the hidden fears, those unexplained fears that beset us all our life and we have no idea where they came from. Psychologists try to reason around this by looking for some secret hidden event that happened when we were children. But most of this is poppycock. Some people have extraordinary fear of heights. Others have fear of water. Some have fear of flying. These are real fears that each of us has to contend with. Nevertheless if nothing happened in one's life to bring about these fears, where do they come from?

Ever since I was a little boy I would sometimes doze off and at the split second I was nearing the sleep state I envisioned myself in a head-on car accident. I see the cars in my mind and they always appear to be old models, but I have never been in a head-on car accident in this life. Yet I am frightened to death to drive with others. This has always been the case. What creates these fears? Where do these visions come from? There are people that have serious problems in their life even to the point of wanting to erase their entire identity. They cannot cope with reality as it has been given them. So they reason that others may have harmed them, and that is why they're so messed up. When one begins to understand the mysteries they realize that most of our problems do not begin in this life. They are a continuation from past life experiences. Some of the problems that people have shared with so-called head shrinks, which they believe have occurred in their life, seem to take the individual back when they were a child. However it's very possible that the true source of the problem was prior to this life. But until you comprehend the mystery of rebirth your mind cannot allow you to see into that realm of a past life. So it takes you back to a child, or as far as it is able to backtrack. And then the individual picks up clues of things that happened to them but they end up placing it on the wrong time frame and the wrong people. Families have literally been destroyed by this conclusion. Sometimes adults become convinced that when they were little children their parent may have molested them thereby bringing these problems forward. The individual may

15

indeed have been molested, however the lifetime this occurred most likely was different, especially if one doesn't recall this event until after someone brings it to their attention.

Another question I had to deal with personally is attitudes! Some people have short fuses and literally blow up at the sound of a whistle. Some are calm and can take abuse for years without ever retaliating. Others are easily swayed into believing anything, while still others cannot be convinced even if the answer is staring them in the face. I always admired my dad and tried to become like him in many areas. No matter how hard I tried, I still never really thought like him. I understood how he thought, and he understood how I thought, but we did not think alike. At times my parents wanted me to become what they believed was right, but I seemed to want to do what I felt internally was right. Where did this strange and unique separation come from? My parents raised me, they taught me, they provided for me. Why didn't I see things as they saw them? It should have been easy enough to follow in their footsteps at nearly every crossing. It became quite apparent that we are all unique by virtue of something that predates this matter life.

We are all personages of the past from the great beyond. We have lived here before! During 30 years of Christianity I would have never dared to think like this, but after years of research and personal experiences, it became obvious that we are not one-timers on this planet called earth. Some have been here many times, others, not so many. I was determined to find the truth about this, NO more spiritual truth handouts. I needed to know the truth personally once and for all.

Many years ago something happened that I have never forgotten. It really scared me. I met a girl and from the beginning it was as if we had known each other forever. The sensation frightened me to the point that I could not be myself around her. One time she told me that I knew her inner secrets, and I never understood what she meant. The experience was too much to handle and I did not see her for many years. When

I met her again as soon as I looked into her eyes I felt a powerful sensation, which words alone cannot express. It came over me that I was married to her, that she was my wife. But how could this be? I was so frightened that I could not even speak to her. I walked away shaking the whole time. I didn't know what reincarnation was, and certainly did not comprehend past lives. I just thought I was losing my mind. I tried to tell my friends of the experience, but I had no words to convey its inner meaning, because I had not yet understood this reality. I just knew that the experience I shared with this girl was beyond this world, but I didn't understand how. My mind was flooded that day with an awareness given to me by a higher spiritual divine power. I was truly overwhelmed beyond anything I could ever have thought of before.

Another experience occurred when I was with a friend in a casino in Atlantic City. While my friend was at the cash register I was standing in front of a unique nickel slot machine. I remembered playing this machine before; in fact it was always my favorite. I was about to call my friend over to explain to him how I used to play this slot machine, until I read the small engraved plaque below. It stated that this machine was an antique last used in 1936. My heart began to race. I said, "*This is impossible.*" I played this machine. I loved this machine. How could this particular machine have only existed before I was born and not in use anymore? I left the casino that day and spent the next three months going through my mind with a fine toothed-comb. I couldn't recall ever playing this machine in this life, but I know as sure as I know anything, I played this machine before. As I began to meditate on the circumstances I actually began to see flashbacks in my mind of being with a few buddies. We were all wearing white Navy uniforms. My goal was to empty the machine out so the nickels would no longer show within the open window in front. I never could do that though. But I remember that I loved playing it. When I played it, where I played it, I may never know? But I know I played this machine before, but never in this life.

These strange occurrences began to verify very slowly to me that we exist beyond the perimeters of the life we are born into. I even recall when I was a little boy sitting upon my swing set, staring at the stars. I used to say to myself, "John, you were here before, and you lived on this planet at another time period." You must understand this was a very strange thought process going on in the head of a boy that was being raised in a strict Christian environment.

The entire concept of past lives penetrated my mind with force. No longer could I perceive that which was taught to me by religion or science. I realized my beliefs had a crack in them. It was then that I came to fully realize that when the Bible speaks of mysteries it very well means what it says.

REINCARNATION A MASTERPIECE IN DESIGN

Reincarnation is not some fanatical view by the Hindu culture and beliefs, but actually a masterpiece in design by the Gods of the shadow lands. It is not the Father that gives us reincarnation. It is the Gods of the matter world who are lords of the lower dimension. But it is the Father's hope that we can finally break away from the clutches of rebirth to return to our original home. So in a sense the Father is using reincarnation as our training while under the rule of the shadow lords.

It is my belief that reincarnation falls under the heading of mystery. And it is one of the many mysteries that have been sealed away from the human race. Jesus introduced the concept of reincarnation through many mystical references. However if you were not prepared or ready to advance to the level of learned student or disciple then you would not be able to receive this inwardly. Mysteries are only given to those that are ready, not to the novice. Jesus hinted at rebirth when he spoke of placing new wine in old bottles.

Mark 2:22 "And no man puts new wine into old bottles: else the new wine would burst the bottles, and the wine is spilled, and

18

the bottles will be marred: but new wine must be put into new bottles."

When you comprehend what is being stated here you then realize this is a gnosis of mystery being brought forth by Jesus. The bottles represent our flesh and blood bodies. The wine represents the spirit of each of our souls. When an old body has perished then the wine must evacuate and enter another dimension. The new wine that is an evacuated soul-projected spirit will need to enter a new bottle upon return. For no longer will the old bottle be sufficient for the new wine. What we are addressing here is the knowledge of putting on new garments when one returns through the cycles of rebirth. Notice another verse enlightening this information.

Mark 2:21 "No man also sews a piece of new cloth on an old garment: else the piece that filled it up takes away from the old, and the tear is made worse."

When you begin to understand using the mystical terminology, then one begins to comprehend the mystery of the cycles. Whereas above we can see that an old garment is your worn out body that expired, what good would it do to enter back into that body? It would just fall apart again, this time faster. When the gnosis of the cycles has begun to enter your concepts you will then realize the true teaching of GRACE. For Moses brought from the shadow lords the law, but Christ brought, from the Father, Grace and Truth. John 1:17

IT IS GIVEN UNTO MAN ONCE TO DIE

As this gnosis becomes more fathomable it becomes necessary that I use some of the verses the doubters will use to refute this understanding. The Bible quotes, "And as it is appointed unto man once to die, but after this the judgment." Hebrews 9:27. Many have used this verse to try to dismantle the hidden mystery of reincarnation. To comprehend the meaning of this verse and others like it we must reevaluate the scriptures and reset the pieces of the puzzle into the order that they belong. We can no longer allow those of the past to try to reconstruct doctrine based on their own deceptive imagination.

19

Once we begin to unravel the mystery then all of these things will come to light as never before.

The Bible is a book that expresses ideas in multiple forms such as: metaphors, analogies and types. It uses symbols initiated by the instructor that have been carefully orchestrated to fit like a glove. Yet one will not be able to decipher this information if they are trying to extract the truth through the written letter. The information must be decoded. In a sense it is like Nostradamus, who because of the persecution of the church decided to encrypt future prophecies through a varied use of languages and metaphors. Much of the Bible is written like this also, except its usage is not as vague. But the mystery is implanted within the written word for the initiate to comprehend. If you are not at that point of evolved growth you will only access its written meaning. So when you see a verse that expounds on a topic like this one, such as: it is appointed unto man once to die and then the judgment. You will then accept its written form and you will use the ideology that man can only live and die one time in the flesh.

Living many lifetimes teach people inner realities about his or her self. They help acquaint mankind to their origin by reconstructing activities in the flesh that will help harmonize the spirits to their true pattern. If you are wealthy and you despise the poor, then you will gain personal awareness by returning and experiencing that which you did not comprehend. For self-awareness is truly the only way to divine expansive character. Without personal awareness you just become a leaf blowing in the wind without prior identity. If you judge what you do not understand then your judgment becomes incoherent. As stated in Matthew 7:5 "Cast the beam out of your own eye so that you will see clearly how to help your brother." Judging only brings a revolving door through the cycles back to the initiator. Judgment cannot be applied unto another. It can only facilitate its true activity through the personal awareness of the individual. If you judge, you will be judged! This is an axiomatic law of the entire universe. Judgment must begin with you the individual. You must gain personal awareness so that you can comprehend its true meaning. If you judge yourself then you cannot be judged. For all judgment belongs to you. You initiate the act so it will come back to you. It cannot affect others. If you become internally aware then you have completed your design, for total awareness reacts only to the one who has gained sufficient understanding to change the creation that was initiated through and by you. The Father does not bring judgment upon his children. For the scriptures taught that the Father judges no one, all judgment was given over to the Son. When you ask who is the Son you may respond, "I AM the Son." We are the children of the Father. The only way for one to comprehend their internal awareness is to grow and learn from activities that instruct us personally. If you have been poor then you can comprehend how to be rich without judgment. But if you have not experienced being poor, then being rich is only half of the awareness necessary to comprehend your entire self.

REAPING WHAT YOU SOW

Ancient Israel was instructed by the Lords of the shadow lands. The physical law that only pertained to the flesh, such as: an eye for an eye, and being stoned without mercy before two or three witnesses. They never comprehended the true meaning behind this decree. As long as they were blinded and kept in prison through the laws of the flesh they could not conceive of this law in its true form. They took it upon themselves to cast judgment upon one another to adhere to this law in its written form. There was a divine instruction that created this shadow law. But until the Messiah would enter on the world scene Israel was imprisoned in their own logic based upon the decisions the shadow lords had given them.

For this law was the shadow of the Law that Jesus taught, which was "reaping what you sow." The divine law that was to be given to the spirit children of God was to instruct that each individual will by law reap whatever it is they personally sow. For the law was set in motion to bring in return all contravention of spiritual & physical law back to the initiator. Ancient Israel was not able to comprehend this mystery, so

21

they were acting out in the flesh what the true design meant in the spirit.

Life is not a complexity of coincidence; wherever it falls, that is where it lands. Life is a designed systemization of events detailing extreme congruency that is perfectly coordinated for everyone's works whether righteous or evil, past or present. The position that each of us were born into was unequivocally created for each of our personal private reckoning. You are not stationed in life one way or the other because you are better than someone else or worse than someone else. Each individual was placed in their distinct class by virtue of the law that ordains all will reap what they sow. Life is to be schooling for each person's training for divine expansive growth.

So this now brings me full circle to answer the question why it is that man was only given once to die if there are multiple lives. If multiple incarnations exist for everyone then what could the Bible mean when it states that it is given unto man once to die and then the judgment?

Your understanding of any verse is predicated upon the ability to ascertain the hidden source behind the written letter. The clues are many when one begins to access the keys to unlock the codes. I cannot reveal all the mysteries; I have only learned a few at present. But through what I have been able to ascertain through life's experiences and some hidden esoteric happenings within my life I will be able to help you identify where you are NOW. Each mystery unfolds according to your evolved growth up till this present time. There is nothing I can say or write that will enlighten you to this knowledge. You will either see it from within yourself or you will not comprehend it at all. I am not handing you a new religion. I am handing you a codebook that will decipher your old religion. You will grasp the necessary elements needed to bring you along the way towards your internal and eternal growth. Your level of divine education will surface when you peer through these mysteries.

I will attempt to simplify these mystical truths using my Christian experience to enlighten fellow Christians to their divine beginnings. I will help you unravel some of the complicated text in the Bible to delve into its true meaning from the Father and no longer adhere to its shadow representation handed down by the gods of this world. All I can say is, it is now up to you to break the codes from within your eternal being. I cannot do that for you.

THE GARDEN OF EDEN

To begin this journey we need to take a trip back to the mysterious Garden of Eden to commence our education in the gnosis of life and death. God had stated to Adam and Eve that of every tree of the garden they may eat thereof, except of the tree in the midst of the garden, the tree known as the Knowledge of good and evil. They may not eat of this tree nor touch it least they die.

Genesis 2:17 "But of the tree of knowledge of good and evil, you shall not eat of it: for in the day that you eat thereof you shall surely die."

We know through this Biblical tale that Adam and Eve did eat of this forbidden tree. So what happened? Did they die that same day? It appears by all Biblical accounts that Adam and Eve not only didn't die, but they went on to live extremely long and very vibrant lives. But didn't God say they would die that same day? Some may interject here and say, "Well, God meant they would die instead of gaining eternal life, and that he didn't mean in that same day." However one would need to ask his or herself, if Adam and Eve were only flesh and blood, how could they live forever? Matter is always decaying; it cannot exist forever. So under this conclusion, whether Adam and Eve took of this tree or not, they would eventually have to die, unless they were not human. Secondly, God told them they would die that day, and they didn't, at least by all apparent circumstances.

The key to this first mystery is that our cognition of what death is must change. Most live their entire lives believing death to be a finality of the biological being. Once this being is deceased then the biological perishes. Some have, through religious indoctrination, a belief of some sort of afterlife but nevertheless

23

each believes death is the finality of the biological matter being. To a point this is true, from our perspective of reality. However, when God told Adam and Eve they would die the day they partook of this forbidden fruit it was meant from the spirit realm perspective, not the human realm.

Let us presume that reincarnation is accurate and add this into our equation. This would then mean we have all lived multiple lives. It would also dictate unto us that we all have an origin that began some time in the ancient past, possibly even before the worlds were created. When male and female were created after the image and likeness of God it was both a spiritual image and matter biological. This would then imply we are all spirit-born children of God who occupy the flesh.

If this theory were accurate it would prove that the majority of humanity has forgotten this. And because of this memory failure the human race see themselves as no more than flesh and blood biological beings that came into existence when their biological parents gave birth to them. Everyone would be under a strong delusion that presents the above scenario, which implies a memory loss.

Take this argument a step further. What would it do to you to realize that you have an origin in the stars as divine beings? We are all Gods of the antiquity and have been in existence for a very long time. We understood peace, love, joy and power of the highest sensation. We knew the glories of the universe as it spread through the reaches of the cosmos. What if today you were privy to information that proved your fountainhead began in divinity?

What we are witnessing through the metaphoric Garden of Eden is the mystery of life and death. For God told Adam and Eve that they would die the day they partook of this forbidden fruit, AND THEY DID DIE THAT DAY!

The story of Adam and Eve is an allegorical description of all humanity when they lived in the spiritual realm known as Paradise. However the written letter, the shadow would only allow you to believe that there was an introduction of two people at some given period of time that some claim was about 6000 years ago. Was there an Adam and Eve? Yes, there was. But their instructions given to them by the Lords of the shadow lands was only a copy of a divine blueprint. When Moses was instructed about the beginning of the race called humanity he never understood its divine meaning. He presented it from a carnal point of view. What Moses never understood is that he was copying down information that would instruct the biologically encased children of their pre-mortal past, but this knowledge would not be known until the Messiah would bring it forth from the Father. From this point I can begin to bring forth this mystery in terms that will be easy to comprehend.

ADAM AND EVE WERE FOUND NAKED

After Adam and Eve ate of the forbidden tree they saw they were naked, without clothing. This is part of the hidden mystery! Their nakedness was the result of the decree set forth, that in the day they eat of the forbidden fruit they shall surely die. But instead of reading that they died, we learn that they realized they were naked. Now what is the parallel? Is the death that God spoke of congruent to them being naked? The answer is absolutely yes!

The Garden of Eden is an allegory that prescribes the connection that humans are actually divine spirits who once wore the proverbial white robes of righteousness. When these divine spirits existed prior to eating of this symbolic fruit they had begun to fall from grace in a sense. There were divine spirits who had begun to challenge the law of ONE! We as spirits began to roam the universe and enter biological vessels to experience the life source of a lower being. We began to do things that were improper for the divine children to engage in while we entered these lower sources of life. We began to feel that the lower source of life was the true life and our existence in the spirit realm began to fade away in our memories. The shadow lands became the reality, and the spirit realm where the shadows originated all but disappeared. When the Serpent told us to take of the forbidden tree it illuminated us to our internal awareness that we were once divine children and that we fell into the grave of the shadow.

God walking in the Garden wanted to know how we came to understand this about our true heritage. "Who told you that you were naked? Did you eat of the forbidden tree?" for it was the shadow Lords that had forbidden our access to this knowledge. But why would God want to keep this knowledge from us? I will explain this in more detail as we go forward, but I first need to set up more of the foundation to this puzzle.

Death then in reality is really the cessation of living as divine immortals. Death is our existing in the material physical world of illusion, shadow! When we partook of the gnosis we recognized our death from the spirit world. This is the true meaning when it states, "It is appointed unto man once to die, and then the judgment." This was the edict that was brought down from the shadow lords. All the divine children that fell from grace by virtue of breaking the law of one, which was represented in taking of the symbolic tree, would die that same day, and be found naked, without the divine robes of righteousness. Spirits would then exist in a world of biological matter and live their many lives while coming under continuous judgment. The Judgment that the Bible speaks of is our awareness of life and death and our willingness to choose. The Law of Karma, cause and effect!

Christianity along with many millions of others have failed to comprehend the gnosis of reincarnation. They attempt to refute this gnosis using the shadow instead of comprehending the mystery. When we dissect the shadow, letter of the law, we can ascertain the mystical teaching of coming under death once and then the judgment. When we ate of the forbidden fruit in the spirit realm, we recognized our failure to follow the Father, and we also became aware of the shadow lords, and this did not make them happy.

Genesis 3:22 "And the Lord God said, Behold the man has become as one of us, to know good and evil: and now lest he put forth his hand and take also of the tree of life, and eat, and live forever. Therefore the Lord God sent him from the Garden of Eden, to till the ground from whence he was taken."

What the verse above indicates is that the shadow lords had been revealed and they were angry. They did not want man to learn the true origin, for they desired to rule over them, and if man were to understand the divine origin their rule would fail. The shadow Lords were given this rule of law because of our fall. They needed to do something quick before they lost control. They then created what was called the "waters of forgetfulness" and caused man to drink of it to place him into a delusion and to forget his past. They then could control these blinded powerful Gods without them ever knowing what had occurred. This was symbolized by being placed outside the Garden and into slavery, wrapped in the garments of biological clothing. The biological vessel or the "fig leafs" that were given by the shadow lords, for clothing, was to keep them ensnared while covering their divine nakedness. Thereby making us unclothed spirits that dwell within the walls of matter flesh, the veil, giving us the illusion that we are physical not spiritual. This was then used to train spirits as humans in the veil of the cycles.

How did all of this ever take place? We on our own came down to the lower world of matter to experience the sensations of the low vibratory rate of energy to learn the laws of the universe and to experiment with it. We had become children led away wanting to do our own thing against the law of one, the Father. We then were separated from our Tree of Life, which is our divine eternal origin, because we were taken prisoners by the lords of the shadow lands, The Elohim, to be taught another way! The term used for God in the Old Testament comes from the term Elohim, which means multiple Gods. That is why the scripture stated, "let US make man in OUR image." And, "Behold man has become one of US to know good and evil." Why would the Gods know evil? The scriptures teach that sin was never heard of until Lucifer rebelled. Who are these Gods? As I continue to lay the foundation of this first mystery it is important that you understand these concepts a little at a time.

For I am sure what you are reading sounds very strange. But again I say, look within your own heart.

We began to experience the lower dimensional sensations of the five senses through animal forms when we fell from the Garden. The longer we stayed in these conditions we began to be absorbed into the matter world of flesh. As time elapsed we forgot our origin and heritage and believed the lower matter world to be the reality and the spiritual reality became a fading concept.

The judgment then becomes a natural law of living in the lower dimensional world and learning from the myriad of mistakes by experiencing a consciousness through a life form that has a temporary existence. And through our many lives and our long arduous journey it was the Father's hope that we could regain our true identity. Jesus spoke of this as one who is rewarded according to their works.

I will elaborate throughout this book three mystical references that the Bible uses to define a hope in an afterlife. The first is "salvation." The second is "eternal life." And the final aspect is "reward according to your works." Eternal life is a free gift! Salvation is an internal awareness! And your reward is your building pool of works to regain the white robes of righteousness, "to become perfect as our Father in heaven is perfect!"

If, within this process at any given lifetime an individual dies prior to their accessing these mysteries, then they will remain trapped within the law of cycles, a type of eternal everlasting death, by having to return to the flesh for more training. So the entire concept of giving man once to die and then the judgment is related from the spiritual not the physical.

We all had died from our greater awareness and are now here experiencing the many lessons of an on-going judgment through death. However neither the judgment or death is permanent, it is our new training. If we continue to physically die over and over again just to have to return over and over again, it does not affect the edict that was brought down from on high. For as long as it takes to regain our origin and identity we are always in a state of death until we are reconciled unto our salvation, which will lead to rejoining our heavenly identity with the Father. So the judgment that everyone fears is not some exact period of time that God plans to take his wrath out on humanity. The judgment is your living in this lower matter form until you return to your fountainhead by discovering the pearl of great price within your internal and eternal being. The judgment is simply school!

If one fails to succeed this time around then they will be placed into the mysterious law of cycles, known as reincarnation. If one finally succeeds in this life or any given lifetime they will then enter back into their divine past and be reunited with the Father. This is known as the mystical ascension! However the resurrection that I will discuss in detail later, is your awareness of this truth from within? This then becomes your true salvation.

THE LAW OF CYCLES

Everything in the matter creation of the shadow lands functions within the law of cycles. If you plant seeds in the spring, grass will grow, by winter the grass will die. However by next spring the grass will appear to miraculously return without having to do anything on your part. This is the cycles of nature. The dead grass will return in all its beauty and luster. The energy that functions as the catalyst of each blade of grass will not recognize that it was here before, but it was. Leaves fall from the trees in one cycle and then return in another. No human caused this to happen. It is all part of the creating process of evolution, which the shadow lands bring into matter life, of that which it parodies from the spirit realm. Everything that the shadow lords have designed within the matter universe parallels that which comes from the Father's world of spirit, except that which becomes polluted. The physical matter universes that exist, all parallel spiritual universes that also exist. For without the electronic counterpart matter could not exist.

29

Winter, spring, summer and fall and back to winter again, the sun shines through the day and departs for the moon to shine at night in all its varied cycles, and then the sun returns. Everything is revolving. All is in a state of continuous cycles. Many will die in the flesh today, and many will be born this same day.

It is the cycles of the matter universe that bring to our attention the concept known as space and time. Matter locks within itself cycles of life and death. When one transcends the matter world and enters the spirit world there is no longer a definition or concept for time or space. Time is only for the awareness of the lower matter cyclical beings that exist at the same rate of vibration. When you incarnate from the spirit realm, which I will discuss at greater length, you will leave a place that exists without time. You will spend your possible 70 or 80-years within the matter world of cycles, and then return from where you came. It will appear to you as if you just left that realm instantaneously. Yet years had transpired while you occupied a dimension with a body. The experience we partake within the cycles brings awareness to the consciousness that creates the illusion that matter is real when in fact it is only a shadow, a virtual reality.

Our spirit consciousness is able to access this lower form of reality to enable to teach us lessons that could not come any other way. Dreams teach us a little about conscious displacement. We enter worlds in our dreams that at times appear real to us in every way. We experience events that seem to actually be occurring until you wake up and realize it was just a dream. However the simulation of experiences that occurred within that dream, whether you believe it was real or not, could bring information to you that can enlighten you in your training process. Nothing really changed, other information was imparted to you that you may use for your edification or not.

When a person dies or evacuates the biological vessel, your life, however long it was, will appear to you in the spirit realm dimension as a long dream supplied by awareness through a consciousness. The experience that you lived through will be all that you take with you once you leave. You cannot take the matter world with you, only the experience. If your experience helped you in gaining gnosis for your internal and eternal awareness then this will be added to one of your mystical heavenly bodies known scriptural as, "laying up for yourself treasures in heaven, working out your karma." These treasures are your works toward the success of leaving this lower dimensional world and they are being placed upon your higher self as a part of identity gained towards perfection. It becomes the fruit borne through spiritual and physical activity in the lower dimensional world. That which you do that is not of the proper vibration, something we would call evil, is placed upon your lower bodies and must be purged through the cycles and/or fire. Be not deceived, everyone will reap what he or she sows, whether good or evil, right or wrong!

Ancient Israel had customs given to them by the lords of the shadows. Holy days were brought before the people to observe and learn. Moses was given the commands to place a people into bondage until the Messiah would come. These commands only affected the lower form biological entity. It only taught a physical awareness of the true. The Elohim recognized the true form of the spirit God, which they had also forgotten, but the beauty and greatness of this form intrigued them, so they placed imitations of what was in the spirit realm into the physical realm. They then designed and coordinated these holy days around an agricultural society. This had to be done to lead a physical people because of the law of cycles that governed the matter universe. The agricultural society was to impart information to the spiritually aware that all life in matter operates under the law of cycles. Thereby it was necessary to illustrate this comprehension to a society that functioned around seasons. Their spring planting season represented planting the seeds of awareness, and then by fall there was a harvest, which mystically referred to those that had bore fruit worthy to take hold upon their origin.

31

It didn't stop there. For within these seasons there would be another planting season and another harvest, this would always continue. So these Holy days were actually physical prototypes teaching a physical people realities that come from a spiritual world. Each Holy day including the seventh day Sabbath was instituted to instruct a carnal people. But in reality they were performing shadow acts that were a replica of something much more vast. This would continue until the divine Son known as the Christ would enter as light enters darkness and possess a man named Jesus. Then and only then could the Father of light be revealed, showing that the shadow was only a replica of the real. And we must leave this realm and return to the light leaving the shadow of darkness.

After Christ was revealed in the man Jesus then the mysteries that were hidden before the world were revealed. Part of the spiritual gnosis that was being mystically revealed through the divine Son, in the man Jesus, was that we were trapped in the infamous law of cycles. And if we continue to remain separated from our true reality we would forever remain in the cycles of hell. A word representing repetition, not burning fire of torment. Never knowing where we came from or what or why we were doing here. Grace that Jesus taught became the knowledge that we all have been given many opportunities to change, whereas under the belief of the shadow lords we were taught instant death to the sinner. Without this knowledge we would always live in fear to entities that had departed from the true oneness of the Father of lights. For Moses brought the law which represented instant death to the unenlightened and Jesus brought grace and truth which represented mercy and hope to the enlightened.

Under Old Covenant law given by the Elohim one was to be stoned to death without mercy before two or three witnesses. Under New Covenant law one was to be given the hope that the Messiah has come to bring us out of this eternal delusion and damnation. Again these words merely signify covering as a veil. Again we see the parallel of how there were new and old covenants, which in the Bible is really defined. New and Old Testaments. The Father of lights wanted us to see that we were kidnapped by beings who operate the shadow universe that claim to be the only God and desire our service and loyalty to them. The Father was sending a ransom to deliver us from the shadow lords. If we continue to live in the negative spirit that has been blinding us we will continue to see God as a harsh stern taskmaster reaping where he does not sow. We will live our lives in fear of ultimate judgment of eternal damnation, when in fact we are already in eternal damnation- repetition, and the Father desires us to find our own way out. The Elohim have no desire for us to comprehend this truth, because their job is to be the friction or the teachers of the shadow. They are only doing what is needed to create the awareness in us that something has gone wrong. Before I go any further in this discussion I want to bring more information within the Bible that teaches the mystical law of cycles.

JOHN THE BAPTIST WAS ELIJAH

One of the most starling facts that Jesus taught his disciples was that John the Baptist was actually the reincarnated Elijah from the Old Testament times. Jesus asked his followers who the people thought he was. Some of them felt that he was one of the old prophets. Others thought he was Jeremiah. There were even those that thought he was the reincarnated Elijah foretold by Malachi the prophet. Elijah was to return before the coming of the Lord, which was understood to be the end of an age.

Before I go further there are a few questions I would like to ask. Why would Jesus even ask his followers whom the people of his day thought he was? Why would anyone even think this unless they had some idea of reincarnation? We of the West in this generation do not usually go around asking people who they were from a past life, do we? Obviously there was a greater belief in the concept of reincarnation in the first century than Christian churches want us to believe. Obviously Jesus understood it!

In the last book of the Old Testament, Malachi wrote that before the coming of the great and dreadful day of the Lord Elijah the "prophet" would return. This wasn't just crazy rhetoric being espoused by the people of that time period. They had implicit instructions given to this effect in their holy books. The Bible stated, "Elijah the prophet would indeed return."

Now I know what the doubters and skeptics will say to this. They will use the scriptures which state that John the Baptist was asked if he was the Elijah foretold to come, and he stated he was not. Whenever anyone is in the cycles of the matter world they usually come under the illusion of Maya, the concept known in the Eastern religious world as forgetfulness brought about by illusion and deception. So just because John said he was not Elijah doesn't prove anything. It only confirms the spirit of forgetfulness! Just because someone is written about in the Bible doesn't imply that they are already enlightened to understand all gnosis. John was a very humble man. He saw himself as a precursor to Jesus; he always willfully played the role of second fiddle. It wasn't in his make-up to think of himself as a great prophet of the past, and secondly, I don't believe he was lying. He just didn't know.

Some will no doubt also use the verse that speaks of John only coming in the spirit and power of Elijah, but that he wasn't really Elijah the Prophet. But I ask you, how in the world can someone come in another's spirit and power if they are only human, and secondly they are already dead? Also, why Elijah? Couldn't John have come in the spirit and power of God? Why does the Bible say Elijah? Why would Malachi prophesy that the prophet Elijah would return? The people of the first century were no doubt waiting for this auspicious return.

The spirit and power of a man is their projected soul-spirit that you will learn much more about in the following mysteries. It is the divine self projecting a spirit from the light into the shadow land. The Bible is absolutely verifying this mystery and my thesis. If Elijah was truly dead and buried then no one could have come in his spirit unless Elijah was reincarnated through another biological entity.

It bears repeating that the Bible is a coded book of mystery. You cannot comprehend this mystery simply by reading this book as some classroom text. This book is not constructed or designed to be read as a schoolbook. It is a conglomerate of thousands of pieces of extracted material from writings over thousands of years. The gnosis of the Bible must be revealed through mystery, not the written letter. The cycles of life are mysteries that are embedded as codes within the pages of this accepted and revered Holy Book.

The disciples of Jesus knew John the Baptist. Men like Andrew, Peter's brother, were even his followers prior to them following Jesus. But the disciples did not recognize John as being the reincarnated Elijah either, until Jesus told them!

After the mystical transfiguration, OUT OF BODY EXPERIENCE, where some of the disciples witnessed Jesus, Moses and Elijah appear before them as spirit entities, they wondered about the scriptures that taught of the return of Elijah. Obviously they were witnessing Elijah standing there in spirit speaking to Moses and Jesus and it had to occur to them, how was he foretold to return if he standing there in front of them? Jesus then revealed the mystery. He said, "Truly Elijah must first come." This indicated that Jesus was well aware of the Malachi prophecy. He then went on to say, "But I tell you he has already come and they knew him not, and did unto him whatsoever they deemed." This was in reference to John being beheaded. Afterwards it states that the disciples then realized Jesus meant Elijah was John the Baptist. Jesus then went on to make it very simple for all the doubters to comprehend.

Matthew 11:13-14 "For all the prophets and the law prophesied until John, and if you will receive it, 'this is Elijah, which was foretold to come.'"

I find it ironic that Jesus had to say, "If you will receive it?" This simply means, that if you can handle what I am about to say, John is Elijah. People don't ever change if something is being brought to their attention that seems to contradict their previous views. They do not want to hear what you have to say! This story was no different! Jesus was attempting to make known to all who had ears to hear that John was the reincarnated Elijah, whether you like it or not.

THE MAN BORN BLIND

At another time Jesus came to a man that was born with blindness. The disciples inquired asking a strange question considering Christians' beliefs today. They asked, "Who committed sin that this man was born blind, the parents OR THE MAN?" What unfolded was a gnosis that should enlighten one about more of the hidden mysteries.

THE SINS OF THE FATHERS

In the Old Testament the Elohim taught embedded within the second commandment that the Lord thy God is a jealous God, who visits the iniquities upon the fathers upon the children unto the third and fourth generation of them that hate him. So the disciple's inquiry about whether this man was born blind due to the parent's transgression was no doubt a response by those that fell under this law. Their understanding was that a person's sins could pass down to the children for many generations. However, asking if the man himself committed sin was totally out of context, because how could the man have committed sin if he was born blind?

Obviously past lives!

Within the Old Testament taught by the Elohim the law instructed that sins could pass down to the children. However Jeremiah ascertained that this law was going to change. He instructed in writings in chapter 31; that no longer will the father eat sour grapes and the children's teeth be set on edge, but every man shall die from his own iniquity. Every man who eats sour grapes, his own teeth will be set on edge. He brought this information to teach about the Covenants changing. He spoke of a time when the law would be written in everyone's heart. This was the mystical reference implying our origin in the spirit realm. For the Elohim gave the matter man the written law that only pertained to the flesh. But the Father though the divine Son brought the spiritual law that would pertain to spirit beings. That is why the law is written in one's heart. This is spiritual not physical.

Moses gave to the people the written instruction from the Elohim. This was the physical written letter of the law, a law that produces bondage and death. Jesus however brought the spiritual law from the Father, a law that teaches mercy and gives life. But why was there ever a law that taught children would have to pay for the sins of their parents? It is because the Elohim were instructed not to allow the people to understand the knowledge of good and evil, which would have brought forth the truth of the cycles. This would in turn have revealed the truth of our divine past. This knowledge could have helped them break away from the clutches of bondage brought about by the letter of the law. However man was not yet evolved enough to break away from the bondage. As it played out only the Messiah, the divine Son could penetrate this hold that the Shadow LAW and the Elohim had upon the people.

If the truth were known there was never a law that judged innocent children by the sins of their parents. It might have appeared that way because the people did not understand the gnosis. The initiator generates all sin and then that sin revolves in cycles coming back to the one who initiated it. It would appear to the unenlightened that the penalty of sin was passed down to the children of later generations, yet in fact it was returning to the initiator who happen to be the children REBORN! So when the law instructed that your sins would pass down to your children, it referred in principle of passing back down to you. Israel was not taught the spiritual law by the Elohim, so they only understood its letter of intent. The mystery could not be revealed until there was enough evolved growth to usher in the TEACHER!

I repeat, the letter of the law only pertained to flesh and blood humans in the grip of the cycles led by the Elohim. The spirit of the law pertained to the spirit in man and this bypasses the law of the Elohim and enters the LAW of ONE the Father.

JESUS ACCUSES PHARISEES OF PARENTS' SINS

Jesus verified the spiritual law versus the carnal law by telling the Pharisees in Matthew 23 that they themselves were guilty of the bloodshed of the earlier prophets. They told Jesus they would have not been partakers of the bloodshed of the ancient prophets. Jesus in anger said, "But I say unto you that you are the children of them that killed the prophets." He then went on to pronounce them guilty. I find this rather strange due to the fact that Jesus was ushering in a new spiritual law. He knew what the prophecy taught in Jeremiah. And he also taught this truth on the Sermon on the Mount. So why was he accusing the Pharisees of sins their parents committed? It becomes apparent that Jesus was saying the Pharisees are themselves the ones that committed bloodshed. They are their parents reborn, the builders of the sepulchers!

When the disciples wondered who had sinned that the man was born blind they were trying to ascertain which law was in effect. The one that taught the children took upon their parent's sins or the one that taught you are responsible for your own sin, thereby having to pay that penalty in a future lifetime. In this particular case the man was born blind so that the Son of Man could glorify the Father by aiding in his healing. The gnosis came out brighter than the sun to them that have ears to hear and eyes to see.

The Father never had a law that blamed innocent children. Although the Elohim may have out of their desire for power punished innocent people it wasn't the Universal Father's Law. In truth everyone reaps what they themselves sow personally. The disciples were learning the gnosis that the Eastern religions call Karma, another name for reaping what you sow.

As more and more mysteries are revealed people will realize that all circumstances in individuals' lives did not come about because of dumb luck. The law ordains everything! These examples above are perfect examples of how the Bible mystically instructs on reaping what you sow, karma. However, Jesus could not even teach the disciples all the mysteries, because in his own words, they could not handle them yet. Each individual will learn them according to their own divine expansive growth through the evolution of life and death and rebirth.

There are many examples of reincarnation and past lives in the Bible, but the written letter is so vague most just pass right by. Most of the teaching of reincarnation was removed from the Bible years after Jesus walked in physical form, by later Church councils fearing loss of control of the people through fear. One such example comes to mind when God told Jeremiah that he knew him before he formed him in his mother's womb. Hundreds of verses give indication that multiple lives indeed do exist. One such area that speaks of a whole nation being reborn in the future is in the book of Ezekiel. Notice closely as you read the scripture below how Israel was prophesied to reappear in the future. However many have taken this to believe that they would be resurrected, but notice closely the terminology that the Bible uses.

Ezekiel 37:4-10 *"Again he said unto me, Son of man can these bones live? So I answered, O' Lord God, you know? Again he said unto me, Prophesy unto these bones, and say unto them, O' dry bones, hear the word of the Lord! Thus stated the Lord God unto these bones: Surely I shall cause breath to enter you and you shall live. Then you shall know that I am the Lord...Indeed as I looked, the sinews and the flesh came upon them, and the skin covered them over. But there was no breath in them. Then he said unto them, prophesy to the breath...So I prophesied and breath came into them..."*

If one takes the time to analyze this verse they would see this is a perfect description of the nine-month gestation period of a mother carrying her young. What we are witnessing is the baby being formed in her womb. After the birth then the breath or soul-projected spirit enters into the child and it then lives.

39

Even the "baby child" is revealed to have come through the womb as the woman who in travail carries the Christ child in Revelation 12. Hosea brings to light another portion of this mystery.

Hosea 13:12-14 "The iniquity of Ephraim is bound up; his sin is stored up. The sorrows of a woman in childbirth shall come upon him. He shall not stay long where children are born. I will ransom him from the power of the grave. I will redeem him from death."

Throughout the entire Bible there tends to be a direct correlation between death and birth from the womb. As above, one is being redeemed from death by being born again. It states, "he shall not stay long where children are born, I will ransom him from the power of the grave." This is a metaphor-ransom from the power of the grave, representing the womb giving forth the fruit of birth. Why would the birth of a child have anything to do with one that is already dead, unless it is reincarnation, a rebirth? It states, "I will redeem him from death..."

REDEMPTION FROM DEATH IS REBIRTH

Our continual redemption from physical death is our rebirth into the flesh through the law of cycles. Obviously we are not really dead, but to the human mind it would appear as redemption from death, *coming from the womb*! There are hidden meanings throughout the Bible, but again I state, if you just read the letter you will never understand.

I could go over scripture after scripture that teaches reincarnation but this would never help the disbeliever to change their mind. Too many are set within a paradigm structure of beliefs and there is no way they're going to change. It is sad that we as humans can be so easily influenced to believe doctrinal error and hold on to it with our dear life because we so fear God and his retribution. I realize that most of what I am saying will be rejected out of hand, and there is nothing I can do about that. However I believed that if I could approach this subject enlightening the mysteries while using the Bible to formulate some of the key elements of this gnosis, then just maybe it would unlock a door deep within you.

Jesus said, "seek and you shall find." And the Apostle Paul made it extremely clear that salvation is not found written in the letter. It can only be found in the spirit. So evidently it was required of all of us to explore much deeper for the truths than religion has ever taught.

CHURCH NOT A BUILDING BUT A PERSON

In seeking hidden gnosis it becomes apropos to ask personal questions within yourself. We need to find the necessary awareness by looking and examining our own heart. We must once again open the door that has been locked tight, because of false doctrine that we accepted through laziness and lack of diligence. The teachers of religions for the last 2000 years are the very ones who have always lacked true understanding of the spiritual word. They appear before the masses with their sanctity and perceived righteousness when in truth they have no idea of the true nature of gnosis. They are the first to condemn those that don't espouse to their corrupted doctrines. They have no understanding of the Father of mercy because they are still following the Elohim of good and evil. The very term Church used in the Bible comes from the Greek word, "Ekklesia." It refers to a "calling out." It is when one becomes an initiate to the mysteries. It literally implies to break away from the norm and to learn a new gnosis.

The corrupted word for church changed into becoming a place of worship rather than an individual. Instead of becoming initiates, one who is ready to internally become aware, many threw out their responsibility in this learning process unto the leaders of a church. They believe that all that is required of them is attending one of these places of worship and everything else will be taken care of. They believe that the leaders of these so-called churches must know what they're

41

talking about, so why question them. But I say, there were few that understood the Old Covenant law like the Pharisees of the first century, yet Jesus rebuked them for their lack of understanding the Father and his mercy. You will come to learn that the Temple of the Old Testament was a shadow of something very important in the spirit. The Temple of the Old Covenant then became the Church of the New Covenant. Yet instead of people becoming aware of the spiritual meaning of the Temple, they turned the church into the shadow worship, as the temple was the shadow worship of Israel. They turned it also into a building.

PARABLES FOR THE UNITIATED

I remember reading in the book of Mark a concept that was the opposite of what I always believed. In Chapter 4 Jesus taught that parables were only for those who were not to receive the mysteries. I had always believed that the Biblical parables were the mysteries of the kingdom. In most of the Gospels information that Jesus taught was brought forth in the form of parables. I never understood that Jesus spoke in parables to throw people off the true trail so-to-speak.

Jesus taught that the parables were given to them that are without, the uninitiated, but the mysteries are given to the disciples, the initiated. So this means for 2000 years people have been trying to ascertain the true meaning of the Gospel by using information that was meant to throw them off and not enlighten them. When the Bible discussed areas where the mysteries were alluded to, the scriptures would then veer off into another direction espousing information of really no importance. It became quite obvious that this happened every single time that any mention of the mysteries occurred. The mysteries were never revealed in the written letter, and this has caused confusion in all the religions.

The parables were used to teach a concept. If one became aware of the internal gnosis then they could understand the parable in its spiritual intent. But if one was not enlightened to see within themselves, then the parable would appear to be nothing more then carnal information with no substance. Many of the parables related concepts within the agricultural thinking of ancient Israel, such as the sower and the seed, and the parable of the vineyard. The embedded codes within these typical parables were to teach the enlightened ones about the concept of birth and rebirth through the planting seasons. If the word of God, which is the internal awareness of gnosis, brings forth fruit, then there would be a harvest where the initiated would access another level in their spiritual training. However if the seed or the word did not take root during the planting season then that yield or lack thereof would need to be tilled under for another planting season. Yet to the unenlightened it would appear to be ultimate failure and death.

Some would see that these parables speak of trees that produce no fruit,which were to be cast into a fire and burned. They would take this to mean God's wrath and vengeance against the lowly sort who failed to produce fruit. They would never comprehend the mercy where God would give more opportunities through new planting seasons.

When a crop has gone bad in the fall harvest the only thing to do is burn that crop to purify the ground for another planting season. It isn't done in anger or vengeance, it is done to pave the way for more opportunities for a better yield next year. Christians have taken these verses to imply that the world would then come to an end through terrible circumstances, and Jesus would return to save some and punish what was left. The term for world in the Bible comes from many different Greek words. The one that implies the end of time usually refers to Age/aeon. It represents an end to an AGE, referring to an end of an astrological age when the harvest is gathered. After every harvest there will be another year to plant, representing that New Ages will come forth. When Jesus walked this earth it was at the end of one age entering another. Jesus then became the master of the Pisces Age known mystically as the fish. This is why the fish is often used as a symbol for Christ.

The Bible taught that the Old Covenant and practices of ancient Israel were to come to an end at the end of the age, not the

43

world. The end-time that was spoken of in the Old Testament referred to the end of the Age of Israel when the Messiah would enter. When Joel prophesied the end of the world Peter understood it to be at his time period. When Malachi spoke of the great and dreadful day of the Lord when Elijah the prophet would enter, it was at this same time. This is why so many have failed to understand these prophecies. They were not meant for our coming age, they were meant for the end of Israel's age leading to the age of Pisces.

THE TEMPLE OF GOD

Earlier I explained that I would give more details on what the Temple of the Old Covenant really represented. There was a mighty reason that the physical temple had to be removed. For if the temple would remain, so also would a great deception remain upon mankind. The temple and the Ark of the Covenant represented the house where God dwells. The only problem was that it was a shadow of the true temple and Ark of God. The Elohim wanted Israel to follow them and worship these beings of the shadow lands so they used these spiritual rites for physical obedience. These beings, as you will come to see, were a powerful hierarchy and a combination of good and evil. They were not the Father, nor the Son. It was the Elohim who came to Moses and all of Israel to gain their following. I will explain in the next chapter where these beings are from and why they are not the true Father. For now I will just keep laying the foundation for you so that you can ease into this mystery without too much difficulty.

Ancient Israel was given all truth in the form of a shadow or copy. Moses was told that the temple he built was a copy of a greater temple in heaven. But the gnosis of this revelation never made its way into the hearts of the Israelites. The Elohim started a line of High Priests through the brother of Moses, Aaron. Aaron and all his male offspring of the tribe of Levi would be the only ones who could enter into the Holy of Holies, in the temple itself. For in this seat sat one of the Elohim, whom the Gnostics called Ialdabaoth, that the people were worshiping. This line of Levite priests was also a shadow of a true line known as the Melchizadeks-Masters of the Ascension. The Levitical priesthood was only a mock copy of the true, a copy of the Melchizadek priesthood. So also was the God or Elohim sitting within the Holiest of all! This was also a mock copy of the true. The Elohim represented the true, but they themselves were not the true. The house that they sat in represented the true, but also it was not the true.

THE TEMPLE OF GOD IS YOU AND ME!

Within each of us sits the Father of all spirits. That is why the Apostle Paul said that if the spirit of the Father abides within you, then know you not that you are the *temple of God*. The true priesthood lines are the true children of the Father, meaning all of us who become initiates are the awakened ones, the enlightened ones. In ancient Israel only the Levite could access the Holy of Holies. This represents the true initiates, those that come to inner gnosis. They will know how to access the inner temple. The majority, even though they may be brought into the temple/church, are still unable to enter the inner temple where the Ark of the Covenant lies. They remain in the outer courts. When we become initiated we can then enter within our own temple and meet our God. We will then come after the order of the Melchizadeks and not the order of Aaron. That is why it states in Hebrews that Christ Jesus came after the order of Melchizadek and not Aaron. We are the true priesthood and once enlightened can enter the Most Holy at any time and access the Ark of the Covenant.

THE SHADOWS COPY THE SPIRIT

Everything in the Old Testament was a mock copy of the true. That is why I decree it as the shadow lands. So the end of this age that we are speaking of was the end of the mock copy, the end of the shadow lands, but only to those that were being initiated. If you are not being initiated then you are still under the control of the Elohim of the shadow lands and must do their bidding. Not even Jesus tried to pull away the followers of the

Elohim that were not ready for the transition. By law until you come to see the Father within then you must obey your captors, the shadow Lords. The Elohim are the Gods of the shadow-materialistic universe. We are all under their control and authority until the Messiah has entered within to illuminate you to your divine origin so that you can break away from your captors by the ransom of enlightenment paid by Jesus.

ASTROLOGICAL SIGNS REVEAL AGES

There are many in the Christian world that will take offence at me using astrological signs representing the end of ages. This is because the Elohim spoke of not using these signs. The Elohim become angry when you begin to recognize your true identity. However Abraham and Job were two key figures in the Old Testament that understood the astrological signs. And so did Moses to a greater degree while living in Egypt. Without the astrological signs we would have never come to understand the cycles, and many other things that now we take for granted. Those of the Old Testament that the Father was spiritually waking up began to comprehend gnosis beyond the boundaries of the Elohim. Even King David did things that went beyond the boundaries of the shadow lords, such as entering into the Holy place and eating the shew-bread, which was forbidden. David was beginning to comprehend the Lord within himself. Once this takes place the shadow lords have no authority over you. Once you understand who you are then you will know that you are a powerful divine being, in some cases even greater than the Elohim angels.

The age that preceded Jesus was an age of Darkness. Christ the Word of the Father was sent here to bring light unto the shadow dominated world. Once this light shines the darkness will fade away as if it never existed. This light was not given to everyone at once, each one only in their own order of evolution. It was only given to those that were ready to evolve by virtue of their past life experiences. For the next 2000 years after Jesus walked this earth in his biological vessel few would understand their origin of the divine light. However a New Age would follow the age of Pisces that would bring in what many have called the second return of the light or Christ. This time it will enter the world at the beginning of the New Age called Aquarius, the water carrier. This is the symbolic sign of internal awareness through the Holy Spirit. We are about to enter a time when the consciousness of humanity will be lifted to a higher evolution. The spirit of Christ will be poured out upon the whole earth.

The astrological signs seem to run in continuous cycles of 12 ages lasting about 2160 years each for a total of nearly 26,000 years. The cycle of Pisces seems to be the end of the 26,000 years of cycles bringing in a time of higher conscious awareness. Aquarius then becomes a new cycle of cycles. That is why there is so much urgency within the religious world. They have not comprehended the true meaning of these cycles and they fear it to be an ultimate judgment that God is bringing upon mankind, when in truth it is actually the ultimate blessing. The Father desires his children to come out from the lower vibrations called shadow lands. The previous ages have brought with them many changes that have literally altered the entire landscape of the earth. Earthquakes, volcanos, pole shifts are just a few of the many earth changes that occur through the age transitions. Thus bringing about the concept that God is punishing his children, when in truth these are just natural evolutionary processes that take place throughout the cycles.

In times past the earth has undergone a toiling which could be represented by the harvest that produces no fruit. Examples of great lands, that we ignorantly call ancient mythology, are Atlantis, Lemuria, Phoenicia, Sumeria etc... This occurred because we of the ancient past failed to recognize the light in any given age. And we were not prepared at the harvest to move forward to the next level. Therefore we were tilled under to appear at another time and generation. We of the 21st century have become very arrogant in believing that our technology surpasses all technology of the past. Our present day scientific knowledge has existed many times in the ancient past. Solomon was quoted as saying there is nothing new under the sun. This is an absolute when you deal with the law of cycles.

Ancient documents of older cultures reveal that we are just now catching up with scientific technology of the past.

SUMERIANS PROVE NOTHING NEW UNDER SUN

Sumerian documents, which existed in Mesopotamia, now called Iraq, show startling information of our planetary system that we still do not understand. It shows another planet orbiting our sun that they claim has a 3600 year cycle and is orbiting in reverse of the other planets. Ages have come and gone and have produced mind-boggling technology as well as scientific knowledge. It has taken thousands of years to recover information that has been lost to earth changes through the ages. Earthquakes, pole shifts, ice ages and last but not least, great floods have been the enemies that we call God's judgment.

Ancient Jewish rabbis were noted for saying that "Worlds before worlds existed before the story of the Biblical Adam." Every time an age ends all that is left are stories usually labeled tales and myths.

Modern Christianity has the shadow belief that God created the sun, moon, stars and the earth on the fourth day of creation which they mistakenly believe was only 6000 years ago. When someone dares to question this lack of understanding, they claim you are rebelling against the great God or you have demon problems, because you fail to see the glory of God's great creating powers. How can knowing the sun, moon and stars have been here for much longer than 6000 years have anything at all to do with the creating power of God? Most do not recognize that the seven-day creation week was a metaphor given to an ignorant and unlearned culture to teach of things that were way beyond the scope of their minds.

SPEED OF LIGHT DOCUMENTS HISTORY

If we take the time to reason things out and quit listening to unlearned men and women espouse ideas that have no relation to reality we would become much more enlightened. If you use simple arithmetic you would see the holes in the idea of a 6000 year beginning of creation. For example, the speed of light travels in access of 186,000 miles per second. This calculates to nearly 6 trillion miles to make up what we call "one light year." We have to use light years to figure distances in space because of its vastness. A light year simply means that it takes light traveling at the speed of 186,000 miles per second one year to reach its destination. It becomes difficult to calculate miles when we talk about billions of light years.

To simplify this, in our galaxy alone it would take 100,000 light years for light to cross our entire galaxy. So wherever our earth is located in the galaxy it would take at minimum 50,000 light years for light to reach our perception from one end of our galaxy to the other. Now this is only speaking of our tiny little galaxy in this universe that is made up of billions of galaxies.

Now with our use of the Hubble Space Telescope we can witness star systems that are beyond the imagination considering distance. The very fact that light takes millions and even billions of years to travel to our perception is proof alone of a universe that at least is billions of years old, not a mere 6000. The stars alone are another proof verifying not only distance, but also how many spirits were created from the beginning. We are talking trillions upon trillions, innumerable without number like the sands of the sea.

Those who continue to make excuses to refute this simple truth will never be convinced no matter what you tell them. Why individuals want to hang onto metaphors as their realities I will never know!

The Bible speaks of mankind as being chosen before the foundations of the world. We have been here for a very long time. That is why ages have passed and histories have been lost way before the story of the Biblical Adam and Eve. There could be a future generation that questions the myth of whether the United States of America really existed, the same as we do about Atlantis today. And I have not even approached the subject of citizens from other planetary systems, which I will address later. A friend of mine came to me the other day and wondered how I could believe in so-called ET's? I simply stated, because God is the God of the living not the dead. God is life. He is not emptiness, just take a peek in outer space and you tell me.

Now that you have read the first mystery of the cycles you are ready to enter the mystical portals of deeper gnosis, to gain a higher perspective of the realities that I am presenting. May the Father grant that your inner reality shine forth like the Son, and blaze forth like a thousand suns. And may your mind perceive the true kingdom of God.

MYSTERY TWO
The Mystery of the Veil

There is a power in the realms of the unknown so magnificent and all encompassing that it literally fills the glory of itself within itself and from without. It is a majestic brilliance of illuminating colors. It has been an unseen force in the portals of mystery, decorated with beauty and harmony and unimaginable luminescence. It radiates itself within the glories of the great beyond and beams its essence to all there is. Unending is its character of development. It is a story of great magnitude, yet it never subsides, and never fails.

From within itself it can create from without itself, thereby bringing its new creation back within itself. An essence that multiplies its greatness and devours the blackness of nothingness, inserting therewith the omnipresence of glory!

The thrills, joy, peace and love that is ever so pure and fantastic that it dances with excitement to extend this illustrious glory and design unto others. It is a love that empties into all atoms and molecules. It is a joy that continues to feel need to share with all it has brought into existence that awesome potential of the one who bears witness to all that has ever been. To that One sacred Holy Spirit that fills the universes with all there ever was. To that one being that we all so humbly call, OUR FATHER!

From this one divine spirit all things came into existence. In the beginning was the spoken Word, and the spoken Word was with God. And the spoken Word was God. From time immemorial there was a beginning to all that we can conceptualize. For the spirit God spoke the dynamic Word, and all things were fashioned. The Word itself became a glory unto itself, thereby declaring Sonship. The Word being one in mind with the Father spirit began to take on a new individualized glory. A distinct separation had occurred yet the Word was in every way like the Father.

Thereby the Father of spirits became the thought mechanism of perpetual creative design. And the spoken Word became his only begotten Son, the creator in process forming two principles of the one divine God. The only begotten Son became the light consciousness of the Father. He in essence became the very mind of Spirit. The divine Son, the Logos, the Word, and the Christ spirit of ages past and ages to come created all things of creation that radiates its shadow unto the matter world. All things of the spirit realm came into existence by the light spirit Son, the voice of the Father of lights.

For God said let there be light, the luminescent brilliance of the mind of the Father. And there was light. The light that shone throughout the cosmos bringing with it goodness and mercy. It was a light that traveled speeds of unknown dimensions, interacting and developing an existence out of apparent nothingness. And the Father declared that the light would represent all truth. And the Father called that truth the first day. Everything that was not of this truth, the very mind of the light of the Father, represented darkness. And this he divided into night! So evening and the morning were the first day. So began the metaphoric terminology of the "seven day creation week."

Out of this perfect realm was created replica deities. From the Father- Aforethought, and the Mother -Barbelo- Foreknowledge and the virgin spirit Son came the replica creation of what was called the perfect humanity. "Piger-adam-us" was the creation by the virgin spirit as the Father of the perfect race. And Seth was his first born son of the spirit world. All of the children from Seth onward would be known as the saints of the Most high written in the Book of Life from before the foundations of the world. (Notice the parallel names from the father Adam and his Son Seth in the physical world!)

Through a process of events many of these children would fall from their original glory and enter the lower dimensions to experience another reality. However the story teaches in the secret Book of John (Nag Hamaddi) that after Seth and after the perfect humanity there was another creation or realm called the fourth realm. In it one was created called the female spirit Sophia.

The story reveals Sophia went on to create a son in which she was not given permission by the great divine hierarchy. This son would not receive the blessing of the virgin spirit, therefore the son was created in error and became contemptible and without purity and divine knowledge.

This being was then named Laldabaoth-Yaldabaoth.

Through this divine error all the matter universes were created by Llaldbaoth as a shadow or replica copy of the spirit world, however because it was also created in error, matter was not given eternal life. It would then deterioate and die thus bringing the sacrifice of light which was the Lamb of God from before the foundations of the earth due to a faulty creation that was called darkness. This powerful God became the God of Good and Evil and envisioned himself in ignorance as being the Only God and there was none other!

The spiritual realm reflected shadows into other dimensions. These shadows took on form by the assistance of the shadow Lord, into a lower vibratory substance. The spiritual universes reflected a pattern that was used to design material universes. The creation, which was designed in its perfect spiritual state, materialized into a decaying state from the shadow projection. The perfect creation reflected its glory and the shadow showed flaws through the material substance that reflected the true. Chaos and turmoil began to operate the lower vibratory dimensions.

This is where the Old Testament in the first book of Genesis changes its pattern. In Genesis 1:1 the Bible indicates that

53

something went wrong and there was a new creation or a re-creation of the first creation. In reality that which went wrong was the material universe. The spirits who entered the reflection of the true design were designing an imperfect matter world using the reflection of the true realm they had left. This is why the Father had to decree, let there be light. The light of the spirit realm had darkened when the shadow worlds were being created. Spirit beings that were blinded by the illusion came into material forms in biological vessels of all different creations of the one divine spirit who led them, and they began to assist in the rule of the matter universe. Afterwards from the second day of creation everything that was created was of the matter universe or a duplicate copy of the spiritual blueprint. The spirit realm of the light was becoming a memory faded into a mirror of shadow.

At this point I will pattern in this thesis my conclusions that are in part based on the Christian Bible as well as the lost writings of the ancient Gnostics. Also I will tie together some of this information with the ancient Sumerians, which came down through the cuneiform tablets. Information that relayed their understanding which they claimed came from the gods of the stars, the Elohim!

SECRET GOSPEL OF JOHN

The Elohim saw themselves as the children of Ialdabaoth, the first son of Mother Sophia who entered the shadows. Ialdabaoth's angels, who had no comprehension of the spirit Father/Mother, ascertained that there must be other Gods, when Ialdabaoth declared that he was a *jealous God and there was none like him.* For how could such a decree have been uttered if there truly was no other God? The lower angels which were created by Ialdabaoth comprehended within the shadows that there were other Gods beyond their realm. One would never become jealous unless other Gods existed, and they were to be kept secret. (Secret Gospel of John -Nag Hammadi)

The Father/Mother declared that he had spoken untruths. The Father-truth and Mother-Wisdom decided to send the Son-Light comprehension into the dimensions of darkness and shadow to reveal to their children, the fallen perfect humanity, that they were being led away from the light. The light that reflected its glory into the matter universes confused Ialdabaoth. He did not understand its origin, for he had forgotten, but he loved its beauty. He began to pattern that which he visualized from the light into the lower realms. The ancient Gnostic writings teach that Ialdabaoth created the lower angels, not God's angels, as servants. However Ialdabaoth experienced some problems, some of his own sons were turning against him in the rebellion known in the Bible as the Lucifer rebellion. The legions of darkness began to war against the legions of Ialdabaoth. The Bible seems to pick up this story when Michael, angel of the father, had been summoned to become the warrior for the Israelite God/Ialdabaoth, and Satan became the warrior for Lucifer. War then began in the realms where peace originated. The gods warred against each other! Planets were then destroyed where civilizations had existed. Another planet had to be chosen for Ialdabaoth to rule over.

Ialdabaoth in his arrogance wanted to create a being that would serve and honor him as Lord God and no other. We then read in Genesis where the Elohim decided to create Male and Female after their image. For the Shadow Lords took upon the image of Man, by also wearing biological garments, thereby making man in the image of the shadow Lords. That is why the angels in the Old Testament were written about taking the appearance of man. Like humans these were spirits living in biological vessels. But a problem had arisen with the creation or genetic splicing of these new beings called human. They would not come to life, meaning there was no life in them. It was then that the Father/Mother was able to instruct Ialdabaoth to give breath to the creature from the Great Spirit force. This breath of the spirit force was placed into the nostrils of this newly fashioned biological vessel. These then became the projected souls of them that had also fallen in the lower realms of darkness and shadow. This declared the allegorical Garden of Eden. These would become the billions upon billions of souls that fell in

55

paradise in the great deception by wandering off into the shadowy world of matter, becoming lost. These fallen souls that were breathed into the flesh and blood veils were every way as powerful as their gods were. They were the perfect humanity. This angered Ialdabaoth. He thought he was tricked and quickly took measures to make sure that the biological beings that veiled these gods would not discover this gnosis.

THE TWO TREES

The Bible declared this event by revealing the two trees in the Garden. One represented the tree of Life, the other the knowledge of good and evil. It was this gnosis of good and evil that the Elohim wanted to keep away from this newly bound spirit.

He then took the two creatures that he created called Adam and Eve and placed them into a physical Garden of Eden. These creatures were led to believe that the Elohim were the true Gods and there was none above them, claiming to be the only God. Adam and Eve were placed into the shadow of their true home. This was patterned from the light of paradise they had left yet had forgotten.

LALDABAOTH = GNOSTICS - ANU = SUMERIANS

The Elohim realized that when Adam and Eve had the great soul spirit breathed into them they had to keep them unaware of this truth. If they found this out they would no longer worship the Elohim. The Elohim themselves were also spirits living inside biological vessels, and they roamed the matter universe in ships that could fly great speeds. That is why God could be found talking and walking in the Garden with Adam and Eve, for God was a man. The Sumerians knew the name of the two sons of the Great Ialdabaoth. They called them ENKI & ENLIL the Sons of ANU, Sumerian Name, the Father of the ANNUNAKI that rules from above. But neither ENLIL nor ENKI were perfect because they were also of the shadow of good and evil. Enki and Enlil were two of Anu's sons/angels and they came to earth to reign for ANU. The EN prior to many of these names stands for Lord. Thereby the angels of ANU were known as Lords. Enlil was known as the Word. He was second in command directly under the great Anu-FATHER. This was a type of the true Christ, but not the real. Enki was known as the Serpent. He claimed to be the firstborn Son and was jealous of Enlil. Enlil and Enki were at odds with each other long before Adam and Eve were formed. These two sons and many others were the children of the great ANU who ruled some of the lower matter dimensions by virtue of their great technological advances. The Great Anu and the gods of the stars come from the Planet called Nibiru, the 10th planet rotating in our solar system. This is their world! (Zecharia Sitchin - The 12th planet)

The planet Earth would rotate around the sun 3600 times before the planet Nibiru would return. This is why scriptures indicated that to God a thousand years is like a day, and a day is as a thousand years. And one day in Hebrew prophecy equaled one year. This was in reference to the difference of Earth and Nibiru rotating the solar star. For one of Anu's years would be 3600 of human years.

When Enlil and Enki came to earth to prepare it, many thousands of followers of lower rank were also sent to work in the mines to look for gold to bring back to Nibiru. These would be called the Anunaki, which is defined as the Children of ANU. These were also living on the planet Nibiru. The Anunaki became slaves to work the mines and serve the Elohim, but they became angered and began to rebel. Enlil and Enki realized that something needed to be done. The Anunaki demanded that others take their place in the mines. So the council/Elohim came together and decided to inter-splice genetically with the creatures on earth. They said, "Let us make man in our image, after our likeness." So from the image of the Elohim they created Male and Female after their kind. For both sexes of the Gods were living in the shadow lands as a mirror copy to the Father/Mother Spirit. The Gods of Nibiru placed their genetic seed into the creatures of Earth, as the Sumerian story indicates.

57

This combination of the gods of the stars linked with the lower animal forms created the missing link that science has always wondered about. At times biological robots were also created that became watchers who relayed information back to the Gods without them having to be everywhere at once, but these were only biological without the true spirit-soul. These robots were also known as demons and looked very much like the infamous gray aliens many have seen today. Actually ancient Sumerian pictographs depict these same entities that many have claimed to have seen. The term alien is actually a play on words from two different languages. (Arabic) ALI=GOD (Sumerian) EN=LORD, thus depicting the name, Lord GOD!

THE ELOHIM CREATED ADAM AND EVE

They attempted the creation of this Adam and Eve by creating seven pairs, using the female gods as the carriers in their womb of the spliced seed. They attempted to create or form a whole race of humans, but this would take time. They learned that two species of the same origin could reproduce themselves. To make a long story short, from this point on the Adam and the Eve were able to procreate. They were not hybrid and they became the slaves to Anu and his children, alleviating the burden to the Anunaki. For the spirit children of the Father could be breathed as soul-projected spirits from their true spirit realm, and they became human. This was revealed in the Bible when the Elohim cursed them to toil and slave for them until they died.

That which was created on the first day took place in the spirit realm that depicted day and night. Day became the Son of righteousness. And night became the fallen son of shadow. This is why we see almost a duplicate creation on the fourth day where it states that the sun was created for the day, and the moon for the night. But this was the creation of Ialdabaoth as the mirror representation. The Elohim as well as all spirits are the creators of the matter universe. Some may wonder why the Bible states that the Word or Christ created all things, and now I am stating other Gods created the material universe. All things of the spirit realm came into existence by the Word of the Father/Mother Spirit. This Word is the divine Son called the Christ, but the shadows are just replicas or copies. The shadow is like the projector shining light on the screen. It would be like God giving you a blueprint to build a house. The design might come from God but you are the one who built and created the house from physical materials. The source of the light from the projector is the real pattern; the screen is only reflecting that source. The Elohim were able to produce matter from the projected light. The material universe became shadows of the true spirit universe. That is why in the Book of Hebrews it states that the law was the shadow of good things to come. This is the matter LAW, the second of the two basic laws of the universe. The true creation is still the creation by the spoken Word, by the divine Son. But the material creation was only the shadow of the true. Now learn a mystery; Christ is the light that dwells within all!

MATTER IS NOT REAL ONLY AN ILLUSION

Understand another mystery now! Matter is not real, it is only an illusion! This is why it is always in a state of decay. It is only an illusion. Illusions give way! It appears real when biological entities are able to vibrate at the same rate that matter vibrates giving us the illusion that matter has substance. This is why Adam and Eve were created vessels to serve the Elohim. Because from the biological vessel's point of view, the matter is the real world, thereby making the illusory Gods, the Elohim also appear real, but all are nothing more than shadows of the true spirit.

However once the spirit within the vessels recognize that matter is illusion and that they are spirits occupying vessels, then the Elohim's rule becomes nothing more than illusions and the Father of light becomes the true source through the divine Son. Thereby enabling one to leave the shadows forever and never again come under the illusion of good and evil. But this takes time, and for some possibly millions of years.

When we look at the creation week a little more closely we see there is something we have never understood. First of all the creation week was never meant to be a literal week of 24-hour days. It was always a metaphor of an unknown period of time. It was used to depict time in the sense that matter all relates to the cycles within the veil of deception. But when you take a closer look at the seven days, you will realize that the fourth day is when the sun, moon and stars were created (which gives us our timetable). This alone indicates that at least the first three days were not literal days because the 24-hour time period wasn't created yet. These were all illustrations to create the pretence to the newly created beings that matter, time and space are real, when they are not. This is why the Elohim described these as days, but in truth they were actually unknown periods of time. Remember only earth gives the presence of a 365 1/4 days timetable based on our Gregorian calendar today.

When we speak of other stars and planets then time and space varies accordingly. How could stars have been created in the period we call days when the days would be different for each star?

LIGHT CREATED SPIRIT; DARKNESS MATTER

When we go back to verse one in Genesis we realize that the Father through the Word created the heavens and the earth as spirit not matter. Using the original Hebrew one realizes that something went wrong. Spirit cannot decay. It actually stated, "God created the heavens and the earth, and the earth BECAME without form and in the void." This shows the first presence of a decaying substance. Spirit cannot change, it is incorruptible. However matter can change and always does. What became without form was the reflection of the spirit that became matter illusion. Matter by virtue of being the shadow of the true became darkness as opposed to spiritual light. It was the Father that then said, "Let there be Light." Now maybe one can understand what the Apostle Paul meant when he said, *man was sown in corruption.* Matter is always in a corruptible decaying state. Understand matter is not evil per se. It is just not real, it is a reflection.

LAMB SLAIN BEFORE FOUNDATION OF EARTH

We can then conclude that the Word, which is the light of the mind of the Father/Mother Spirit, came into the realm of the shadow as the divine Son. It was to bring back awareness to the divine children that fell from the spiritual *garden* by entering the corruption of decaying matter, which brought the illusion of good and evil. When the divine children fell the Elohim patterned their worlds after the blueprint of the spirit. The spirit was all that could truly reveal the light patterns of illusion. This is why everything in the Old Testament brought about by the Elohim was mock copies of the true. There was no other source for the blueprint of their designed world except the light that the Father sent into the shadow lands. The light or divine Son had been crucified by the illusion of matter. This then brings to light what the scriptures indicated when it spoke of *the Lamb that was slain from before the foundation of the earth.* Thereby the Father needed to resurrect that light by sending it into the illusion. Bringing awareness back to those who murdered the Divine Son, the Holy Word and Law of ONE by the sword of ignorance. The slain Lamb from before the world was when the children left the light and entered darkness. Darkness-matter crucified the light-spirit. The resurrection was when the Word revealed the light back into the Darkness/shadows.

In Genesis 1 and John 1 it speaks of the Light being brought forth by God and that the light was God as well as being the Son of God. The Father/Mother spirit created a harmonized reflection, one that could bear witness to the light's origin. The Son's duty was to bear witness that there was a Father other than the Elohim, thereby decreeing the origin of the light that created the reflected worlds of shadow. But until the Son came into the matter illusion world no man or god, while living in the

61

biological vessel, had known the Father, or heard his voice, because they had all forgotten their origin. Yet the scriptures state that Moses spoke to God face to face. This is proof that Moses did not know the Father; he knew the illusion of the Father. Moses knew Anu's son Enlil-angel of the Lord-Anu-Laloabaoth. Moses knew the Elohim/ANUNAKI!

SEVEN ISRAELITE GODS

Seven shadow lords ruled ancient Israel. *JEHOVAH/ENLIL all one in the same* ruled Moses, Joshua, Amos and Habakkuk. *Iao* ruled Samuel, Nathan, Jonah and Micah. *Sabaoth* ruled Elijah, Hosea, Joel and Zachariah. *Adonai/ENKI* ruled Isaiah, Ezekiel, Jeremiah and Daniel. *Eloi* ruled Obadiah and Haggai. *Oraios* ruled Malachi, Nahum. *Astaphaios* ruled Esdras, Zephaniah. These are the Lords of God, the Angels! (Nag Hammadi)

When we recognize the light then we can see the distortions of truth all throughout the Old Testament when the Elohim claimed the one true God. Here are some of the examples. Ialdabaoth was a jealous God. The Father has nothing to be jealous of. For the Father is spirit, and he is life, without him nothing would exist! There is no ego to pump, no whistles to blow. The Father just is! Secondly, the Elohim told Israel not to kill. This was given them as their sixth commandment. However, when the Elohim became angry they instructed Israel to kill the Elohim's enemy. This is not fitting a role of a Father in any sense. This creates abnormality and confusion. And the Father is not the author of confusion. Thirdly, the Father told us to love our enemies, and do good to them which despitefully use us. The Father would never command his children to wipe out a nation as the Elohim instructed the Israelites to do to the Canaanites. Next, the Father, in the book of Hebrews was said not to dwell in Temples made with hands, this is to say of this earthly realm, as buildings. But the Elohim instructed Moses to build a Temple for God to dwell in and one of the Elohim sat in the Temple's Holy of Holies.

THE ELOHIM AND FATHER ARE DIFFERENT

The scriptures teach that flesh and blood cannot please the Father, for he is spirit, but only the flesh and blood works of the Israelites pleased the Elohim. The Elohim did not teach salvation or mercy, only judgement, but the Father taught both of these and said he judges not. The Elohim taught when one sinned they were to be stoned to death. The Father taught, judge not or you will be judged- everyone will reap what he or she sows. Each person's iniquity will be required on his or her self. When you displeased the Elohim they would very seldom forgive, no matter how many tears you shed, like the case with Esau, who was tricked by his brother Jacob! The Father's forgiveness was endless. Jesus said, forgive 70 times 7 times. The Elohim kept the veil up to separate us from our true origin. The Father rent the veil in two. The Elohim set up a priestly line, the Levitical priesthood. The Father already had a priestly line, Melchizadek. The Elohim said they create evil. The Father has no part with evil.

There are a myriad of references in the Bible that teach the Elohim and the Father are separate powers. Furthermore Jesus himself said that he came to reveal the Father, this was the duty of the divine Son. The Elohim never revealed the Father because they tried to usurp his authority and claim themselves as being the only Gods. And Ialdabaoth set himself above all that is called God or that is worshipped, so that he as God sat in the Temple of God showing himself to be God. But the true Temple of God is the spirit-veiled child, which lives in biological bodies. Whether you are an ancient Israelite and live by the teachings of the Temple or a modern day Christian that live by the teachings of the so-called church, if you have not the testimony of the Father then you are not of the Father, the one Jesus came to reveal. You have been separated and blinded. He must be revealed so you can enter the Holy of Holies within yourself, where the Father of all spirits dwells. For deep within us reigns the true spirit of righteousness that needs not be

63

jealous in any form. What God do you worship? The one that takes vengeance on his people or the one that sends the light to save his people? You can't have both!

THE LUCIFER REBELLION

Does the Bible indicate there was a rebellion among the Gods? There is a twofold teaching that needs to be revealed here. Who was Lucifer? Lucifer had great power as a divine Lord and one of the hierarchies, reigning as an archangel. Lucifer was known as the god who tried to set himself above all that was called god or worshipped. He was then cast out of his first estate and made to rule within the matter creations. He caused a great following to serve him. Lucifer had his own angels, all the beings of light that fell in the day that the gods warred against one another. MARDUK was the leader of the rebellion. This was the first sign that everything is duplicated in the matter world from the spirit world. This was the first enactment of the law, reaping what you sow. Ialdabaoth left the Father/Mother Spirit and entered into the shadow worlds and claimed he was the only God. Marduk, as one of the high-ranking angels of Ialdabaoth, then rebelled against him, leading a huge army, which became the black legions. Marduk, one of the Chief warriors, was known by the Sumerians as Enki's son, was responsible for giving the name to the planet Mars, and through our mythology we know Mars as the *god of war*. So also was Marduk a god of war. It was then that the proverbial war in heaven took place that I will explain in more detail towards the end of the book. So Lucifer is a representation of both the shadow rebellion and the spiritual fall from paradise. Lucifer is Anu-Laldabaoth!

WHO ARE THE ANGELS?

As I return to the Bible I will take up where I left off to tie this picture together. In the creation week we have always been taught that everything was created within these 7 days. Yet you notice that there is no mention of the angels. Why are they not mentioned? Leaving something this important out either implies editing or a mystical secret was kept from mankind. What really are angels anyway? What is their purpose? There are millions of people who believe in angels either through religious dogma, or literal experience of contact with these divine entities. It is necessary to understand that the term angel means nothing more than a messenger sent forth. There are angels that exist within the spirit realm as spirit entities. There are angels that also have biological bodies. Angels have one characteristic that humans do not have by virtue of the veil. Angels are able to access powers from within themselves that we have forgotten due to our transition in the lower dimension.

The Bible declares that man was created for a little while lower than the angels. It means we have the same characteristics as angels but while living in the flesh and blood garments, we do not know how to use them. Jesus said that at the time of entering beyond the veil, we would become like the angels. This does not mean we are changing into angels, it means we will recognize that we are already like the divine gods from antiquity. There are some angels that are light bringers and some that work for darkness. Some are in the veil or have been, others have never experienced the veil of flesh. There are two types of Angels, the original perfect ones and Anu's angels.

WHO ARE THE FALLEN ONES?

The question then remains, are we the fallen ones that the Bible makes mention of? In the Old Testament there was a Hebrew word that will define these questions: Nephilm. It simply means those that fell from above, or those that have fallen to earth. In the 6th chapter Genesis it speaks of the sons of god intermingling and marrying the daughters of men. Also in Numbers 13:33 it reveals that Giants are the children of Anak or ANU. When the gods from above, meaning the Planet Nibiru, began to have sexual relations in Genesis 6 with the human daughters, offspring were created that the Bible calls Giants. "There were also giants in those days, and even afterwards..." The Hebrew word for giants is Nephilm. The Nephilm are the Elohim/ANUNAKI from Nibiru, the Giants are the Children of

ANAK born to human women via intercourse with the Nephilm. These are two of the Nephilm types. The humans on the other hand were the subjects of the Nephilm by reason of being created by them. But the law of one revealed that these other beings were not to mate with those of their creation. The humans came under control of these gods because humanity was deceived in paradise and became blinded to their true origin. And then sent to be under the rule of those that caused their fall by free will choice. Do not forget this. The Nephilm in essence kidnapped humanity by tricking them after we were trapped. However in turn we are to follow these captors until we understand how to break free from bondage! So in truth, both human and the Elohim are those that fell into darkness!

Genesis 6:1-2,4 "And it came to pass, when men began to multiply on the face of the earth, and daughters were born unto them. *That the sons of God* saw the daughters of men that they were fair; and they took them wives of all which they chose...There were giants in the earth in those days; and also after that. When the *sons of god came unto the daughters of men,* and they bare children to them. The same became mighty men, which were of old, men of renown."

Numbers 13:33 "And there we saw the giants/Nephilm the sons of ANAK-(ANUNAKI- ANU)"

The Nephilm are beings that have much greater technology than earthlings have. Plus they are able to use internal powers that we lost. Mind communication, levitation, healing, etc... But they have and continue to share that technology and the knowledge of some of the internal powers we already have, with the human race whenever they see fit. All technology comes from the Nephilm. Nothing originates from earthlings. Somehow someway we are given this knowledge, as the gods deem fit or by inspiration of God within. We would still be cavemen if the ANUNAKI and other higher evolved races had not increased our awareness at different times throughout the ages. Studies have shown that there are villages with people who have never seen civilization, and these poor people remain

66

for thousands of years as if they never passed beyond the cavemen status. However when one of them was removed from these pathetic groups and brought into civilization it was only a matter of time that they could relate to the higher status in life. This is all caused because we have been blinded, not because we can't learn!

The Lucifer story was given to mankind to teach everyone about their fall from paradise. Our fall took place before the first day of the creation week thereby necessitating the need for light. The proof of this declares that we all existed before the creation of the world. Earth just happens to be our training ground now but we have existed on other realms, dimensions and yes, Planets.

Ephesians 1:4 "According as he has chosen us in him BEFORE THE FOUNDATIONS OF THE WORLD..."

The Father of lights, through the divine Son chose us before the matter universes existed.

Ephesians 4:6 "One God and Father of all, who is above all, and through you all, and in you all."

This is why the divine Father of all spirits is not the God of the Old Testament. The true Father is in all, and above all. Nothing exists without him. And yet no one can know the unknown Great Spirit unless they learn of him within their own self. He is a part of all including the Elohim. No entity can ever stand up and claim there are no other Gods. For the Father of ONE is in all, and there are many Gods. And we are all Gods. However, we are all ONE!

FUNDAMENTAL THEOLOGY?

As we return to the Bible to discuss some fundamental theology I believe it is necessary to establish this mystery to unveil the forthcoming gnosis. In the Garden of Eden the Bible teaches us that the serpent was the one who caused the great fall. This is both true and false. The Bible actually shows that there was a duality within the mystery to define our fall from

67

before the world. What happened millions, maybe even billions of years ago, realizing time is not calculable in many of these events, was kept away from the knowledge of the human race for a reason. It is my conjecture and will continue to be throughout this entire book, that the Father of Lights was never planning on destroying his children. But in fact had figured out a most ingenious way to save them without ever having to interfere, except sending the divine son into the shadow worlds.

The Father designed a method using our fall to lead us back through the very sin we had committed. If knowledge of good and evil caused us to fall in the first place, then knowledge of good and evil will be the formula to get all of his children back. The serpent was then both our friend and our enemy. Training for self-awareness became the real tool.

I believe all matter world elements are the fallen ones. Everything and everyone that lives in the shadows are the fallen children of the Father. The Father could never attach himself to sin of any kind, because the universal spiritual vibration is perfection. So he allowed some of the shadow realm to take on the authority of the Father to establish laws and rituals, until the divine Son could be witnessed from within each and every child.

THE GNOSIS IS ABOUT TO BE REVEALED

Adam and Eve represent the two-flamed beings of the Father/Mother God. Each spirit entity represents the Father/Mother and has the two-fold nature about his or her self. When God told Adam he was incomplete without Eve, this was acknowledging the first mystery of man. Adam and Eve, like each of us, are a complete whole entity that divided when we fell. We are all complete divine beings with both characteristics of the Male and Female. This was enlightened when the Elohim said let us make man in our image. They then made male and female in the image of God. The mystery was to teach us that in the spirit realm where we came from we were twin beings, of the one nature. When the serpent, which was our need to experiment with things, spoke to us, we then left the perfect realm of spirit and got lost in the shadows. When we did this we divided into separate beings that lost the oneness of the whole. When we entered into the flesh we lost our complete identity thereby decreeing our loneliness in the flesh. Adam was incomplete until his other half was brought to his side. And then the two could become one, but only in the flesh. They were still separated by the veil. Paul mentions this when he declares those that marry become one flesh. This was symbolic of our true spiritual union. But the marriages in the flesh will not remain after you leave the veil, because they were only illustrations or mirror images of the true union of spirits. That is why at physical death the marriage is then decreed over!

SPIRITS PROJECTED AWAY FROM LIGHT

When we fell we projected away from the pure soul spirit that the Father had created out of himself. For this pure spirit could not be defiled in any way. We had to project away as light is projected away from the projector. When we did this we separated from our tree of life, and entered the realm of good and evil. Our pure soul spirit no longer had control over the lower projected soul, thereby causing our kidnapping by the Elohim that could control the shadow world, and all of us in it. Our eating of the forbidden fruit manifested this; for the day we ate of the forbidden fruit we would surely die. And we did as a result of coming into a lower dimension creating our downfall from the perfect spirit world. Again it was only an illusion. And as such we died by losing all memory of our eternal fountain of youth, while being wrapped in the garments of decaying matter.

We forgot our heritage and lost our true origin. The light was taken away and we have remained in darkness of the shadow worlds. When the Elohim gave us fig leaves to clothe our nakedness this was to teach that we were being clothed by a decaying substance, the biological matter. From that day forward as long as we walked in the flesh and blood we would wear biological clothing to cover the fallen projected-soul spirit, which the Bible calls the spirit in Man. Without the Christ, the divine light, we would never recognize our true origin. We would then be forever damned in the lower shadows of hell or the symbolic grave of death. This is the true eternal damnation. This is the ongoing judgement! It is being trapped within the cycles within the veil.

The Father's plan from the very beginning was to save all the fallen children; his decree was then established, *"Let there be light!"* The reason the Bible speaks of an inheritance given to those that are to access eternal life, is because we are already the true children of the Father. The Bible states, "Flesh and Blood cannot inherit eternal life." *If we are not already the true spirit children of the eternal Father/Mother spirit; then we have no inheritance, there would be no eternal life.* We are the perfect humanity from before the foundations of this world!

If spirit beings could be led astray from before the foundations of the earth by seeking the knowledge of good and evil, then experience would need to become our new teacher for divine awareness. We can now experience the deeds of our actions as well as the rewards for doing right, by being placed in vessels that occupy a lower conscious awareness that can experience things that spirits cannot. By wearing biological garments we can experience death. When death hangs over one's head then your experiences become real even while living in illusion. If there were no penalties for your actions, then there would be no concept of unrighteousness. But one must remember good and evil only exist within the matter illusion. Once you return to the Father's realm the concepts that exist are Father/truth, Mother/wisdom and Son/enlightenment. When we fell in the garden we could not have had the awareness needed to teach our inadequacies unless we experienced our decisions. When we live in a matter world defined by our lower dimensional setting we can then experience the results of what we do, right or wrong. This then becomes the pattern designed to perfect gods.

THE SHADOW WORLD IS THE REAL HELL

Life in the matter world truly then becomes the hell separated from heaven. When God said let there be light, we were roaming around in other dimensions of our own making, and we became lost from the mind spirit awareness of our Father/Mother guides. We were in darkness unable to visualize where we had come from. So Jesus' sacrifice was to teach us that the ancient Son, the light of the divine mind of the Father was slain by our leaving the light and entering darkness. Then Jesus' resurrection was symbolic to teach that the mind of the Father, the light would overcome darkness. So the Father's plan to restore the light to all his fallen children is the true meaning of Jesus' sacrifice.

The Father has never had a plan to destroy anyone. Christ the Lamb slain before the foundations of the earth was to instruct how the plan would eventually cover all. As in Adam all die, as in Christ all shall be made alive.

THE DIVINE SON ENTERS THE SHADOWS

The Only Begotten Son came into the shadow lands to define us as being the true children of God. The SON, the LOGOS was 'US'. When The Father/Mother spoke the Word/SON, the light of God's mind-consciousness, was separated to share their identity and source as a sign of what we are all like. When our projected-soul spirit separated from the true pure soul presence we were as a fallen SON separated from the FATHER. This light of the pure soul spirit would have to enter into the fallen projected soul spirit to bring awareness back to the source. We would then take hold of this light, the CHRIST child in all of us, and begin to mature using the pure source as a guide, while melding together within the divine Son, making us co-heirs with Christ and heirs of the Father.

Once this takes place we can then reunite with the Father our pure-soul spirit which I will discuss more in the next two mysteries, the I AM and the Christ.

71

The Father is where the idea, the mind originates. The Son then speaks the idea in the WORD form. Then the matter creation, which we have become as a result of our fall, will be the idea created in spoken Word. This is how higher evolved beings can create using this power. It is how we can also create. Many have taken this beautiful parallel and tried to place an erroneous concept in it called the trinity. The true divine tripartite is the Father/idea, the Son/spoken Word, and the holy spirit/action- the power in US. If we do not play the co-creator's role by bringing into manifestation what the Father desires through the Son, then there is no trinity. The spiritual Father, the spiritual Son and the spirit made matter. The Father is really our portion of the pure soul-spirit he created out of himself. The Son becomes the projected soul-spirit from this Father. And the Holy Spirit is the matter creation that we find ourselves in now linked with the FATHER. This is what is meant when it states that GOD or god's spirit dwells in the Temple of God. The Temple that houses the projected soul spirit of the Father is the human being. And when the divine Son is revealed, your spirit- the spirit in man then becomes the Holy Spirit, thereby revealing your higher presence, the Father.

FREE WILLED CHOICE GIVEN

The spirit Father is a force, an energy that is everywhere omnipresent and omniscient throughout the cosmos, and without form continues to grow and increase in knowledge, glory and wisdom. As this awesome force thinks it materializes its reality through its creation. But because of darkness that projected its duplicity in the spiritual realm it was then necessary to establish what one may call, "a line drawn in the sand." Life and death would then become the battle cry heard in all dimensions and universes.

This would distinguish between good and evil within the shadow lands. The light became the only hope, and the only way, "Walk you in it." Those that respond to the light would be called the children of the Father/light or God-Good. Those that reject the light would be called the children of the devil/darkness. Devil equals "darkened evil!"

The history of the human race has witnessed duplicate realities to teach a veiled people of their true realities. God manifested unto us the spoken Word so that we could comprehend these ancient mystical teachings.

Human beings were not placed into the flesh to experience the spiritual. On the contrary, they came here to the lower vibration dimension as spirit beings to experience through the flesh.

The Father through the fall of his children devised a plan to allow his children to experience realities cut off from eternity within time and space. We could then continue for as long as it takes to recreate experiences over and over again. To replay events until we finally understand something is out of sync here.

As we live through the continuous cycle of cycles we can be brought into this fleshly realm hundreds or thousands of times, if need be, to become aware of our true source of light. The Father in his ultimate mercy is allowing us to take as much time as each and every one of us needs and at the same time, not really taking any time, spiritually speaking. It will all be accomplished in instantaneous fashion. Why? Because time and space do not exist within the spirit realm. We are occupying one of many dimensions at the same exact time to learn and grow. The Father is forever patient, he needs not be jealous, and he has no need for timetables. He is not a hard master ready to strike at a moment's notice. We are here learning lessons, but this is only the beginning of the mysteries. What we see here on this plane of awareness is only one of many dimensions that we individually exist in at present.

When I began to comprehend some of these mysteries it was like a light turned on within me, no pun intended. It began to make sense out of a huge list of confused ideologies. It feels as though one always knew this to be true and wondered how did we forget. I realized that humanity was experiencing the many aspects of life and death for more profound and greater reasons than religion and science was offering. Yes, Christianity would always speak of a loving God who wanted to save us, but then in the next breath they would talk about an angry God who would punish, avenge and destroy.

WHAT DO HUMANS NEED TO BE SAVED FROM?

It only made sense to inquire about what we were being saved from. It appeared we were being saved from an angry God who wanted to save us. Talk about a paradox! Well, please forgive me, I would never want to live with any being, including a God, who was like a mad scientist. This reminds me of when a person who is an alcoholic comes home and beats his wife and children. Then the next day he wakes up and apologizes and reconfirms how much he still loves his family. And then the next night he comes home again and beats the hell out of them again. This is not love. Granted these are human weaknesses, but what is God's excuse? As I examined these issues it led me back into the Garden to realize that something was terribly wrong with the God concept that Christianity and other religions were espousing. In fact the three main religions all came from the same source.

When you seriously read the account of the Garden of Eden and Adam and Eve you have to realize that something is really crazy if we continue to believe what religion has told us. Looking at it from religious viewpoints, why would God place two humans in a beautiful Garden paradise and then allow some evil serpent to enter this perfect realm? Almost as if God knew nothing about this. And this serpent literally screws up their lives and all of humanity. Supposedly this serpent of great and mighty wisdom had the ability to sway gods, and now here he is messing with two mortals that don't have any power to protect themselves from this onslaught of deception. And then religion tries to tell us because the poor helpless humans gave into this god, now all humanity comes under a curse for the sin that two people committed that frankly the world has never known. As my head began to spin, I had to wonder???

Let us get real here for a second! We can spout our religious rhetoric about how great and loving this God is, and that he wants to save us from hell. But why didn't this loving God stop the evil serpent from spinning his damnable web in the first place? Furthermore, *why did God allow the serpent into the Garden?* I thought it was off limits to evildoers. The Bible seems to indicate that as soon as Adam and Eve made one lousy mistake they were history. It is like the OLD umpire saying, "Yer outa here!" But the serpent on the other hand, is allowed to roam paradise freely hurting and destroying anyone he desires. It doesn't add up using religious rhetoric!

Using the age old accepted ideas that most are familiar with, it would sound something like this: We learned that there was a war in heaven. Lucifer and his minions fought against all that was good and righteous. However God became angry and decided to banish these evildoers for all eternity. Except it appears that he never banished them after all. These beings have been around for possibly hundreds of thousands of years. They have been allowed to deceive these poor helpless creatures at will without ever having to pay for their crime. But humanity is the sucker that got stuck between good and evil. And because of this, humanity is now paying for the evil they were lured into, as if they could have ever fought it in the first place.

Putting this in even greater perspective, we have come to believe that humans were created as possible replacements for those that fell in the heavens. So in actuality one would suppose that God decided to create humans based on this scenario. However these newly fashioned and formed beings had no savvy to ascertain the wiles and deceit of a devil/god.

Now this all-powerful wonderful God took this newly formed creature and placed it in a type of utopia, a Garden of Eden, Paradise. This brand new creation was no match for the gods. They were puny, fleshly, material based creatures. Then this all-loving creator decides, let's send the evil one into the

Garden to see if he can cause these peons to screw up because he did such a grand job ruining spiritual beings' lives.

ARE WE BEING BLAMED FOR ADAM'S SIN?

Are you starting to get the vision here? A loving Father who would decree to send his only Son to save these poor creatures would have never allowed, or sent evil into his domain to cause this type of havoc. He could have never allowed the serpent into the Garden in the first place. Orthodox Christianity teaches that Adam committed what is called the original sin that follows forward unto humanity causing everyone to become sinners no matter who you are or what you do. How could a sin committed by one man be passed down to everyone else? Remember through the last mystery we discovered that sins could not pass from one to another. Everyone is responsible for their own sins.

In reality then Adam and Eve represent us all as an allegory, a story of events that depicts all humans. And each of our sins from the past are placed right back where they originated. This is the mystical reference to the Adam and Eve story. Each of us has to resolve the problems of our own actions, and the story of Adam and Eve was actually the reference point.

Also orthodoxy teaches that Jesus died erasing the Adamic sin. Yet if you do not verbalize that you know this Jesus then you're going to suffer the wrath of God and enter a hideous torment for all eternity, for a sin that someone else committed.

Please understand I am not here to ridicule your faith. What I have been telling you applies as much for me as it would anyone else. I used to believe many of these same so-called fundamental truths, but I began to ask some serious questions. If you do not become internally aware then anyone could snow ball you into believing anything.

WHO IS THE SERPENT?

The serpent in the Garden did not enter to deceive poor helpless humans who had no power against the Gods. The serpent represents a two-fold nature of the deception in Paradise and our inner awareness of our fall from paradise. The serpent in retrospect becomes our free willed choice. The serpent was sent into the Garden to reveal to us who we really are, that we are like the Elohim who understood both good and evil, and that we cannot really die. When we were in paradise we were one of the gods, we were not poor helpless humans.

ALL HAVE SINNED

The Bible declares, "All have sinned and come short of the glory of God." It wasn't because someone had sinned for us; it was because we sinned from the beginning. Everyone that has been veiled has sinned, only the Light has never sinned. I will explain this mystery later!

It is my belief that the Planet Earth as well as many other planets were training grounds for the fallen ones. It was established to help us regain our eternal identity from our Father and at the same time become like him through free willed choice. We have existed for a very long time. I'll keep repeating this!

We have all been sent to various dimensions within the shadow realms of the kingdom to train for higher levels of consciousness. There are high-ranking Lords, Emissaries, Angels, etc... who reign within the shadow kingdom under the Father of all spirits. But the world they reign in is good and evil; not the perfection from above that is with the Father. We all have to come to that perfection again before we can enter beyond the shadow. Our friction of force between two natures, good and evil, regains this perfection that can only come from the shadow lands. These shadow lords that exist have also gone through much of the training that we are going through. Remember that it is not the Father's will that any perish.

LIFE THROUGHOUT THE COSMOS

What we see here is a universe that is teeming with life in all dimensions. There are evil beings as well as righteous beings that have been training for this perfection. There is no better way to express this than to state that the shadow lords are of a higher evolution in their growth process than we are. That is why they can so easily run the show without our being able to interfere. But some of those that entered a higher evolution of consciousness began to sin even greater. Their sins led to greater darkness. Thereby we have the scriptures that teach of Satan and the demons. These are characteristics given to those that had entered a higher awareness and rebelled from a more perfected state. They seduce others by their characteristics such as: greed, lust, envy, jealousy, hatred, self-centeredness, dishonesty and lack of concern. These have the ability to lead others in humanity to approach life with these same characteristics. However those that are rising to higher levels of perfection have opposite characteristics. They are becoming more like the Father. Such as: love, joy, peace, goodness, gentleness, kindness, long suffering, temperance etc...

There are angels that are very loving and are becoming more and more like the Father. They reign from the spirit realm. Some have become masters! They have discarded their biological vessels and received better vessels for their duties. You see, within the shadow realm still exists the spirit realm. It would almost be like a underground flowing river. The earth on both sides is the shadow realm and the river is the spirit. If you were to enter the spirit by passing through the shadow it would be like leaving the veiled body, but now existing in the spirit realm for a time being. I will explain more about this in the mystery of death and spirits. So righteousness does not necessarily exist just because you enter a spiritual realm. This explains how there can be beings of darkness living in the spirit realm within the shadow. You can enter the spirit realm yet still lack the light!

78

YOU MAY LIVE NEXT TO A SHADOW LORD

The patterns I am setting up are to show that there are powerful spirits both good and evil who live in the veil as well as the spirit realm. They are of a much higher evolution than the average person. However there are also elementals, but I will not touch on them that much in this book. If you are beginning to comprehend this mystery you will understand that evil beings do not necessarily have to be spirit entities in the sense of being outside our human dimension. These beings are also involved within the cycles, reaping what they sow. The only way to bypass the cycles, no matter what dimension you exist in, is to overcome and become perfect as your Father in the proverbial heaven is perfect. It takes schooling and training!

Then you can bypass the cycles and pass the four lower bodies, which will be explained later. I have to take these things one step at a time for you to comprehend the necessary elements needed to understand these mysteries.

You will come to understand that angels and devils can exist within the human form-the veiled presence, as they can from the spirit form-the unveiled presence. They can incarnate within these worlds just as you and I do.

BIBLE IDENTIFIES LUCIFER AS A MAN

Ezekiel illustrated in chapter 28 that the ancient king known as Tyrus was actually Lucifer. Notice below this description of Tyrus as Lucifer.

Ezekiel 28:3,8,9,12-15 "Behold thou art wiser than Daniel...They shall bring you down to the pit, and you shall die the deaths of them that are slain...Will you say before the one that kills you, I AM a GOD? But you shall be a man and no God in the hand of him that kills you...Son of man take up lamentation upon the king of Tyrus...You have the full sum of wisdom, and perfect in beauty. You were in the Garden of Eden. Every precious stone...was prepared in you in the day that you were created. Thou are thy anointed Cherub that covers...You were perfect in the days that you were created."

We are witnessing a two-fold example of this man called Tyrus who is the incarnated Lucifer. As well we are recognizing that Lucifer is like all of us. We were all in the Garden of Eden and we were perfect from the day we were created, until we fell into these lowly bodies and would then see death as a mere human. It finishes off by showing that Lucifer would be destroyed in the fire. This is mystical language that all will either be purified through the cycles of fire or ascend to their throne. Notice Isaiah describes the same setting from a different viewpoint but establishing that Lucifer as well as all of us are incarnated as spirits living in the flesh. But there is an important key here, who was it that claimed to be God in the Garden of Eden? Well, it wasn't the serpent. Think about that for a while!

Isaiah 14:12-16 "How are you fallen Lucifer, son of the morning? How are you cut down to the ground, which did weaken the nations? For you have said in your heart, I will ascend unto heaven. I will exalt my throne above the stars of God. I will sit also upon the mount of the congregation, in the sides of the north. I will ascend above the heights of the clouds. I will be like the Most High. Yet you shall be brought down to hell, (the veiled ones) to the sides of the pit. (earth) They that see you would not uphold you, saying, 'IS THIS THE MAN THAT MADE THE EARTH TO TREMBLE, THAT DID SHAKE KINGDOMS?'"

I find it very interesting that these verses seem to indicate what the Gnostics would call Ialdabaoth. And what the Sumerians called Anu. Although these names may intertwine with one another, they may also have representations of other beings known and unknown. These beings that appeared before man as being great and powerful are no greater than we are. Once they are veiled they are like us, just mere men and women. These scriptural stories are to teach all of us about what we really are. Lucifer was always known as the shining star of the dawn and may have represented also the first born of the Sumerian Enki as Marduk. Marduk tried to overthrow Enlil. And also represented Laldabaoth and Enlil. That is why there are a myriad of references in the Bible that show how the first born son always seems to lose his inheritance to the second son. I find this remarkable when considering what the Sumerians taught concerning Enlil and Enki. Enki was the first born of ANU, and Enlil the second child became the favorite. Again patterning designs set in the heavens. Were the Gnostics correct in saying that laldabaoth claimed to be the only God, and there were to be no other Gods but him? Is this not what the scriptures say about Lucifer? Did not the god that spoke to Moses claim to be the only God? Did not Moses and the Israelites believe in God all their lives while living in Egypt, but when Moses left Egypt he met a God whom he did not know, and had to ask his name?

IS GOD PLAYING FAVORITES?

Let's review this equation from another aspect that has been accepted by orthodoxy. Why would God allow the evil beings that roam the spirit world to remain for thousands upon thousands of years, but the poor helpless humans are going to burn in hell after a mere 70 years, if they are lucky? Is God playing favorites? If these beings are that powerful and roam the world of darkness to destroy, then why does God allow them to keep going? Why didn't God destroy them as some feel he plans to do with us? This sounds very fishy one way or the other, if you ask me!

All right, how about another angle! Would God decide to destroy his first children, the sons of darkness but save these poor creatures called humanity that are even more easily deceived? Now some may reply to this, "Jesus sacrificed for us." Then why didn't God have a sacrifice for his first children? We are all his children! If he doesn't care for his first children then what makes you believe he really cares for you?

The Father loves all his children whether you are in darkness or light, you are his children. The Bible unravels this mystery by saying God is both the God to the Israelite and the Gentile. There is neither Male nor female, Greek or Jew, everyone is equal. Jesus did not appear on this planet to save only a few while the many were destroyed for all eternity. Jesus came to show everyone their origin, so all could be saved. However, neither Jesus nor anyone else can take us out of the problems we made for ourselves. You can repeat his name a thousand times and it will accomplish nothing for you. Jesus came to show us the way out of something we created for ourselves, and then he said, "Follow me, as I follow the Father." He was telling us what to do, he wasn't doing anything for us.

A blueprint was given to ancient Israel that shadowed the true plan of salvation, but it could not save you. There was no eternal life or salvation in this blueprint. The shadow Lords are unable to offer anyone this. Only your Father has eternal life to give. When Jesus walked this earth he understood this gnosis. He never tried to do away with the blueprint. What he did was impart gnosis about what the blueprint means spiritually. As the old law taught an eye for an eye, Jesus revealed that one was not to take vengeance by his or her hand. So why did the law teach an eye for an eye? Because the shadow lords saw the spiritual blueprint of Karma, reaping what you sow and they tried to parallel it in the lower matter world. It was a physical manifestation teaching that by law you would reap unto yourselves what you have sowed. But since the lower matter veiled beings could not correctly understand how administration of Judgement would be handled they were instructed to act out the punishment in the flesh to give a physical awareness to the spiritual law.

The shadow Lords didn't care because they know that we really don't die, you just leave the veil. This is why the Bible teaches, "Vengeance is mine, sayeth the Lord." It is not because God is personally going to punish you. It is because within the laws are embedded reactions to every action. Everything you do carries with it a return trip of that which you caused, good or evil.

Ancient Israel was given this blueprint to act out in the flesh what was to be later understood in the spirit. As long as darkness covered Israel they would never know the true meaning of their own laws. Jesus came to teach the spiritual interpretation of the law. Once you were internally enlightened by this indoctrination you would then recognize the spiritual law written within your heart, as Jeremiah the prophet said would one day occur.

Humanity needs to understand that we all come from a very big family and we are all brothers and sisters in the light. We must begin to truly love one another! If you fail to recognize this internally then you are still in darkness that is divided from the light.

THE BIBLE CAN BE DANGEROUS IF MISUNDERSTOOD!

This book that we have today called the Bible is an historical document of events that took place over a very long period of time. But it is a very dangerous book for the novice, because it is incomplete. The Bible shows patterns in the flesh that if understood would reveal the spirit. The problem is that so many take the Bible literally and it becomes a book of damnation. They start preaching a fire, hell and brimstone type of God that is angered and setting out to destroy humanity in the worst of all conceived ways, unless you happen to be some of the lucky ones who can quote the name Jesus. If you can go into this book and recognize some of the spiritual parallels within the written letter, then maybe you will begin to understand some of the hidden mysteries.

CAIN, ABEL AND SETH

In the Beginning we learned that Cain and Abel were the two children born to Adam and Eve. Cain killed his brother Abel. This short little topic ought to be ringing some bells in your ears if you have been following this gnosis all the way through. The purpose of much of this documentation was to enlighten the truth seeker through analogy and metaphor by using allegorical stories.

Notice the Bible seems to indicate Cain was the firstborn. Eve had declared, I have received a Son of the Lord. The Gnostics believed that both Cain and Abel were the offspring of the shadow Lords. The Sumerians teach these were Enki's two sons. Even though the Bible stated that Adam knew Eve, it may have not had the same meaning we have all been taught, or it was added to dispel the truth. I will explain why! What did Eve mean when she stated she had received a son from the Lord? Was Cain the son of one of the Gods? As the story plays out we learn that Abel was born second. Some have even believed that Abel was Cain's twin. But the identifying factor in all this is when Seth the third son was born. Genesis 5:3 reveals that when Adam had Seth, he had begotten a son in his own likeness, and after his own image. Why is the description here parallel to the description with man being created in God's image and likeness? Was this to verify that Seth was truly the first-born Son of Adam and Eve's likeness, whereas the other sons were made in the image and likeness of the shadow Lords? Seth was the first born son to Pigeradamus in the perfect humanity.

It is possible to ascertain through these scriptures that something has indeed been revealed through the strange use of terminology. When we see more of the parallels it is possible to see the whole picture come to light, as above so below.

In the flesh Adam and Eve represented the Father/Mother Spirit. Cain represented the first-born son's betrayal and entering into darkness. Abel represented the second son of the light that was slain by darkness. Seth then became the reality born in the flesh to become the Word made manifest in the flesh. Seth's Word would be the enlightenment towards life. Walk you in it!

ANALOGIES AND TYPES

I cannot emphasize this enough; the Bible is a coded book of mystery teaching an ancient knowledge that belongs to our heritage. From the line of Seth came two groups of people: the promised ones, who actually can be anyone and the bondage ones, the Israelites. From the lineage of Cain came what the Bible refers to as the Gentiles, but these could also partake of the promise. Abraham was the Father to the promised children. Moses was the Father to those who were in bondage, the Israelites. As we put this gnosis together it becomes quite apparent that many things were revealed through shadows or types. Abraham represented the promise, but when Jacob was born, God changed his name to Israel. And it was Jacob/Israel who first went into slavery in Egypt. The bondage was to teach of our captivity within the veil. The promise was to teach of our origin through internal gnosis and our freedom. When you understand this story then you can understand where Joseph the first-born son unto Rachel plays into this scenario. Joseph became the light manifesting within the hierarchy of Egypt. For his brothers who entered darkness thought Joseph had been killed. Just as when we left the Garden we thought the light was slain. But it appeared later manifested into the flesh for our hope.

Joseph, as a representative of the light, loved his fallen brothers dearly, and was able to save them from disaster. But again all these were just types and parallels of what took place before the foundation of the world. Throughout the entire Old Testament these parallels continued to manifest through real people who were living their lives in the veil. These types also revealed through the different races and nations that there was more than one type of god who fell from the beginning. There are many types of gods who live throughout the universes masked by their veil. But there would come a time that the light would so shine that all would understand eternal life belongs to everyone, not just this group or that, or this race or that. When the light of the Word of God entered the man Jesus it was revealed that in the light there is no separation. There is neither Jew nor Greek, nor Male or Female, nor Bond or Slave, all are to become one in Christ the light, the manifestation of the

Father. This was the true Gospel; everything else was a deception.

So Adam and Eve set forth two separate races, those that represent the fallen ones from above, the darkness, and those that represent the children who fell under their power. Understand I am not speaking of races in the sense of color. I am talking about representations of higher things. There are two types of the fallen gods, those who have the power and those that come under that power. In humanity you see these same two groups; those that have the power and those that come under the power.

The mystery of the veil teaches us that we are all veiled within the shadow lands. The veil hides the truth from humanity. Even the Apostle Paul spoke of the veil when he said the reading of the Old Testament would never take away the veil. This reveals that even if you followed the shadow lords perfectly you would still remain in bondage. There was no salvation in that law. You would still be veiled! The removal of the veil can only occur upon gnosis, internal awareness. This takes the Father's consciousness through the divine Son. In the Gospels it taught that when Jesus finally succumbed to mortal death the veil that separated the partition between the outer temple and the inner most holy was torn in two pieces. Gnosis, inner knowledge tears the veil away from inside your temple. When you become aware of the light of the Father then you may enter beyond the veil and see the Father face to face. You then become a priest after the order of Melchizadek, as Jesus did. You are then of the High Priesthood of the Father. As the Apostle John stated, when you recognize the light of Christ, then you will know you were not born of flesh and blood, nor of the will of man, but you were born of God.

The terminology here is clear, the word "were" means past tense. We were born as spirit children of the Father, and that will be revealed when the veil is torn in two by the light of this same Father.

THE MYSTERY OF THE VEIL: WE ALL DWELL IN PHYSICAL TABERNACLES!

We are children of the Most-High Spirit Father/Mother and we dwell in physical tabernacles in the wilderness of shadows/Sin. Paul taught that if our temple were to cease to function and perish, we would still go on day by day. The real being of who we are is inside this veil of flesh. It isn't the flesh. Flesh and blood have no inheritance of eternal life. This belongs to only the preexisting family members. And since the Father is spirit, so are we!

Another Biblical story that brings to light this awareness is the story of the prodigal son, about a Father who had two sons who were to receive their inheritance. One of the sons rebelled against the father and took his inheritance and spent it unwisely. Afterwards the son realized he had erred and returned to the father. The father opened his arms and welcomed him back, and reset his status as it had been before. Notice the parallel? Both these sons had already been with the father to gain their inheritance, but one left. I think that is clear enough.

Even after this entire thesis that I am bringing forward now, many will still be subjugated to the veil and believe we are nothing more than flesh and blood humans. I repeat to all that believe this from a religious viewpoint, "Flesh and Blood has no inheritance of eternal life." Flesh and blood is only a shadow creation of the real. It is an illusion, it is not real, and it is decaying matter that will forever cease to exist once this body dies.

We were created perfect but the dishonor came when we fell and lost our divine nature by being veiled in fig leaves.

Ephesians 3:3-5,9 "How that by revelation he made known unto me the mystery...Whereby when you read, you may understand my knowledge in the mystery of Christ. When in other ages was not made known unto the sons of men...and to make all men see what is the fellowship of the mystery, which from the beginning of the world has been hid in God..."

WE ARE THE MYSTERY THAT WAS HIDDEN FROM BEFORE THE FOUNDATION OF THE WORLD

As you read more of Paul he declares in Ephesians 1:4 that we are the ones chosen before the foundations of the world. We are the mystery that has been hid in God, but now revealed to us through Jesus our Christ.

Paul revealed this great mystery in one of the most powerful Gnostic scriptures in the entire Bible.

II Corinthians 3:14-18 "But their minds were blinded; for until this day remains the same veil which is not removed by reading of the Old Testament; which veil is removed away in Christ...Nevertheless when it shall turn to the Lord the veil shall be taken away. Now the Lord is spirit and where the spirit of the Lord is there is liberty. BUT WE ALL WITH UNVEILED FACES BEHOLDING AS IN A MIRROR THE GLORY OF THE LORD, ARE CHANGED INTO THE SAME IMAGE FROM GLORY TO GLORY, EVEN AS BY THE SPIRIT OF THE LORD."

Paul is declaring that if you looked into a glass and saw beyond the veil that covers your true identity, you would then see the same image of the Lord whom you seek, for we are the SONS OF GOD.

What we all seek is behind the veil, inside this very flesh and blood, the true "I AM" of the Father of all Glory.

MYSTERY THREE
The Mystery of the I AM

The term 'I AM' was given to Moses at Mt. Horeb, when he asked the angel of the Lord, "Who shall I tell the people sent me?" And the Angel said, "I AM that I AM. Thus shall you say unto the children of Israel, 'I AM' has sent me unto you." The name 'I AM' is an identifying mark on all of the Father's children. Jesus said, "Before Abraham was, I AM." Jesus took this name while describing himself many times.

He used the name often to express his personal connection with the Father. This identification wasn't just for Jesus or the Elohim. It is a name given by divine right to all the Children of life and light. The name of the Father is a lineage name, it is also the name of ONE. If someone came to you and asked who the Father is, you can respond, "I AM!" This is a great mystery! Once you begin to use the keys from within to unlock this mystical teaching of life then the simplicity of this dynamic proclamation will make itself known. Thereby you will understand the separation of the Father and Son and yet realize their ONENESS.

HAVE I BEEN WITH YOU SO LONG THAT YOU DO NOT KNOW THE FATHER?

When the Apostle Phillip asked Jesus to see the Father, Jesus responded by saying, "Have I been with you so long that you do not know the Father, for if you have seen me then you have seen the Father?" This magnificent response did not set well with the religious hierarchy of Jesus' day! How dare Jesus compare himself to the Great God! Jesus understood full well the mystical relationship between the Father spirit and projected soul- Son. He knew he was the offspring of his Father *and he also knew he was the Father!*

Christ is the light of the Father, or what one may call the mind consciousness of the omniscient all-spirit force. Jesus was one of many spirits that were created before the world existed. But Jesus entered the shadow lands like we all have, and the veil also masked his divine glory. He along with the rest incarnated into many lives prior to the lifetime we have come to recognize him. He learned to overcome and become as one with the Father. Remember Jesus asked in prayer in the Gospel of John before his ascension, "Father give me back the glory, which I had with you before the world was." Jesus is like each of us. He is our brother of the shadow and he is also our spirit divine brother from before the foundations of the world. And yet as all of us have, he lost that glory to regain it through the shadow worlds of trial and error, good and evil- overcoming.

This is a primary reason for his sacrifice. If Jesus was anything other than what we are then his sacrifice and overcoming the world was done in vain? What use would it do any of us? It appears, from the records, that Jesus was the first of those training on the earth to regain his divine heritage from those that had fallen from the Garden Paradise. He was then able to set a standard, A WAY, back into eternal life- *by following him.*

JESUS THE MAN WAS LIKE EACH OF US

Jesus never personally claimed he was different from any of us. Only some of his so-called followers claimed that of him. If Jesus ever thought he was a divine being special from the eternal, and different from each of us, then why did he say, "Don't call me good, there is only one good and that is God"? There are many that believe Jesus was a God who incarnated into the flesh. This is both true and false according to how you perceive this truth. Jesus like all of us is one of the Father's spirit-born children. He entered human life like we all do. I will discuss the virgin birth later. What Jesus declared is that there was only one Spirit that is true and righteous. When we occupy these lower vessels for training we are sown in corruption of the shadow world. We are by virtue of our descent into the flesh only a shadow of the true. We live in the realm of perception of good and evil. As we live in the flesh we are separated from the Father as a son journeying away from his home. We are on a quest for the Father, but while living in the lower world of matter we have to take on a separate identity to evolve into a divine spirit that will be pleasing to the Father and equal as well as an individual.

Jesus continuously recognized the separation as well as the oneness with the Father. While Jesus walked in the planes of the shadow lands he was training to ascend back to the Heart of the Flame of God just as we all do. He could claim no greater authority than any one of us could while in the flesh. If Jesus had never fallen into the shadow world and only appeared one-time as a God manifested in the human flesh about 2000 years ago, then why would he have ever said, "Don't call me good"? Why would the man Jesus separate himself from the Godhead of perfection? This would almost be a slap in the face to perfection and the Father if Jesus were a single entity called GOD as the second of a triune Godhead.

SON OF MAN AND SON OF GOD

Jesus' life went down in history being known by two epitaphs; one was Jesus the Son of Man. The other was Jesus the Son of God. The Gnostics believed that Jesus was known as the Son of Man primarily because it was believed that the Great Spirit is human. They believed that theology should actually become anthropology. They then believed that the Son of God represented Ialdabaoth as being Jesus' actual father and he was the God that impregnated Mary, thereby making Jesus the Son of Ialdabaoth. I understand their thinking but in this area I do not agree, unless Joseph was the reincarnated Laldabaoth. No matter how you might view this, man is both God and Man! We have seen how the Elohim created vessels in the past by genetic splicing and impregnating women. We have lived amongst the evolving Elohim as we have the evolving human. Was Jesus, the biological human, the offspring of an eternal

91

source? Yes and no, for his spirit within was eternal but his garment of flesh was temporary.

For the Gnostics also teach that the Elohim were angry when they recognized that the light or the Christ had entered Jesus. This is why they wanted him killed because he would turn against the Elohim that seeded him. It really matters not who seeded the vessel we abide in. It is the projected-soul within that truly counts and that belongs to the spiritual Father.

I perceive that Jesus was the Son of Man because of his lineage within the line of David. Jesus' ancestry was human. However Jesus' ancestry was also God or divine spirit, at least from his origin. So Jesus' birth and bloodline in human form represents him being the Son of Man. Jesus' divine origin represents him being the Son of God.

Jesus often said, "My Father which art in heaven," and we know that the Father is the true divine power, not Ialdabaoth. For when the God of the Old Testament was in power no man had known or seen the Father. However this implication also reveals, just as the lost Gospel of Phillip in the Nag Hammadi fragments, that if Jesus said his "Father in heaven" this also revealed that he had a human Father. Why distinguish between the two?

THE FATHER EXPERIENCES THROUGH US

Jesus like all of us has the eternal spark of the great I AM presence. While living in the veil Jesus was human just as we are human, yet at the same time we are all gods! Try not to be confused by this. When we come into the biological vessel separated from the Father we exist in a temporal state of mind. We live and die and most have no conscious awareness of their true identity. While living in this state of consciousness we are the children of good and evil. Laws were created based on these perceptions. We live and rule in worlds that follow decrees that could only apply to flesh and blood entities. We died from our heavenly existence to live in these forms to experience a training process that will yield tremendous growth and knowledge over long periods of time. These experiences that we all gain go into the oneness of all. The Father is experiencing all realities through his divine children. We in essence become the experiences of the Father in lower form. It is obvious while living in these realities that we are not what we conceive God to be. We are human! However as Jesus told those that were confronting him, "YE ARE ALL also GODS!" We may all declare this as the right of our origin, not our present state of existence.

It reminds me of the story of Anastasia, the daughter of Czar Nicholas and Alexandria. All her family had supposedly been slaughtered during a revolution to wipe out the last of the Roman Emperors. Nicholas was possibly the last of the long ruling line of "Caesar," which resulted in the shortened name Czar -'C-ZAR.' It was supposed that all of the family had been killed. However years later a young lady appeared claiming to be the daughter Anastasia, although very few believed her. Today any of us could claim our royal heritage of the Father but who would believe us? As Jesus said, you are all Gods, but who believed him? Religion today would claim this is blasphemy and you are a heretic to believe this. Therefore we present good deeds and works before the Father so we may return to the light with our own proof gaining our reward.

So let's begin with the first of the two epitaphs of Jesus as the Son of Man. To fully comprehend the name 'I AM' we first need to clear up misconceptions in the scriptures. The virgin birth needs to be brought to light or else Jesus being the Son of Man would be discredited. I had to rely on my inner wits using the knowledge of multiple sources of historical evidence and finally coming up with a conclusion that makes sense. The Gnostics most definitely received much truth, however not all their understanding was totally correct. It is very possible that Jesus was born of Ialdabaoth, as the Gnostics believe. I am trying to reason this by using many documents such as the Bible and some of the newly discovered and transcribed "Dead Sea

Scrolls." If this was the truth then it is possible Joseph was the reincarnated Ialdabaoth.

If you truly understand this mystery either of these explanations would suffice. So I will present what I believe as the best of both possibilities, always realizing I could be wrong. I have been wrong before, and I will be wrong again. This is how one learns. Stick your neck on the line and all the information comes from a thousand different sources.

VIRGIN BIRTH CONTRADICTS THE COVENANTS

I believe the virgin birth contradicts the Old and New Covenants as well as the Bible. It appears that the Dead Sea Scrolls reveal much of what the Bible was trying to teach on this subject. Granted there were so many ideologies that came out of the first century you don't really know who was passing down the truth, versus those small communities that had their own ideas. If my thesis is incorrect then the Bible is even more inaccurate than one might first believe.

Back in the days of Moses there was a teaching that a great prophet would rise from among the tribes of Israel. This was a prophetic reference by all accounts to Jesus the Christ. Later this knowledge would be interpreted by the Israelites that a Messiah would come to restore the Israelite Kingdom on earth. This Messiah would come from the direct bloodline of King David. The New Testament confirms this in several places throughout the Gospels and the book of Acts.

The question is, why King David's bloodline? All through the long struggle of the ancient Israelite tribes the Elohim placed rulers, kings, judges, prophets, writings and laws to reign over the people. It was the government that ruled Israel. This was their protection against the enemy known as the heathen, the Gentiles. The Elohim were the Gods of the Hebrews. When the Elohim set up a leader over the people, this leader would become the *Anointed One* by the Gods who ruled in secret. The Anointed One actually became the representative of God. The people accepted the Anointed One's words as if God was speaking to them personally.

Notice in Exodus 18:11-13 "Now I know the Lord is greater than all the Gods... And it came to pass on the morrow that Moses sat to judge the people."

The term Christ comes from the Greek word, Christos, and the Syriac word for Messiah, meaning the Anointed One. To better understand this theology you need to become aware of the Israelite mind being ruled by the Elohim. The Israelites knew of the many Gods that ruled over them, and they knew of the one that was greater than all.

Notice also Exodus 15:11 "Who is like unto thee O' Lord among the *GODS*. (Hebrew for Elohim)"

The Israelites were looking for another Anointed One! They were never seeking one of the gods to impregnate a woman. They were looking for a male born of a woman by the male representative of the tribe of Judah. It was through David's bloodline that the next ruling King of Israel would come. They believed this individual would overthrow the world powers that controlled Jerusalem at the time, in this case the Roman Empire. This was their projected Messiah, but looking for this Messiah was tantamount in believing God was entering personally, because the Gods gave great power and authority over to the Anointed One. So therefore the stories as they came down through the generations turned a man as the Anointed One into a God. The Hebrews gave great honor to the prophets of the past.

THE MESSIAH WAS TO BECOME KING OF ISRAEL

The Messiah, the Christ was to be the Anointed King of Israel. As long as Israel had a king they had their Messiah, the Anointed of God. But these prophecies extended into a time period where there would be no ruling King of Israel. The people would then longingly seek this predicted return of the Messiah-Christos-Anointed One.

Zedekiah was the last king of this lineage that came through the bloodline of King David. He fell to Nebuchadnezzar, king of Babylon about 585BC. Israel was without a king and a Messiah for nearly 600 years until Jesus walked this earth. Jerusalem had been sacked, burned and destroyed. And although a new Temple was built in Jerusalem twice, one by Cyrus the great king of Persia and the other by Herod the Great, the people never received their own king from David's bloodline. To interject a point here that I found fascinating, both Nebuchadnezzar the destroyer of the Temple and Cyrus the builder of the Temple were Gentile leaders who the Elohim claimed were their servants. The Elohim came to both these men to show them who they were and they both were impressed and became faithful to the Elohim's commands. This was another area that shows the Elohim were not as partial as one may believe. The Elohim ruled everyone!

As Israel awaited their Messiah it never occurred to them that their Messiah would be any different than any of them. Remember Israel recognized these Elohim as being like them but with great powers. These were beings that looked every way human, but with extraordinary miraculous powers. Israel's perception of God was quite different than our perceptions today. They saw God as more of a superman than a spirit. They were never looking for a divine spirit birth. They were looking for a man who would rightfully claim his kingdom, born from the bloodline of David. They believed this man would gain his status of Anointed One from the Elohim as soon as he became King of all Israel again.

One of the greatest proofs that Israel was not seeking a divine God as the Messiah is that they rejected Jesus because he never did take back the kingdom of Israel and rule. Till this day there are people who reject Jesus because he never fulfilled his status of being the Messiah. This is understandable when you realize what the Hebrews were looking for.

THE SPIRIT OF THE FATHER REIGNED IN THE OLD TESTAMENT

There are many today that are still waiting for this coming of the Messiah. There were a few in the Old Testament that understood some of the prophecies concerning the savior. They ascertained that a Messiah would enter that had understanding that would lead to eternal life. Men like Abraham, who gained the status as being the Father to the faithful, and some of the prophets of the Old Testament, were receiving incredible knowledge from the divine world that was bypassing the Elohim. All my years in Christianity and Biblical study I always found it incredibly strange that Abraham and his offspring were given an absolute promise for eternal life through the Christ. But as the story continued Jacob, the grandson of Abraham, was given the new name Israel, and through circumstances was led into Egypt where the offspring were in bondage for more than 430 years. After the Elohim took Israel out of bondage they made a covenant with Moses and all the children of Israel. This covenant was actually contradicting the promise. They set up a ritualistic covenant and laws of the flesh that never taught of the true eternal reward and salvation as was meant to come down from Abraham. It became obvious that something was wrong! What occurred is that a nation was chosen by the Elohim to be their loyal servants, or should I say slaves. But the promise went beyond any human covenant. It was a spiritual blessing that benefited everyone. This is what Paul was trying to teach in his letters to the Churches.

Even though the Elohim had great control the spiritual promise was finding its way through the same ones the Elohim were controlling. I have learned that truth and freedom will ultimately reign because the Father is greater than the Elohim.

SECRET SCHOOL FOR VIRGINS-MAIDENS

Israel never comprehended the mystery of the promise. They only viewed things physically because that is all the Elohim would allow. When we view the Biblical confusion of the virgin birth it is important to use some information gained from the Dead Sea Scrolls. Some of this information declared that Mary along with many young girls was trained from childhood to become the chosen one who would give birth to the next reigning Messiah. The scrolls indicate that these virgin girls were young maidens. They were trained in a secret school until about the age of 13 or 14. Afterwards they were matched with a man of the lineage of David. The group known as the Essenes, which existed during the time of Christ and revealed by the scrolls, hoped through this process that the girl would find favor with God and become the mother of the next Anointed King.

The guardians of this secret understood the Messiah would be born from the tribe of Judah. They diligently prepared these girls for this service so they could fit the mystical description. They believed the Messiah would be born of a maiden, a young girl, which in those days obviously implied a virgin.

MYSTICAL SCHOOL OPERATED BY THE ESSENES

It never occurred to the Essenes that operated these mystical schools that one of the Gods would impregnate the girl. There was no reason to believe this. For the Messiahs of the past were always human beings given the authority of the gods! But they also knew the Messiah had to be born of the lineage of David. The Essenes understood the mysteries of our eternal spark. What purpose would it fulfill for God to supernaturally intervene to impregnate Mary? First of all, God the Father is spirit. Spirit cannot impregnate flesh, only the seed of like can conceive unto like. Like produces like! This could be why the Gnostics believed that Ialdabaoth was the father of Jesus because he was also of like species to man. The Elohim could and have impregnated human females because they were the progenitors of the human race. However the Father is spirit; and spirit would be unable to interact with the flesh as a component to impregnate. Spirit is spirit, and flesh is flesh. The two shall always be separate. Light and darkness cannot intermingle, they can however coincide with each other!

Mary received the seed of man to give birth to a son. Christian churches believed centuries after Jesus walked this earth that the Adamic sin was placed upon all humanity. This was their excuse to believe that God personally had to intervene in a birth of this type. They understood that Jesus was the Son of God and in their minds this meant he was God's literal physical child, which in truth makes no sense. They taught that if Jesus were born of the male lineage of Adam then he would also be under the curse of the Adamic sin. However they ignored the prophecy that he had to come from the lineage of David, the seed of man, that being Adam. Even the Apostles taught that Jesus was of the fruit of the loins of the seed of David, or the blood lineage.

ADAMIC SIN GOES AGAINST ALL PROPHECY OF THE FUTURE MESSIAH

The concept of the Adamic sin goes against all scriptural prophecy of the coming of the Anointed One. If Jesus was not born of a human family, by the seed of the male carrier, then how could Israel have ever known where to look for the coming of the Messiah? He could then no longer legitimately be recognized as the Son of Man! It would mean the entire Old Testament prophecy that pointed the way both physically and spiritually would be bogus.

Mary was flesh and blood of the seed of man also, and she was chosen to give birth to Jesus of the human race. Why didn't the church leaders wonder about her having this Adamic sin carried through her genes? Actually they did! They believed that only the seed of the male lineage was tainted by the Adamic sin. This meant that these church leaders willfully rejected the prophecy that taught that Jesus was of the male lineage and fruit of the loins of David. Thereby coming up with a supernatural virgin birth. If Jesus wasn't the born son of David through blood then why did the church ever accept him as the Messiah? What proof would they have had? Many have come in the name of God producing great miracles but the Church never considered them as the Anointed One.

What if we were to eliminate the Adamic sin in this theory? If the Adamic sin is not true, that would imply that a child had to be born without sin. However we have learned that all have sinned by virtue of the fall from paradise. So we must conclude either Jesus was a soul-projected spirit eliminating any need to be born unto imperfect parents, or Jesus was somehow special, unique, different and had abilities none of us have. If the latter was true, there was no need for God to personally intervene, because Jesus was special, different, and unique. He wouldn't have to come under the same tests and conflicts we all endure, because he was different from us. He also did not need to be born of a human woman. Why bring a God into the flesh if he is a being representing himself as human only. It would only be a lie. He wouldn't have to be born. The birth process only applies for humans evolving through bloodlines. And Jesus didn't need a human bloodline, because as many think he was of God's bloodline and not really human.

There is a problem with this theory based on the Messiah's role to save mankind. He was supposed to be tempted as we are. It is said that he overcame the world, and that we must do the same. Jesus said, follow me! Well, that would be easy for him to say. He had it made with all those special abilities. If Jesus were unique and special and the only other God, then his life of sacrifice would only amount to ceremonial exercises to put on a show. We couldn't do what he did because we lack his spiritual aptitude. We would be doomed before we ever began. The church leaders thought about this one also. They concluded that since we can't do what Jesus did, then he did it all for us. I will address this nonsense later.

DOCTRINE OF ANTICHRIST

The Apostle John taught that if you didn't believe Jesus came into the flesh then this would become the doctrine of antichrist.

So the question remains, was Jesus a God or a man? He was both, and so are we.

If we look at all the possibilities only one answer appears to fit this dilemma. Jesus was the Son of Man by being born unto flesh and blood parents. And Jesus is the Son of the Father by virtue of being one of the divine spirits of the antiquity, like all of us! If the Gnostics are correct that Jesus was the Son of one of the shadow lords, that still creates no dilemma, because many humans are also of the bloodlines of these aliens, the shadow lords. The Elohim created the entire race of ADAM, before men began procreating within themselves. After reading the book entitled "Holy Blood, Holy Grail" by Baigent and Lincoln, as well as "Bloodline of the Holy Grail" by Gardner, there seems to be an indication that there is a secret society, which exists right up until this day that claims they have divine blood from the Gods. They have kept records of their entire genealogical line. They also claim their heritage as the bloodline of Jesus. This would then make Jesus the Son of Ialdabaoth by virtue of the entire bloodline being of the Elohim. It was known by a few in the secret society that the term Holy Grail actually means divine bloodline, translated from the words 'San Graal-holy blood,' and not a chalice or cup as many have come to believe. They claim the divine bloodline to be the reigning kings and queens throughout Europe. When one closely scrutinizes this bloodline of kings in Europe they realize that all of the powers of Europe within the last 3000 years are blood related and directly tied to the throne of England, which appears to be of the direct bloodline of King David.

The truth is that the spirit of the Father existed alongside the Elohim then and today. And within these darkened periods of time, even though many did not realize it, the spirit intervened to proclaim truth and light within a darkened people. However many would not understand until light shone from within them. That is what was meant when Jesus said, "Abraham desired to see my day," and he did. And it is also what was meant when Jesus said, "No man has known the Father but the Son."

LIKE PRODUCES LIKE SEED AFTER ITS OWN KIND

The Bible itself has strange contradictions concerning the subject of the virgin birth. One is whether Joseph was a part of this pregnancy or not. Jesus came to reveal his Father. His Father was spirit. Spirit will not impregnate flesh. The law teaches like produces like! Seed after its own seed! Either Jesus was the born son of the shadow lords or Joseph was his human Father. Either way, like had to produce like. The Father did not impregnate Mary! The true projected soul that is in all of us is of the Father; it is inside the human flesh. We are all gods incarnate! Why would the Father need to impregnate Mary with material male sperm of a human genetic composition, when the true spirit is separate from the flesh? Flesh and blood is not divine, either for Jesus or for us. That is why he said, "Don't call me (the biological container) good!" And the Bible states, "Flesh and blood does not please God. For God is spirit and we worship him in spirit and in truth."

We have learned that the vessels are the carriers of the spirit within. The vessel is sown in corruption by the very fact it is the shadow of the true. The light came into the shadow to reunite everyone with their Father/Mother Spirit. Jesus was a soul-projected spirit into the vessel born unto Mary. It matters not how the vessel came into being concerning the Father. What is important is the spirit. But in this case Jesus' vessel was to be of David's biological bloodline. For a spirit being to impregnate Mary, would tell us that flesh and blood can be as perfect as spirit. This is impossible due to its process of decay. When you look at your reflection in a mirror, which one is real? Can you interact with that image on the mirror? Of course not!

Flesh and blood is the veil that covers. Why would the Father waste his time perfecting the veil that hides the truth? The Father declared flesh and blood does not please him. This would include that the flesh and blood of Jesus didn't please the Father either. Yet we have been led to assume that the

Father went out of his way to impregnate flesh and blood. The Father wanted the son to become perfected using the inadequacies of the veil. Thereby Jesus learning obedience by those things which he suffered. The Father does not need the veil and never has. For the Father to produce a flesh and blood offspring would imply the Father is more concerned with the veil than the spirit. And this goes against everything Jesus taught.

DID GABRIEL BRING MESSAGE OF VIRGIN BIRTH?

Many will turn to the scriptures that speak of Gabriel the archangel telling Mary of this miraculous birth. This is where I believe editing had taken place. Remember Gabriel also went to Elizabeth and told her about the miraculous birth that would usher in her son John the Baptist. But no one assumed that Zachariah had nothing to do with this. In reality Elizabeth giving birth was more miraculous than Mary giving birth, because Elizabeth was older and barren. Mary was young and filled with youthful vitality. Now we have to divide this concept into two conclusions. Since the Father did not impregnate Mary, then Mary could not have remained a virgin after birth. And if the Elohim impregnated Mary then the act would have been the same as if Joseph impregnated Mary, thereby concluding she could have not remained a virgin. If we wanted to get technical about this one might think, well, maybe Jesus was a Test tube baby. Either way try to follow the line of reasoning. Once we take away the status that Mary was a virgin after the conception then we can ascertain the truth in this area.

If Jesus was not like each of us then what purpose or ability would he have to bring salvation to anyone? His sacrifice would mean nothing unless one believes that Jesus took all our sins upon himself, thereby leaving no responsibility on us. This is what the church leaders declared and it was a total lie, as you will soon see. If Jesus could have taken all sins upon himself we all should have been saved immediately and entered our heavenly existence. The very fact that we are all still here is proof that never happened. Now some may state, "Well, you have to say you love the Lord and say his name, and then you are saved." That's fine with me, but I still look around and I see these people who claim they're free of all sin and the Lord has saved them, still living in the same rat race suffering sickness and death and injustices, suffering all the inequalities of life, and they are still sinners. If this is what one gains from the shed blood then who would be interested? And if it is something you gain later my question is, why wait? You should be with the Father like Jesus is, instantaneously. Under this understanding Jesus died for us; he covered the penalty of our sins. We are not supposed to be dying for him, are we?

Before I go into more depth with this subject I want to address what will become an issue with the subject of the virgin birth. Isaiah 7:14 states that a sign would be given that a virgin shall conceive and bear a son. There is no other place in the Old Testament that implies this miraculous event. But was this meant to be miraculous, or was this taken out of context?

The Hebrew word used in this verse for virgin is used only twice in the entire Bible, Genesis 24:43 and Isaiah 7:14. Genesis was referring to Rebecca at the well waiting for Isaac. The term Virgin represented her being a young maiden, a young girl. In the Strong's Exhaustive Concordance, this word comes from the term "ALMAH" (5959). It means lass, (as veiled or private) damsel, maiden, virgin. It is referring to a youth, a girl not yet of age or maturity, which also implies virginity. The other form of this same word also represents males who are youthful and not yet of mature age. The more popular term for virgin in the Bible comes from the Hebrew words, Bcthuwlah Bcthuwlem from Strongs. These words mostly apply to what we consider a virgin today. This Hebrew word represents a girl who keeps her virginity, and those who bring tokens of proof that she remains a virgin. But this is not the word used in Isaiah!

In Isaiah 7:14 it states that a virgin/young girl would conceive... Conceive comes from the Hebrew word, 'hairy.' It simply means to become pregnant. It is purely a flesh and blood operation. Nothing divine is mentioned outside of the normal act of giving birth. Here is what was said in this verse. "A young girl before the age of maturity will become pregnant and bear a son." If the Dead Sea Scrolls are accurate, Mary was only 14 years old when she conceived Jesus.

There is nothing especially divine about this conception. So if the Bible states a virgin shall conceive, it is the act after the fact. Historically many young Jewish girls were already being prepared for marriage by the age of 12 and 13. So this was not odd considering the belief system of this day and time!

If the virgin birth was correct then the ancient prophecies proclaiming the entrance of the Messiah were nothing more than fabrications and lies. It makes one wonder why the two most mystical followers of Jesus, John and Mark, never mention the virgin birth at all. I believe these verses were edited to take away the true meaning of the mystery. I believe the early church that claimed all authority changed certain words and placed them out of context and created the illusion that something more was happening than was first implied. In fact the book called the "Gospel of the Nazirenes" seems to prove just that.

I have read many accounts dealing with the unauthorized changes by those who claimed their spiritual power from above. They continued to make changes in the Bible all through the 16th century, and even today changes are still being made. They debated this issue of whether Jesus was divine or human for ages. The conclusion was that Jesus was very different from any of us. They lacked the true gnosis of inner realities that would have enlightened them of the mysteries. Jesus was more advanced in spiritual training, but he was still like us.

It follows that if a man were predestined in the ancient Judaic traditions, his genealogy would stem from the Father. If Joseph had absolutely nothing to do with the conception of Jesus, then how was Jesus of the seed of David?

Matthew shows the genealogy from David all the way through Joseph. What good does that do if Joseph had nothing to do with it? Why would Matthew show Jesus' ancestry from his physical father Joseph, going back to King David, and then write about the miraculous virgin birth where Joseph had nothing to do with it? This is a major Biblical inconsistency.

Furthermore, why did God need to personally impregnate Mary to bring forth a son, when he could have just materialized him into a human? Why go through the birth process at all? Why did Jesus ever have to grow up as a child? Why did any of these things need to take place? I think it is apropos to illustrate in no uncertain terms that God is not interfering with the evolutionary process of humans. Humans are born, they die, and they are born again. It is an evolutionary process. Neither Jesus nor Adam was created by fiat; they were born using analogies of creation. The Father allows for the cycles of matter through the shadow to continue to evolve.

As stated earlier, the New Testament warns through the Apostle John that the spirit of antichrist is when one fails to believe that Jesus Christ came into the flesh. What does this mean? It simply implies that if Jesus wasn't born like we are all born then he wasn't human, and this belief results in the indoctrination called antichrist. You either believe that Jesus came in the flesh like we all do, or you believe he manifested himself from the godhead to appear as human. But the latter would decree no need for Joseph and Mary, and that Jesus never really came in the flesh.

What is the spirit of antichrist and why is it so damning to the soul? What you are about to read you may have never realized in your entire life. If you believe that Jesus was different than humanity and he was not really like all of us, then there could be no eternal life or salvation for anyone. Why? Because if Jesus is the only Son of God and he is the only one to exist along side the Father from all eternity, then humans have no eternal life awaiting them. And there is absolutely nothing Jesus or the Father could do for you. The true Christian

Gnostics understood plainly that Jesus taught that flesh and blood has no eternal inheritance. If all we are is flesh and blood entities then we are doomed for all eternity after this life ends.

JESUS BEING THE ONE AND ONLY IS THE DOCTRINE OF ANTICHRIST

That my friends, is as damning as you can get! If people want to continue to believe that Jesus was a one and only separated from us for all eternity, then he can't save you anymore than you could save yourself. His entire sacrifice for enlightenment would have been in vain! The attitude of antichrist places Jesus into a framework of being a one and only and Jesus never taught this. Men and women over the years created this concept because they never understood the mysteries. Their only interest was containing the cattle and keeping them subjected to the rules and laws of humanism. The laws of the shadow lords! If you don't have the abilities Jesus had, how could you ever follow him? Jesus stated, "He that does the will of my Father is my disciple." How could you do the Father's will if you didn't have the same ability, *if you were not connected?* This is why flawed individuals of the ages took away the truth that Jesus taught. That we are rewarded according to our works. They changed it to, Jesus did it all for us.

How many times have you heard the cry, "Jesus saved me!" and "I am of Jesus, he loves me and he died for me?" Everyone is content to eliminate their own responsibility for their deeds because of these flawed doctrinal changes that occurred after Jesus left the earth. If we were really honest about the power of this great creator God, then why didn't he just make us like him? Why do we have to suffer and live in this world called hell trying to figure out what we are doing here?

First of all, the Father did create us just like himself! And secondly our hell that we have here in this lower realm is by our own creation. We chose to take the symbolic tree of knowledge of good and evil and depart from the tree of life. Therefore our training is now of this path!

CHRISTIANS DENY THEIR OWN RESPONSIBILITY

When the deception, "Jesus did everything for us" began to take hold upon people's lives another deception soon followed. Not only did millions fail to recognize their spiritual origin, but they then lost the truth of what becomes of us after death and salvation. They lost the knowledge of once again becoming God. I have asked Christians what they believe they are going to become once they enter their Father's realm. They have no idea except to think they are just going to sit around playing harps, wagging their tails like dogs before the creator, just praising his name. Their uncertainty is so great that most Christians would do anything in their power to save their human life rather than entering this utopia. Yet I ask, why would they not want to be with the Father, and instead choose to remain with all the suffering? It is because no one in their right mind wants to go some place and do nothing for all eternity, whether it is utopia or not. They failed to understand that if we are active here living and working and becoming, we will be even more active there. We are Gods in the making, not androids. The concept of android comes from this doctrinal error that teaches you are not responsible. This knowledge was lost!

Jesus was every way human as we are. He was the First-born son of Joseph and Mary. He was the first among those that died before the foundation of the world. (Revelation 1:5) He set the standard creating the WAY so that we could follow. He did not come here to do anything for us. He was illuminated to teach us what lies within us, the truth, mysteries of the Kingdom of God. All we have to do is tap into the same power, the 'I AM' presence that Jesus tapped into, and our pathway back home would be established.

The changes I have spoken about were brought into the Christian churches to take away the power from the people and place it upon egocentric humans. They needed to teach a philosophy that decreed that man was forever separate from the Father, and the church was the only avenue that could unite this vast gulf between man and God. They taught the two would never connect. We would forever rely upon a secondary source for eternal life. The Mother church and now all its breakaways in Christianity have become seduced by this doctrine of damnation, which will always keep unenlightened people prisoners to their own fears. They teach that man is no more than a second-class citizen of the kingdom, and is worthless. And the people's only hope was to remain within the church and rely on the misconception that Jesus would do everything for us. The comprehension of what the church really was had been lost. People did not understand that the organizational church in the New Testament was only for the babes in Christ who were not yet enough spiritually minded to exist on their own.

As Paul stated, "For when you should be teachers you still need one to give you the milk of the word. For you cannot handle the meat, you are as babes in Christ." The organizational church was only to be a mother to wean the child off the milk until one was mature enough to take the spiritual meat of the Word for themselves.

I truly hope that I have been able to clarify this subject to enlighten you concerning your true origin and that of our Messiah. For a savior to truly intervene he needs to reign from within and not from without. We need to have already been connected to Jesus or he can never be connected to us.

Now that we understand the principle of the man Jesus it is time to understand the principle of the Christ. The two are separate and yet the same, again, another mystery. Jesus said, "Many will come in my name saying I AM the Christ and shall deceive many." What could he have possibly meant by this? There have been many conclusions based on this verse, but only one will really fit. Jesus said many would come in my name. This means they will represent the man Jesus. It goes on to say that they will claim he is the Christ. Then it states that these who claim such will deceive others. What is the deception? It is when one sets up Jesus the man as the only Christ, because this is also antichrist. The truth is *Christ is the spirit of Sonship.* Without it you cannot be the Father's offspring. If only one could claim the spirit of Sonship then only one can be a Son.

JESUS IS NOT THE ONLY BEGOTTEN SON, THE CHRIST IS!

The Son of Man known as Jesus was NOT the Only Begotten Son. Christ the Light, the spirit of Sonship is the only begotten Son. He is the Word, and the Logos. The spirit of Sonship united with the projected soul of the Son of Man, Christ, was the mediator between the Father and Jesus. The Christ became the middleman and intercessor to unite Jesus the fallen projected soul with the light of the Father, the 'I AM' presence. The presence of this Christ must be in each of us to reconcile our division with the Father brought about by the fall in paradise. This presence proclaims our own Sonship with the Father. If this same Christ is not brought within each of us then we cannot ever be the children of the Father. The Christ then becomes the "light of all men." John 1:4, Christ is the key within to unite us all back with the Father, so we can lay hold of our eternal treasure. The tree of life is our very own inheritance of the Father.

Christ is the conscious mind of the Father that reveals Sonship in his darkened children, bringing them back to the light. We then become like the Father in spiritual nature. That is why Jesus said, "If you have seen me, then you have already seen the Father." But if Jesus was the only one to proclaim these words we can have no part with the Father.

110

Some have misunderstood the meaning of the second return of Christ as being a physical return of the man Jesus. What many do not understand is neither entrance of the Messiah was to be translated physically. The first entrance was the Christ bearing witness within Jesus. The second entrance is the Christ bearing witness within us.

Christ is our link to the inheritance that we left behind. The Apostle Paul declared, "Christ in us, this is the mystery."

Who really is the Father? The Father is spirit! Spirit is everywhere always existent. The spirit reigns in all dimensions and universes. It is the power that brings life and light to all that exists. Each of us is a portion of this Great Spirit. We are evolving to become part of this Great Spirit again united as one, and with it we will bring our very own identity as the spirit of Sonship reveals.

The Father as our portion of the one is gaining its own identity through each of our own efforts. This unfolds in its greater mystery to reveal what Jesus meant when he said the Father does the works through me. When we are brought to awareness of the Father through the divine Son then we can allow the portion of our I AM to perform through us the deeds necessary to give identity back to our Father.

WE ARE MULTI-DIMENSIONAL BEINGS WHO EXIST ON DIFFERENT PLANES AT THE SAME TIME

We do not experience the realities of our portion of the Father through only one lifetime or dimension. We live many lifetimes gaining awareness through much experience. We also live multi-dimensionally. We live in many dimensions at the same time learning this awesome potential. As the Father separated into trillions of parts through the sparks of light, so has each of our portions of that same Father divided into many aspects. Later I will discuss our multi-dimensional aspect. I have literally walked into many parallel dimensions where I exist in

111

other realities alongside this one. This is how we became lost in the first place in the shadow lands. We separated from our pure divine self, the Tree of Life, and entered dimensions that swallowed us up causing us to forget where we came from.

The Father declared that his children were lost in the unknown dimensions of the shadow and spirit. At this point he sent forth his spoken Word to give back the recall needed so that his children could become aware again of their true reality. Therefore the Word became each child's portion from the Father to gain back that awareness.

CHRIST AND THE FATHER IS OUR PORTION OF THE INHERITANCE

Christ the light then became the co-heir with each separate projected soul spirit of the Father reestablishing our inheritance as the heir of God. As the light blends in with the projected soul-spirit then our multi-dimensional selves will transform into the oneness of all, giving us back our true identity as one of the many sparks of the grand design. We in essence return to our portion of the Father, and once again become one with the Great Spirit.

Romans 8:16-17 "The Spirit itself (the Divine Son) bears witness with our Spirit (Soul projected Spirit) that we are the children of God. And if Children then heirs, heirs of GOD, (Inheritors through the Tree of Life) and joint heirs with Christ (The Divine Son) If so be that we suffer with him, (Incarnations into the flesh) that we may also be glorified together."

The inheritance that belongs to the children was given to us from before the foundations of the world to legitimatize the fact that we were the created offspring of the Father. We as the projected soul spirit, the fallen son, need to reconnect with the divine source, the 'I AM' presence, the Father. Once this connection takes place then we become both the Father and the Son. As Jesus said, I AM in the Father and the Father is in me! The two become one!

When we put this scenario into perspective we see the parallels to each source. First the great Father/Mother Spirit created, or projected out of themselves children of the same make-up and composition with total perfection. We became the Son/Daughter of the Great Father/Mother. When we the son/daughter projected away from ourselves as multi-dimensional beings we became the fallen son separated from the daughter and of our higher selves. Our higher selves in essence then became known as our "personal" Father/Mother Spirit, which was the son/daughter projected essence of the great replica Father/Mother divine.

THE "I AM" IS US!

So our higher self is the 'I AM' presence. It was then that the Great Spirit declared, "Let there be light." The Great Spirit projected out of himself his very own mind consciousness. It then portioned itself out among all the fallen children to become the radiant light of life. As we are all property of our higher selves we become the Son and daughter of the Father and Mother. When we fell we became blinded to our real source of our light. So the Father projected out of himself a carbon copy that could be divided amongst the fallen children to become a light source revealing each of our higher selves. This carbon copy would be known as the Only Begotten Son, the Word, the Logos and the Christ. The carbon copy was actually the Father and the Son. John spoke of this in the first chapter of the gospel stating, "In the beginning was the Word, and the Word was with God and the Word was God."

But how was the light portioned out? Each of our higher selves is also a carbon copy of the Father, but it lacked true identity. It is our higher self that projects its own mind consciousness into the fallen son and daughter. We are receiving our own portion of the light. This is why the scriptures teach we are co-heirs with Christ, and heirs of God. We truly are both the Father and the Son, but in our fallen state we have not become aware of these two principles. So our higher self upon our acceptance

113

sends the light into our fallen state to gather back what is theirs.

When the son accepts the mediator, the light of our Father's consciousness, we then accept the light of our higher self. As we enter this union we become one with the Father bringing an end to the separation that has kept us in blindness. We are then upon the union of the Christ reestablished as the divine child of the Great Father/Mother Spirit. As the spirit divine SON, the Christ is melded together with the fallen projected soul spirit. It then unites the two as one thereby creating the marriage of the Lamb. *So the marriage of the Lamb is the divine Son uniting with the projected soul son and blending the two as one spirit.* Then the Son becomes the Father and the Father becomes the Son.

For 2000 years mankind has rejected this wonderful knowledge believing it only belonged to Jesus. But Jesus said, "The things that I do you will do also, and greater things shall you do." He understood that we are all the divine children of our Father, whereas those who claim to follow him do not believe this. Jesus said, "I AM the resurrection and the life." He rightfully claimed what was his. He knew he was the 'I AM' presence and the Son. He said, "I can lay down my life and bring it up again." How can anyone do this unless there is a separate entity involved in this process yet both belonging to the one? Jesus was attempting to teach us what we can all do when we recognize what he also recognized. This is why the name 'I AM' is given. It was to personalize our unity with our Father. The name 'I AM' is first person. If you use this term then it belongs to you. You would not say 'I AM' in referring to someone else. Who is the Father? I AM! Jesus said, "I AM the way!" This means the Father is the source for the Son. But the Son is also the Father. Jesus said, "Before Abraham was, I AM." This meant the Father, our higher self, existed before the human called Abraham. Abraham the man was before Jesus the man, but neither was before the 'I AM', yet they were both the 'I AM'. That is why it stated, "Abraham desired to see my day, and he did."

What transpired many eons ago was our separation from our self, which is known biblically as the *Tree of Life.* The Father in essence becomes the life energy of the tree and the Christ becomes the vine and we are the branches, but all are one. Our Father along with a myriad of dimensional aspects of our self is our personal guardian angel. This is how the Father watches over each individual. It states that our Father knows what we need before we ask. How are all these things possible? It simply shows that our higher self is the one that is aware and watches over us while we exist in this blinded state. We are the projection of our higher self. You can bet our Father keeps his eye on us. Some may wonder, is our personal higher self different than the Great Father/Mother Spirit? The answer is NO! Each of us are a portion of the whole, each of our portion is exactly like the entirety. We were created in the image of God, the Elohim created the biological and the Father created the spiritual. The material/biological represents our fall from paradise as our carbon copy of the true source; the spiritual represents our oneness with the whole. Our portion of this great creation wanted to gain its own identity so it left its Tree of Life, the I AM to find it on its own. We failed to gain our identity while living in the state of perfection in paradise. Therefore we must gain our identities now while living in the shadow/carbon copy world, by using the friction forces of good and evil and learning to overcome and become perfect as our Father is perfect. We are the body of God -- one body, one mind, one spirit.

The Father is neither good nor evil but instead he is perfect. He is pure knowledge and wisdom and abides continually in truth. We live in a carbon copy world that relates only to polarity. Where there is good there is evil. Where there is right there is wrong. Where there is up there is down. Where there is a North Pole there is a South Pole. Everything in the matter universe is under the laws of polarity. Matter could not exist without it. But spirit is not under this law. There is no right or wrong, good or evil, up or down, North Pole or South Pole. The Father is Truth, Wisdom, and knowledge. It is pure with no occasion for defilement. Now please understand that I am not saying there is no right or wrong. I know there are religious organizations that finger their way through material like this just to try to find an Achilles heel. They have no desire for the truth but want to find something to accuse the messenger. As we of the biological live in the matter world we come under the laws of polarity. I assure you that if the polarity of the poles decided to shift I don't care how spiritual you are you would feel the negative effects of such a disaster. Remember karma, reaping what you sow is based on the laws of polarity. We must overcome the lower world to return to the higher world. Once we return to the Garden of Eden these laws no longer exist. Law of matter only exists within polarity not truth. Law of matter only pertains to the sinner not the righteous.

THE DIFFERENCE BETWEEN LAW AND GRACE

This is where many become confused as to the difference between law and grace. The Bible teaches that eternal life is a free gift. It also states that one is rewarded according to their works. Many in the Christian world have taken this to imply that if one is under grace and not law then there are no works involved. This misunderstanding was created because many did not understand the difference between the covenants of the Old Testament and the New Testament. When Paul spoke of one being saved by grace and not by works, he meant the works of the Old Covenant law. The matter LAW, the one Moses was given by the Elohim. There were two laws given in the Bible, the first was physical pertaining to the biological vessel as well as the material universe, and the second was spiritual pertaining to the soul-spirit. If one continues to follow the physical they will never access the spiritual. Using that method they would be locked in a type of prison. When one ascertains the true meaning of their origin then they come under the law of the spirit. Jesus took the entire humanistic law and translated into the overwhelming spiritual law. Love God with all your heart, mind and soul, and love your neighbor as yourself. There are no rituals, no complication, no feuding over which day is right, or what food you can eat, or where you worship. It simply defines love!

THE SPIRITUAL LAW PERTAINS TO SPIRITS. THE PHYSICAL LAW PERTAINS TO THE FLESH AND BLOOD

If you practice the spiritual law you cannot come under the physical law. It is impossible. So our works are those things we do that fit in the entire spiritual law. If love is not the central theme for your life, nothing you do will ever suffice. I don't care how many Hail Mary's you say, or how often you go to Church, or how diligent you are to obey the Old Covenant laws. If there is no love then your work is in vain and will lead to remaining within the cycles, which is the true meaning of death.

Eternal life is a free gift based on the fact that it is already ours. We were created eternal. Nevertheless we projected away from our eternity into the lower body of flesh and we experience the death sensation continually for our lack of knowledge, yet at the same time we are here to grow.

WE MUST PASS TESTS TO ADVANCE SPIRITUALLY

For anyone to advance to higher levels of spiritual growth we must pass tests. When you go to school you can't just jump from one grade to another by fiat. No one can pass the tests for you. If you fail you will not advance. Why is it so hard for people to realize that we are here taking tests? And if we fail these tests we cannot advance to higher levels of learning. Can you imagine what it would be like if someone were training for a test so they could enter the field of medicine? But they decided to have someone take the test for them. Now they are operating on you with no prior education or understanding of the necessary elements needed to engage in this kind of work. How would you feel? Both the individual who bypassed their work stage and the recipients of this tragedy are going to be the ones that suffer the most. Why would the Father want anyone who is not adept to handle responsibility to enter his realm recklessly all because someone else took the test for them, namely Jesus? What good is it going to do you or anyone else in the Kingdom of God if you slid in on someone else's coat tails?

We are rewarded according to our works as with anything in life. We are here to learn lessons. If you were training for a 100-meter dash in the Olympics, your reward would be determined by how much effort you place in your training. You will not win the gold medal by fiat, or by anyone else's efforts.

I know the arguments that are used against what I am saying. People scream out stating that the Apostle Paul said eternal life is a free gift that you can't earn lest you boast. What Paul said is absolutely true. You can't earn eternal life. Eternal life means you are already a born son of the Father, who is eternal! That would be like saying we go to work to earn our flesh. No, our flesh and blood was a free gift upon our birth in this physical reality. It was the inheritance we gained from our parents. We go to work to advance in this lower matter world, not to earn our flesh and blood. If we are to advance in the spirit world we must also train and work for this end. We are earning our advancement in spiritual life; we are not earning eternal life that was already given.

To understand the mystical argument Paul was bringing forth is to thoroughly understand the three segments I spoke of earlier: eternal life, salvation, and the reward for works. To be saved means to be redeemed unto awareness. To be saved implies that someone needs saving. Someone is in trouble. True salvation is knowledge that leads to truth. And truth will set you free. There is a truth that will set you free from the bondage of hell. Salvation is our awareness of our origin and of this truth. It becomes the resurrection unto eternal life. Many believe you must die to be resurrected, but the Gnostics understood that we are already dead. If you die in the flesh before you are resurrected then you are still dead. So one must first be resurrected before they die and then they will never see death. The resurrection that Jesus taught was our eternal awareness of our higher self. I AM the resurrection and the life; he that comprehends this although he may die will never see death. Once you comprehend the mystery of salvation you will understand that you never die, you just change and enter another realm. This awareness will teach, although you may die in the flesh, you don't really die. This is what Jesus meant when he said. "He that believes in me, (the Christ) though he were dead, (our fall from paradise) yet shall he live. (Our awareness) And whosoever lives and believes in me shall never die…" (just a transition)

Once you recognize that the spirit of forgetfulness has blinded us, then the truth of our 'I AM' will manifest within ourselves. What I AM saying is salvation is not eternal life but the realization that you are eternal.

EARTH- WATER- WIND- FIRE = BAPTISM

When one has been saved it is because they are initiated into the mysteries of the kingdom and their awareness is reopening to their ancient reality. Once you have been initiated into the mystical doctrine that teaches the "OLD MAN" perishes for the "NEW MAN" to live, then the divine SON the Christ begins to take effect within you. John the Baptist revealed the physical initiation called the water baptism. This was the physical sign that the projected soul spirit was buried in the flesh and blood body, which represents water and earth. The OLD MAN is the individual who has been dead within the veil. The NEW MAN is the awareness that we are life eternal. Jesus brought the Baptism of fire and wind. The flesh and blood is the EARTH. The projected soul spirit is the WATER. The divine spirit is the Holy WIND, and the initiation that changes the OLD MAN into the NEW MAN is the FIRE.

Millions and millions of people have been initiated into the physical baptism, but very few in the last 2000 years recognized the spiritual baptism of fire. One must become the NEW MAN to enter the Holy of Holies, which exists within our temple body. In ancient Israel only the Levitical Priesthood could enter the secret chamber. That meant that over 90% of all Israel could never enter the secret chamber. This was a shadow to teach us today that over 90% in the church have not been baptized by fire and are still living outside the veil. Less than 10% of all initiates understand how to enter the secret chamber. Water Baptism will never bring about the change. It was only designed to bring your awareness to the physical Jesus and his Christ. However once you are baptized by fire you will recognize the Christ within yourself. And then as a high priest you will be able to enter the secret chamber of the Father.

Baptism by fire is our true salvation; the other is just a sign of the true. One represents the shadow, the other the spirit. The fire is when the divine Son melds together with the fallen projected soul and takes complete charge. If you do not believe that the same Christ, who was in Jesus is also in you, then you have not yet been initiated by fire, only by water.

When the fire of initiation has saved one then they will place into effect the results of their communion with the Divine Son. The works that are now accomplished is the Father, our 'I AM', living within us doing these works. So by grace we are enlightened by the effort that is placed within us by our Father doing the works. We are the manifestation of those works and this was decreed within the parable of the talents and pounds. It takes effort and works to advance into the kingdom.

When we were asleep living in the Maya of death, before we knew the Ay AM we were in ignorance to our heritage and origin. But when one has awakened they must begin to accomplish, they must respond. You cannot go back to sleep. If you are awakened that you are a spirit born child of the perfect manifestation known as the Father, then you must begin to exemplify this character. The Apostle James said, "Faith without works is dead."

This reminds me of how I came upon the mysteries in my life. Each mystery came veiled in ways I least expected. God didn't just hand me the mysteries on a silver platter. I had to first recognize them and then work with them according to my knowledge. I then had to learn to be patient, allowing circumstances to reveal each and every point needed to ascertain my personal awareness. Mysteries are revealed from within you, not from outside you. That is why the Bible states, "No man need teach you, the comforter will teach you all things."

MYSTERIES ARE REVEALED INTUITIVELY

Each mystery that I have learned came to me through personal life's circumstances. As I accepted them I would then learn more truth. When I rejected them I stopped learning all together until circumstances led me back to the origin of gnosis. I continue to learn more mysteries nearly everyday. I can only reveal what I have learned within my area of acceptance. Each individual must learn intuitively and recognize the truth from within themself. There are no such things as spiritual truth handouts. If you do not become internally aware you will lose what someone else gives you. I still receive many questions from people who are trying to advance on my knowledge. I try to help them, but I realize that unless it becomes internal they will not comprehend. This is the problem with religion. People place their trusts with those that are freely handing out gnosis that they themself never truly comprehend.

I realize there are those that will say faith is all that is needed for salvation. Yet I ask, what is faith, and did Paul teach that it's acceptable to sin just because you are not under law but under grace? The answer was, "God forbid." Salvation is our resurrection and our awareness of what we really are. But if we do nothing about this awareness, will grace alone keep us enlightened? The answer is emphatically NO! Knowledge is no substitute for experience!

In Paul's day there were many that were still affiliated with the laws of the Old Covenant, which were the strict adherence to the Holy Days, the ten commandments, the rituals of cleansing, sacrifices, tithing, etc... Paul understood that these physical ceremonies given to them by the shadow lords were mystical representations of the spiritual law of life. However the adherence to these laws could only pertain to the purification of the flesh. You must learn their meaning so you can purify the spirit.

LETTER OF LAW = VEIL/ SPIRIT OF LAW = GNOSIS

The letter of the law will still keep the follower under subjection to the veil of deception. Paul knew that when one began to enter beyond the veil they could begin their journey into eternal life again. Those who continued to try to impress God by following these physical rituals would cease to understand their spiritual meaning, as in case of the feast of Tabernacles. One had to comprehend that this feast represented our bondage in the tabernacle of the flesh. However if you keep celebrating the physical manifestation, then you will forever fail to understand its gnosis, and will remain in bondage of that very tabernacle. Once you understand gnosis there is no need to celebrate its shadow unless it is being done to keep one in mind of its truer meaning. In reality the physical law kept you in bondage and the spiritual law of gnosis removed you from bondage.

Under the Old Covenant there was no reprieve for sin. When one broke the physical law, they lost their physical lives. The spiritual law on the other hand is to teach us that our Father through grace continues to allow us redemption from death by giving us more opportunities to overcome our shortcomings. Under the physical law you were given one opportunity. This is why many today do not comprehend the mystery of the cycles through the veil. Even though they may not comprehend the difference between the Covenants and they may not even be religious.

The physical law works with those that are blinded by the veil and the spiritual law works for those that go beyond the veil, to the enlightened ones. The physical law seduces us into believing that we are mere flesh and blood beings. The spiritual law teaches us that we are spirits who live in the flesh and blood containers.

Those that feel nothing needs to be done because Jesus did it all for us have completely misunderstood the mysteries. John wrote in the book of Revelations; "To him that overcomes will I grant to sit with me in my Fathers' throne and he will go no more out." The last part of this phrase refers to being able to leave the cycles and not having to return anymore. Jesus stated in the sermon of the Mount that we must become perfect as our Father in heaven. We must have good works!

WE ALL CAN AND WILL OVERCOME

The Good News is that we can overcome because we are given multiple opportunities under the spiritual law of liberty. We overcome as a result of many lifetimes that add to our heavenly body the riches of character. We are all being perfected by our personal I AM presence as we live through the cycles in the veil. But we must understand this so we can provide access for our heavenly Father to work through us. If we live in continual ignorance we will stop the activity that is from above so that it can be brought down below. We see a world that is still basically cut off from the Father because people are still living in ignorance.

The good works that we store up lifetime after lifetime are added upon our higher bodies storing the treasures that we build in our heavenly places. All the fruit that we have ever acquired will never be lost. It is always added into the spiritual realm where moth and dust do not corrupt. When we can obtain more good fruit than bad fruit then we will have balanced the law and become 'overcomers' to enter our next phase of training with the Father.

Much of our good effort that is produced towards this end is by our enlightenment of the fact that we are already the children of the Father and our 'I AM' presence is our share of the inheritance. We must use this presence of our Father, our higher selves by using the name 'I AM' properly.

USING THE POWER OF THE NAME 'I AM'

When we use the decree 'I AM' we engage the engine that propels the activity in our lower world. As we comprehend the deeper meanings behind this we will understand the metaphysical and the paranormal within our lives. One of the areas I will discuss later is O.B.E. or going out of your physical body. This is how much of what you need to learn will be granted to you. When one enters the spirit world by going out of body they automatically ascertain truths that were never recognized before. When one goes out of body they will learn that their thoughts are actually energies that create, and put into motion the action necessitated by your decree. While we live in the three-dimensional world our thoughts also create these energies, but its effect is much slower due to the vibration we exist at.

Our thoughts are energies that move freely throughout the cosmos. They are generated by our projected soul's consciousness, which is connected to our 'I AM' presence. When we think negative thoughts, that defines our lower aspect bringing in the energy veil or evil that changes the perfect creation of thought from your higher power. We change what is flowing positive into negative by the energy veil. When we think and speak in negative terms we are creating that field of wrong energy around our lives. If we continue to think in these terms we will create the image from the fourth dimensional world and bring it into our three dimensional plane.

Years ago psychologists called this, "self-fulfilled prophecy." It means whatever you think will be brought into your reality. They may not have realized why this takes place but they understood that it did happen and they were quite correct.

Tony Robbins is an example of a person who has changed the lives of millions of people. He teaches them to change their perspectives, which will engage a process that will slowly change their realities. Taking small steps will eventually create within your life the desired circumstance you have centered your attention on. He relates his own private circumstances to show how this revelation works with anyone. And it can shift one's life in another gear, hopefully it will be a positive change. Tony Robbins is tapping into the correct use of one's energy whether he knows this or not! It then becomes reality. Whatsoever one might think will automatically bring into fruition in the lower matter world those thoughts through the use of the creating energy power of the I AM.

It may take baby steps with much patience. Recreating thoughts to reprogram one's life from the direction they were leading after many lifetimes is going to take some time. But continual mental changes that direct its force toward that change will eventually occur- *this is LAW!*

This operation works as the result of using the most powerful name in existence, I AM. If you say I AM healthy, then you set in motion the matrix needed to fulfill this command. It is like setting your life on autopilot. Eventually you will arrive where your life is being programmed. Yet on the opposite hand if you use the name 'I AM' negatively then you will engage this force to operate on the lower three-dimensional level. Examples are: I AM sick. I AM poor. I AM too young. I AM too old. Whatever you think will assert its power over your life. *This is power given unto the gods.* Thank goodness the vibration is slow here or there would be nothing but chaos on this world! Could you imagine if all of our thoughts became instant realities?

Our use of this simple pronouncement is the difference between destroying and building. When you use this term (I AM) even unintentionally you are calling upon the power of your Father, to create within your world that energy that was requested by your thoughts. We are co-creators of the Father. We are the lower being of a higher manifestation. However when cut off from the Higher Source and lacking the power of the Divine Son, our creations are usually negative. We have great powers within our reach and this is why Jesus said, "Greater works shall you do than me." We can tap into the creative energy power at will once we are re-aligned with the Matrix.

Your mental picture is more powerful than you have ever believed. We are spirit beings, and our thoughts are living creating particles. You can with your mind create positive or destructive forces around you. All you have to do is concentrate on the mental thought that you want pictured in the three dimensional plane and the energy of your projected soul spirit will begin to manifest it into your world. However I must warn you, any destructive use of this power will go against your karmic debt, reaping what you sow. Wrong thoughts could even bring someone's mortal death.

ALL POWER AND CREATION IS WITHIN US

We are the masters of our own reality; there are no excuses for anyone. The key to success using this power is to redirect your mainframe of thoughts and imaginative characteristics around LOVE. Loving our Father and loving one another are the two central commands of the great 'I AM'. When we put to use this power of love towards our Father and one another then we can individually change circumstances throughout the world and the entire cosmos. Our love must be real though. Believing God wants to save you and destroy another is not the love of the Father. The Father told us to love our enemies, and do good to them which despitefully use you. If we teach that our Father is going to burn people in hell for all eternity then we teach hate and vengeance, not love.

Love is the heart and soul of each of us. Love is our lifeline! The very pure soul spirit called the Father and our higher selves is made up of only one type energy presence and that is love. When one fails to use the power of love they cut off their higher presence, and enter the world of the energy veil where your soul-projected spirit will produce evil of all kinds. Love is the toggle key and brain central for our higher operation. It is the sunshine for the plant. Without it we would just wither away and die. Love is not an idea or an emotion; it is an energy source. Denying love towards anyone separates us even further from our 'I AM' presence. We then enter a deeper darkness that blinds us more than we have already endured. Murderers, rapists, drug dealers are just a few of those that have entered a deeper darkness and are losing their identity. Many of them are struggling deep within the lower astral world. I will explain this later.

We entered darkness when we left the Garden because we failed to have perfect love. Now we are here to learn how to love one another again using the method that brought about our fall.

LOVE IS THE KEY

Love is like the password for a computer program, without it you cannot operate a specific program. The energy that operates the program will remain dormant and non-functional. However, if you enter the proper password then the lights begin to flash and the program begins to operate. When we use the password of love then our higher selves kick into gear and operate through us below.

When our spiritual program is operating properly we can then access the perfect world of our Father and use it in the lower dimensional world. If we continue to operate non-functionally by programming wrong information into our central brain, then our pure source will be cut off and we become cluttered with debris and foreign material, like a computer virus. Our lives will then pattern this faulty energy as the energy veil, and evil will more heavily surround us.

It is important to use the name I AM in total harmony with the Father. It is the creating power of GOD. Jesus used it to perform miracles. He said often, "I AM the resurrection and the life." He was patterning this thought to become a reality.

Each person can use this decree and have the same power Jesus had. But it is not supposed to be used as a show. Those that use this power just to prove it to others have cut off the

127

law of love and their higher presence. Usually but not always, the power will cease to function with the wrong motives. You do not need someone to prove to you they have this power. You have the same power! If someone asks you to produce a sign to show this power then it will do him or her no good. You should do as Jesus did and decline to show them. This power is not meant to glorify you the lower form, but to glorify the Father your higher presence.

Too often Christianity had taken Jesus' own words to apply to him personally. I have stated all through this book that Jesus' mission was to reveal that his power was also with us. Jesus taught us to walk the walk, follow his path and example. He didn't come to give us a free ride. If it were possible for God to give back everyone's tree of life with his or her own identities then it would have happened a long time ago. Evolutionary growth is a process we must be a part of. If we cannot pass our own tests now, then we cannot handle the responsibility for our future.

JESUS REVEALS GREAT GNOSIS

What grand purpose would there be to just say the name Jesus? Some may and most will not. Why would one be saved and another destroyed over such simplicity? Notice what Jesus told the young man in Matthew 19. The individual asked Jesus what was needed to attain eternal life. Notice the response, and recognize that Jesus never said, "Just say my name and say you love me."

Matthew 19:18-22 "Jesus said, you shall not murder, you shall not commit adultery, you shall not steal, you shall not bear false witness. Honor your father and mother, and you shall love thy neighbor as thyself. The young man said to him, All these things have I kept from my youth. What do I still lack? Jesus said unto him, If you want to be perfect, go, sell what you have and give to the poor. And you shall have treasure in heaven; and come and follow me."

I find this to be one of the most revealing scriptures given to Christianity direct from Jesus' own mouth. Let's break this information down. The man asked, "What do I need to do to gain eternal life?" Nowhere in Jesus' answer did he say that if you do all these things you would have eternal life. Why? Jesus said, follow the moral code of loving one another. This man was raised under the old law all his life. He stated, "I have done all this. What do I lack?" Recognize that obedience to the moral code was not enough for this man to attain eternal life. It was good for the flesh, but it still didn't redeem his spirit. Jesus then said, "If you will be perfect..." Why does this ring a bell? Earlier I stated that Jesus referred to the Sermon on the Mount in stating we must become perfect, as our Father in heaven is perfect. Then I stated to become perfect would take many lifetimes. And as we live throughout many ages we will produce fruit that will be applied to our heavenly body as treasures in heaven. Notice that Jesus says the same thing. If you will be perfect, go sell what you have and give to the poor. This is an act of good works and it will be added to your heavenly body. Jesus confirms this by stating, "You shall have treasure in heaven."

Throughout all this he never says the man will have eternal life. He ends by saying, come and follow me. He didn't say, just repeat my name and say you love the Lord. He said, follow me! The reason Jesus never told him that doing these things would gain eternal life, is because eternal life is already with us and it can't be earned. Our identity, our training must be earned and neither Jesus nor anyone else knows how long this will take before one returns to their I AM presence. All Jesus could say is follow me, and keep adding good fruit to your heavenly treasure.

Jesus made it very clear that this young man needed to add more good fruit to his treasures in the heavenly pool of righteousness. Just following a physical moral law was not enough in itself, for this individual was to sell all he had. Then the new treasure could be added to his continual building causal body.

Some have asked me, do I believe in following the Ten Commandments. My answer is simply this. If you are obeying the spiritual law of Love, then you are already fulfilling all law. There are great aspects that should be adhered to in the physical Ten Commandments, but adhering to a physical law can be accomplished while not adhering to the law of love. I maintain that one must adhere to the overall law of love and this will fulfill all laws. Example, one who doesn't kill has fulfilled the physical law, but one who hates has broken the spiritual law whether he or she breaks the physical law or not. But if you fulfill the spiritual law, you can't break the moral code physical law.

There is another interesting aspect embedded within these verses. The young man could not do what Jesus told him to do. He was a very wealthy man and could not let go of his physical treasure to add spiritual treasure. This is what I AM trying to point out, just following the physical law doesn't really do anything towards adding spiritual treasure in heaven. There is more involved!

The disciples wondered who would succeed under this kind of request. Jesus then said, with God all things are possible. Even though we may make many wrong choices God is always forbearing and ever patient. Jesus did not condemn this man to hell as one might believe. Jesus realized this young man was not ready yet for this leap of gnosis. He knew that his greatest test would be to rid himself of physical treasure to gain spiritual treasure. Jesus understood that this young man would have many more lifetimes. This is how all things are possible with God when he is dealing with a flawed humanity. More and more opportunities will come later. The true Father is not a destroyer but a creator, and he works beyond the shadow worlds and their lords of both space and time.

Our 'I AM' presence is our hope to have all things become possible even in an impossible world. We can use this incredible power anytime we choose. Our proper use of the 'I AM' is our building block for the future. If we use this power rightly then the Father, our higher presence, will shine in our lives within a dark world. Our lives will become more spiritually abundant and even physically if our karma allows.

The matter shadow world is our training ground to enter the spirit world refreshed and perfected. Do not become overly concerned or frightened if things do not go well in your physical life. It is all part of your 'I AM' training to return to the Father of light. Sometimes we just need to take a step back and view this world as a gigantic classroom in the solar system, and we are all galactic travelers visiting temporarily.

MYSTERY FOUR
The Mystery of the Christ

I felt it was only logical that I place this mystery in the center of the seven mysteries. The book of Revelation reveals that Christ stands in the center of the seven candlesticks. Also, as I have explained thus far, Christ is our mediator, our intercessor, which occupies the middle plane between our 'I AM' presence, the Father and the projected soul-spirit, the son. He is the center of our higher consciousness. The subject of Christ is most beautiful indeed, yet it is a subject that has been greatly misunderstood!

Romans 8:11 "But if the spirit of him that raised up Jesus from the dead DWELL IN YOU..."

Romans 8:10 "AND IF CHRIST BE IN YOU, the body is dead because of sin; but the spirit is life because of righteousness."

Romans 8:16-17 "The spirit itself bears witness with our spirit that WE ARE THE CHILDREN OF GOD, and if children, THEN HEIRS OF GOD AND JOINT HEIRS WITH CHRIST, if so be we suffer with him, THAT WE MAY ALSO BE GLORIFIED TOGETHER."

Romans 8:26 "...for the spirit itself makes intercession for us."

Romans 8:27 "...because he makes intercession for the saints."

Romans 8:34 "...who also makes intercession for us."

Romans 8:19 "For the earnest expectation of the creature waits for the manifestation of the sons of God."

Many times I have mentioned that Christ is the light of the Father! What does this really mean? What is the light? God said in the beginning, "Let there be light!" This light was the force that created all things. Without the light nothing was ever created. The light was also known as the WORD!

I have attempted to disclose this information on the mysteries from as many angles as I could perceive. I know how very difficult it is to allow new ideas to enter one's mind, especially after we have been preconditioned to view this information from another perspective. I realize hundreds of questions will come forward considering this topic. It has been my intention to try to answer these by addressing this subject in different and unique ways. It may seem that I am repeating myself, but in reality I am mystically setting up this information by approaching the illumination of this gnosis from multiple views. If you are not cognizant of other's ideas it may sound repetitious. However the individual that recognizes where I AM coming from will see the Inner Light, while others may ignore it. This subject that I am addressing is not complicated for those who are becoming aware, but it is brand new information to those that are reading it for the first time and could become quite confusing.

Although you have already read about the Christ and the light of the Father from the previous chapters as a set-up, I AM going to discuss it again from another angle. Remember most have never conceived of the idea that the Christ is a separate entity to Jesus, and yet still one in the same. You are possibly learning this concept for the first time, and I go and throw a monkey wrench in the works with an entire new concept that teaches Christ is in all of us, not just Jesus.

I realize that for anyone to comprehend this gnosis it will take a personal paradigm shift of previous thinking and observing. This will then create within one their own identity through personal gnosis, enabling them to add this truth within the framework of their previous understanding.

133

Those that have been raised a Christian will realize that I AM not changing many of the old views you have come to love and cherish, but in reality I AM delving into its truer meaning. Much of what I write about is going to ring bells within your head enabling you to realize there is great familiarity with the concepts. The only difference is that I AM bringing a newer understanding to those age-old philosophies.

I understand Christians have been educated within the early concepts that came out of the churches centuries after Jesus walked this earth. I know that to attempt to break through those rock-solid ideas it will take something very familiar that you can personally identify with. Thus creating a slow shift in your thinking process without too much discomfort. There will always remain those that will attack me for what I AM saying. Yet I feel, what better company to be in than Jesus himself. The religious hierarchy attacked Jesus continuously, so I have no doubt they will attack me. People become very frightened when they see someone espousing different ideas, especially religious leaders that feel they could lose control of their supposed flock.

JUST HOW DO I GO ABOUT REVEALING THIS

It was quite gut wrenching to figure out how to approach others with this new information. I wanted to lay a ground work for Christians to understand this thesis, because I was raised in Christianity for 30 years before I broke away from the organizational aspect of it. There are many books on the market that reveal quite a bit of what I will bring forward, but very few will piece this information together with the Bible. Many recognize the Bible has some serious flaws in its work, so they end up rejecting it altogether based on those conclusions. I don't believe the Bible should be rejected, I think it should be understood. And I don't simply mean its content; I mean its structure. How the Bible has been arranged and the type of people it was written for all need to come into account before drawing conclusions on its content. Being Christian helps me to discern between the mystery versus the faulty conclusion. And it is my hope that I can share those conclusions with other Christians. However, this book wasn't just written for Christians. It is for everybody.

I know diehard atheists that have begun to learn these mysteries internally. They were not involved in religion at all! They were led through circumstances that changed their views completely. Two of those circumstances were near death experiences, and out of body experiences. Anyone that has had the fantastic opportunity to peer beyond the veil has been given a great blessing. So neither religion nor Christianity holds all the cards to understanding gnosis. We should never become so arrogant to selfishly ignore others' strides towards perfection no matter what angle they come from. What saddens me is that there are many who will stake their lives on what they perceive the scriptures say and will condemn others for not agreeing with them. This is the height of arrogance! I have met Christians from all over the world who espouse their unrelenting belief in something they believe is in the Bible, yet it was nowhere to be found. Why did they believe something that wasn't there? How does this take place?

Many take their beliefs from others they respect for their knowledge, especially those that are a part of a Church hierarchy. They were taught to accept the word of these professional theologians and not dare question them. Gnosis is not a degree that one receives from college. It is not a piece of paper that you receive with a bunch of letters tacked onto the end of it; it is an internal awareness. No one can hand you gnosis; you must become internally aware. I AM giving you information, but if it does not become an internal awareness, then it will soon perish and die with other information you receive. The reason anger sets in when someone's beliefs are being attacked is because the individual does not have the knowledge internally, only externally. They can't defend their beliefs. Fear sets in because they begin to wonder if they were lied to. They simply have no way of knowing. The truth was never theirs in the first place, they are just borrowing it from someone who handed it to them on a silver platter.

How can you defend your beliefs if you do not understand the internal workings of those beliefs? That would be like trying to convince others you know Einstein's theory of relativity is correct, but you have no idea what it is. If someone challenges you, then you have only one way to respond and that is anger or embarrassment. You must comprehend what you believe in or it is not really your personal beliefs.

Many believe that if a Priest says the Bible indicates something then it has to be correct. He is a man of God, surely he would know? But it doesn't matter if he knows or not, it matters do you know? When you study the foundation of the Bible, you begin to recognize that it is a catalog of ancient writings from multiple periods of time, spliced together and interpreted through many different languages that were put together by men and women, not God. This doesn't mean that some of its information is not accurate or from the inspiration of God. It means the bits and pieces have been put together by others that decided on their own what to believe. I find it ironic that the Bible we have today, that Christians claim is authentic, was put together by clergy, under the authority of King James. Very few indeed realize that the Catholic Church was responsible for what was passed down to King James. They are the ones that decided what was to be a part of the original canon, meaning inspired scripture.

When the reformation took place under Martin Luther some of those books were taken away. What we have in reality is a book that the Church of England deems sacred that was passed down from the Catholic and Eastern orthodox councils. Yet the Bible is an incomplete work that houses thousands of edited manuscripts, scrolls, etc... And portions of the documents have been extracted and reedited for contextual use. When the average person picks up the Bible, all they really have is a book of confusion, unless they know its foundation and mystery.

Understand this is not your fault, and it doesn't mean you are stupid. You are picking up a gigantic work of books that have been reedited for someone's belief structure. These stories go back tens of thousands of years but are realigned to make one think it has only been 6000 years. Now maybe we can understand why Jesus said the comforter would teach us all truth and reveal all mysteries. He never mentioned the Bible as the source for truth when he spoke to his disciples and was about to leave earth!

SOME WILL SAY I HAVE NO FAITH

I know some are going to scream, "God inspired this book, don't you have faith?" Please understand faith has nothing to do with it. If you would just do some simple homework you will find what I AM saying is true. I recommend the books "The Gnostic Gospels" by Elaine Pagels and "Reincarnation, the Missing Link to Christianity" by Elizabeth Clare Prophet. These works are phenomenal explanations of the early church and who really designed our Bible. Faith without works is dead faith. If you do not prove for yourself the origin of this multi-sectioned book and realize how people for their own various reasons edited this work, then do you really think faith alone will save you?

The Book of Jude had a quote from the book of Enoch. However the early church did not allow this book to be part of the Bible. If it was good enough for Jude to write about as the inspired word, it seems it should have been good enough for us. Actually the writing of Jude is Enoch's work nearly word for word through the entire book. There are many books that the Bible quotes as inspired works. Even within the last 100 years another book was found called the Book of Jasher, which was mentioned in the Old Testament and causes the story of Moses to take on a new light. In fact when the truth finally comes out you will learn that Moses, the supposed author of the first five books of the Bible, actually copied them from a larger version of ancient Sumerian cuneiform tablets. You may even find out that Moses himself was an ancient Egyptian Pharaoh; possibly Akhenaton.

Our Father is not the author of confusion. (I Corinthians 14:33.) There are those that have written entire subjects dealing with the contradictions in the Bible. Some of these ideas may be picking at straws, but there are many that are absolutely accurate. I brought to your attention a simple contradiction in the Mystery of the 'I AM'. It stated in the book of Matthew that the genealogical line of David was placed into scripture to assure Jesus' bloodline comes from David, and then it writes about a miraculous virgin birth where the bloodline was insignificant.

The Bible is a wonderful book of mysteries and the nice thing about mystery is that even with incomplete information it will still shine forth. If people keep trying to live according to the letter of the word they will indeed remain confused and angered. And if someone doesn't agree with their thinking they will attack, gossip and malign that individual bearing the message, rather then attempting to refute the message itself. For 2000 years religion has indeed accomplished one very important thing. It brought deep fear into the minds of innocent people. When people have incomplete conjectures then fear is their only avenue to express their shock and lack of knowledge. I would never want to live in the world with the God that religion has created. God is our Father, not a taskmaster! He is our hope, not our threat! He is our guide, not our enemy! He is our light, not our darkness! Nevertheless if people continue to view God from both sides of the coin they will never gain the vision of the great deity of light and love.

The light is the very essence of the Father. It is his consciousness, his power, his mind, his thoughts and his personality. The light is the energy source of our Father.

THE FATHER AND THE SON ARE ONE

In the gospel of John it teaches that the light came forth from the Father as a separate entity and yet was the very same God.

This at first may appear to be a complex theory, but is actually quite surprisingly simple when you can break the code. If we continue to read only the letter it will appear very paradoxical. If however you shift your consciousness just a tad into the consciousness of the Father then you will truly understand this harmony.

MOVIE STAR WARS REVEALS MYSTERY

The Father is a power, a force if you will. The movie Star Wars centers on the theme of a powerful force that is always present. And the trained Jedi Knight is able to use this power. This movie is not so farfetched as many might believe. It expresses very well how the powers of light and darkness tap into the same power, but for different reasons. It shows how the Father/Darth Vader of Luke Skywalker fell into Darkness, and it took his trained Jedi knight Son to help him return to the light. The power here is called the 'FORCE' but in reality it should be known as the 'I AM' presence. The fallen Father is each of us that have fallen as the projected soul spirit of the Father as the fallen child. And it takes the divine son, the trained one, the Christ to enter our world of shadow and fear to bring us back to the light.

I remember at one point in one of the trilogies Yoda the Jedi Knight said we are spirits living in vessels. He taught Luke that our flesh was only a container that carried the light of our true reality from within. This is one way mysteries can shine forth in the least unsuspecting way. Another area where Yoda advised Luke was right on target; he taught how we need to battle our fears to gain access to the force. Yoda went on to show how our fears are only illusions, they're creations of our mind. I will explain this mystery in the later pages of this book.

The entire lesson brought forth from these movies was, to become adept as a Jedi Knight you must go through training that would unlock the hidden force from within, to tap into the ever existing power. There is no closer parallel to the truth.

The force that is being tapped is our Father. This force is everywhere, omnipresent and omniscient. It is in all dimensions, all universes, all life is sustained by this force. However, unless you are trained sufficiently you cannot access this power properly. The Son, the accomplished one, Christ, then becomes our teacher of the light, like Yoda was Luke's teacher. He is our two-edged sword of truth! He is the trained Son of this great force. The Son came to teach us how to lay hold of our destiny, our heritage. We are to become Jedi Knights! I truly hope that using a movie to explain this important topic doesn't offend too many, but like I said, I will approach this with information from many different sources and angles.

CHRIST IS EACH ONE'S PERSONAL TEACHER

Christ the teacher, the master melds within our conscious awareness; our minds, so we can pass the ultimate tests that will challenge us in the future. This teacher then becomes the totality of the consciousness of the Father, the force. As we work and grow within this light directed by the teacher of the force, we become one with the teacher, the divine Son and the force, the Father. We are in reality using the Great Force's mind in directing our success.

As you allow this Son to teach you then the spirit of the Father can declare, "This day I have begotten you, you are my beloved son, and I AM well pleased." This is your call to your equality with the divine Son, the Christ as co-heirs. At this point you will have blended with the teacher- the divine Son and then you can say, "If you have seen me then you have seen the Father."

As you blend within the light of the teacher you take upon the power that directs its own force. You are then filled with the same power Jesus had, including alchemy, creation. You can learn to use this same power to return to the garden of paradise, your Father's higher consciousness, uniting with him again. You would gain back the glory you had with him before the world was.

Jesus said he was about his Father's business. This should be our fundamental decree also. When you link up with the consciousness of the Father you will be about your Father's business. Your purpose would cease to be of the flesh and centered more on the spirit, which is your true being and inner awareness.

MALE AND FEMALE EQUAL AMONG THE GODS

Our Father is the energy source that created everyone in his own likeness and image using his WORD. We were perfect sons and daughters of God when we left our first estate. When I use the Male term: men or sons, I AM not trying to be sexist. I AM revealing the mystery using terms that are already recognizable and used by the ancient mystics and the Bible. The mystery was revealed in these terms to help us gain an inner awareness of the gnosis of eternal life through a lower consciousness. However during the days of Jesus he was speaking to people that did not understand the equality of men and women, so he had to address these mysteries using male type analogy. In truth he taught that the Father and Mother Divine existed as a replica of the Son and Daughter.

Men and women are co-heirs together and later I will discuss the polarity of the twin flame of the Father/Mother Spirit. Each of us has both characteristics of male and female, because each of us is miniature Father/Mother Gods. That is why the scriptures teach, "Let us make (hu)-man(s) in our image," and in the image of GOD (both) MALE and FEMALE were created. Obviously God's image is both genders.

WE ARE THE BRANCH OF THE TRUE VINE

Each of us entered different conscious awareness in varying levels of degrees. It was then that we became a branch of the true vine. However we became lost in the mystical portals of divinity. We became the prodigal children leaving our home, as light is projected away from the projector and onto the screen. We began to see the screen as our true reality, and failed to comprehend that we were a projection from a truer source. We became blind souls of a greater aspect.

The source of the light that projected us onto the screen was eventually blocked by the wrong creation of energy known as the energy veil. We became solid due to the lack of light, and we manifested into the shadow of light and took upon the characteristics of shadow and darkness to be our real world. We were then locked in this portal of mystery unable to ever see our true source again. We became darkened children! We had no idea what we were doing here and no clue where we came from. Thus bringing the question, "Why were we born?"

At this point we were the spirit-born children of God living in the matter world perceiving it to be true. We could no longer see the projector or our true source of life. We looked up but it was blackness. We became lost children roaming in the shadows of darkness within our multi-divided consciousness, not having any idea where we started or that we were a divided being. We saw our human families and the life and death scenario as the true reality of all existence; everything else became a myth!

The Father was saddened! He knew that our only hope lie with him! But the Father could not come to us because he is one spirit and is everywhere. We would never understand our personal relationship with this force. We could only perceive him as a great source of power and glory, but with no connection to us. The great force needed to design a way to enlighten us to our origin. How could this ever be done? How could this spirit change our darkened reality to reveal our Tree of Life that we left behind in paradise? How could this force ever get through to his blind children?

THE FATHER CLONED HIMSELF BUT NEEDED IDENTITY

The Father concluded that there was a way! He could out of himself create a source of light that could become a separate force that could act as an intercessor for the lost souls. This was the decree, "LET THERE BE LIGHT!" Yet how could we receive this light personally? With each manifestation or creation of the central Force the Father could within itself reveal the light to the fallen projected soul. When the Father created these spirit-children he unleashed from without himself the glory of his own design and makeup. The sparks of light were the Father's offspring but they lacked individuality. They were a perfect creation of truth, wisdom and beauty. They were every way like the Father except they lacked identity. The Father actually cloned himself but he wanted each clone to gain his or her own awareness and identity through experience. When we chose to experience realities in the knowledge of good and evil and not the Tree of Life we had to separate from our source, the cloned spirit of the Father. When we did this we got lost.

Because each of our higher selves is the clone of the Father, we are in essence all of ONE. We all have the eternal awareness of each other as ONE. The Father signaled the clones to manifest out of themselves the light, or another cloned spirit of their essence. This light, the only begotten son, was then sent into the screen of life where we have existed since the projector sent it. And once the light of the higher presence was perceived it could then interact with the lower aspect of the soul to reunite them with their higher power. The reason the light, the Christ is the Only Begotten of the Father is because it is still the perfect manifestation of the Father, whereas we fell. Nevertheless once we are rejoined with the light we will become begotten of the Father.

Just as the scriptures revealed about Jesus, "This day have I begotten you." THE ONE TRUE SOURCE IS GATHERING HIS IDENTITY FROM THE LIGHT SENT FORTH!

This was accomplished to help all the fallen children reunite with their personal 'I AM' presence. We were all created from the source as copies or replicas of that source, but we lacked individuality. We had not been truly born. We were only created. We were like the child in the mother's womb, but we were not yet born. The Christ was born as the only begotten son so that it could unite with each of us to make us the begotten of the Father through this light.

WE ARE NOT TO BECOME ROBOTS

The Father never had any desire that we should all be alike in the sense of a robot or automaton. He wanted us to have an eternal design like his own but with external identities. He desired uniqueness, but each of us had to remain with the same makeup of our true source, or else we would become something far different than what was intended. The way humans are today is not what the Father intended; it is what we have become separated from our source.

The Christ spirit is the spirit of the higher consciousness that must possess the lower soul. It is the resurrected light of our Father to save the children from eternal damnation or being blinded by the veil, of living in the delusion of the cycles within the veil.

CHRIST POSSESSES JESUS TO BEGIN REVELATION

Jesus was the one chosen 2000 years ago to become the vessel that the Light of Christ would enter and literally possess. As the two united they became one thus bringing about the name, Jesus the Christ. These two names solidified the fact that the projected fallen son had now united with the divine Son of righteousness and the two became one. From all those that had died the mystical death from the Garden, the slain Lamb from before the foundations of the earth became the first born among those that had died. Gnostics had been accused of being pagan sun worshippers by the church, however when one recognizes the truth one realizes we are sun worshippers from our origin. The problem entered when unenlightened individuals worshipped the physical sun by giving obeisance through ritual. They did not understand the metaphor behind being a true sun worshipper. The great central sun radiates its glory throughout many realms and is a spiritual sun that hosts the glory of God. That is why in Malachi chapter 4 verse 2 it states, "But unto you that fear my name shall the SUN OF RIGHTEOUSNESS arise with healing in his wings." Notice the spelling of the word SUN, not SON!

PAGAN SUN WORSHIPPER OR DIVINE SUN WORSHIPPER?

The SUN of Righteousness is the divine SON united with each of us; it is the LIGHT of the FATHER. In Old Testament times Sons of God were also known as the STARS. Stars are all brilliant SUNS. When we look into the heavens we are witnessing the shadow manifestations of all the children of the Father/Mother Spirit. We are the lights of the heavens! We are the named ones in the heavens! We are the brilliance of design! We are the ones that have shone brightly with the glory of God. We are the countless innumerable multitude shining brightly in the heavens, trillions upon trillions and countless trillions. But until we can escape the veil and cycles we will forever look up and only witness a manifestation of our very own glory.

The earnest expectation of the creation awaits the manifestation of the Children of God. We are children being born again! This is why galaxies spiral like the child in the womb. And stars are born from galaxies! As with the manifestation some stars lose their light and luster and begin to burn out, and some even fade away. However others grow brighter and become the great lights of the heavens.

Yes, the Gnostics were SUN worshippers and so AM I, but we are spiritual SUN worshippers. So Jesus' path was to lay a foundation for our divine reality to shine like the sun. He set the way within the last cycles of ages to present for us a WAY by the Bread of Life, the WORD, the LIGHT to become part of our own beings. As accusations continue to flow against the early true Gnostic church, the truth will finally be known that the true pagans are those that continue to worship the flesh as the all in all. And they fail to see the SUN of righteousness as the ALL IN ALL. Truth and wisdom are the divine counterparts to all GNOSIS. And as we begin to fear the SUN of righteousness, which interpreted means to 'divinely respect', then we can be assured of the proverb that teaches, "Wisdom begins with the fear of the Eternal ONE!"

As we continue to comb through our past with the true revelation of Jesus the Christ we understand the true importance of his life. That Christ didn't come here for his benefit, he came for ours by teaching us how to become aware internally.

EMMANUEL BROUGHT AMONG THE CHILDREN TO DECLARE THE KEYS TO SONSHIP

In Jesus' last incarnation in the cycles of the veil special care was taken by those that carried the mystical scepter to provide a young maiden to give birth to the keys of the Father and unlock the mystery of man. She was instructed to call this child, Emmanuel, meaning God with us, representing our true divinity from before the world now made manifest through Jesus. And also for his physical counterpart he took the Greek name Jesus, which meant savior! So entered the child who was born of the Father through the realization of the Christ uniting within as the divine SON/SUN, the only begotten Son of God, thereby decreeing, "ABBA FATHER," his very own united SONSHIP!

146

CRUCIFIXION WAS TO PROVE VICTORY OVER DEATH

Christ then became the light to the world that was slain from before the foundation of the earth. It shone upon the soul of Jesus to guide our way back to our origin. Jesus wanted to exemplify this light greater than any other could. He allowed the cry, "Crucify him," to annihilate his flesh to prove that the light of our very own being is greater than death. His sacrifice was to declare our SONSHIP that would inevitably save us from our fallen state. However his sacrifice never removed our sins, as if someone came as a sacrifice and instantaneously washed them all away. His sacrifice was to teach of our origin so we would recognize the Divine SON/SUN within that would inevitably cleanse us from our lack of Gnosis, which was destroying us. Our sins/fall is washed away by the divine power from within once acknowledged and acted upon, not because we sit around verbalizing the name Jesus. Jesus did show us the WAY and by that he becomes our savior, but he said 'FOLLOW ME!' Jesus never once said, "You just hang tight and I'll get this done for you."

GRACE DOES NOT REMOVE SIN, IT GIVES THE SINNER TIME TO CHANGE

For centuries many have looked upon the subject of grace as some sort of stain remover, when in reality it doesn't remove the responsibility. It makes us recognize what our responsibility is, so that we can change. Under the Old law the sinner was instantly put to death. There was no room or allowance for change. Grace actually removes instant death for the sinner allowing more time and opportunity to change. Do you recognize how easy it would be to interpret the true meaning of grace, as to take away responsibility? When in truth it gives us more time to own up to our responsibility. Obviously if one only had one life to live then there would be no grace! Because sometimes life's situations do not leave enough room for change within the perimeters one might be given. Grace is

147

our hope through the cycles to come unto perfection. Grace is our forgiveness through multiple opportunities, whereas ancient Israel was given the law that taught immediate punishment. Grace came to offer hope to the sinner.

Grace is like a judge giving someone a pardon from a death sentence so that person could be reformed. Grace does NOT mean giving a pardon to a criminal so the criminal can keep doing what they have done. Grace does not give us the right to sin. This is where karmic accountability plays a far greater role than teaching that someone has been instantly washed clean from all their responsibility. When one realizes they are responsible for their own crime they will be less likely to commit that crime again. However when one believes they have no responsibility for what they do, and that Jesus paid that for them, they will be more likely to commit the act again, because they never learned their own responsibility in the act.

Every act that does not honor the Father brings with it a payment in full that is due sometime in the future. There will be those that get very angry at what I AM stating. They will claim that I AM denying the sacrifice of Jesus, but understand that I AM not denying his sacrifice; I AM explaining what it really meant. Jesus said, "Become you therefore perfect as your Father in heaven is perfect." How could one ever achieve this if they feel they have no responsibility in their own spiritual acts whether good or evil? Perfection is the result of hard work and perseverance. It cannot be achieved by fiat.

UNTIL THE CYCLES AND VEIL PASS ALL COME UNDER LAW

If we did not play a role within this creed then there would be no cycles, no veil and no inheritance. Notice what Jesus said in the Sermon on the Mount!
Matthew 5:18 "For verily I say unto you, till heaven and earth pass, one jot or one tittle shall in no wise pass from the law, till all be fulfilled."

Once you comprehend the mysteries it will become much easier to understand the mystical meaning in these verses rather than struggling with the letter. Notice closely what Jesus was trying to expose. "I AM telling you that until the shadow lands have been brought to nothing by the light, you will all remain in the cycles through the veil, but once the light is revealed then the shadow will disappear."

Jesus came to fulfill the law, not destroy it. He came to acknowledge the shadow Lords and state that there is one greater. One that we can unite with that will take us away from this ignominy. But until we enter the light the shadow law will remain. The physical heavens and Earth, will continue to exist until every last one of us have reentered the light, every man, women and child in their own order. Overcoming is a long process and one that will vary for each one of us. But until the shadow land is no longer needed, the "shadow law" will remain in effect.

Now learn a greater mystery! Whenever a life-stream contravenes a law, it will orbit like a planet orbits a star and returns to its origin. There are two laws; one applies to the human being, the other applies to the entity inside the human being. Each law works within one another, but one is real, the other is an illusion. This is why Jesus taught, "In the Old times it was stated that if you killed someone you were guilty of the judgement, (this is the Law given to ancient Israel.) But now I tell you that if you are angry with your brother without a cause then you are guilty..." Jesus understood the law of thought energy. Killing is a physical act and it will bring physical judgement. But the spiritual act is far greater than the physical act and this is what brings about the law of cycles in the spirit realm. It was the attitude that one must pay later. It was the thoughts that engineered this terrible atrocity. One's karmic judgement will be decided spiritually by one's thoughts, not action. If you hate you have already committed murder. Whether the act expressed that hatred or not is immaterial. The fact that you sent forth energy of hate, it will return to you sometime in your future. Again, let me emphasize the Father is not sending this back to punish you. You committed the act out of free choice. You sent that energy into the higher dimensions where all vibration is accumulated, to your spiritual blueprint of your four lower bodies: the physical, mental, emotional and memory body.

This energy has to rotate within the law of cycles. This was the ultimate fairness of judgement, so that "NO" one would ultimately suffer for another's wrong deeds. We create our own realities. It was our thought sent into motion and it will be our thoughts that return to us, because we are all spirit projections of the true Father. So it is the thought that you are responsible for in karmic accountability. All penalties incurred by the human being, will bring about another type of judgement. This is why we have man made laws just as ancient Israel had carnal laws. This is where our captors the shadow Lords become our gods. This is why the Bible states to honor the decisions brought down by humanistic governments and that God placed these governments over us. And these carnal decisions, we are told, are actually God's decision. But it is not the Father's decree; we have not been under the realm of the spiritual Father since we left paradise and our personal Tree of Life. These decrees to obey man-made governments were set up to become responsible and accountable in the flesh, not spirit. Notice that when people murder people, the Father does not come here to set up court for judgement. Men and women under laws pertaining to human rights become the judges. But the decisions brought forth, whether one is guilty or innocent, have no bearing upon our karmic accountability.

It is your thoughts that ultimately are registered and this will return like a planet orbits a star. There is no proper payment for one that commits a terrible act against his fellow man, unless it be returned to the initiator. When someone kills for example, how does taking that individual's life in return ever repay the agony that so many will endure by one senseless act. The thought that created the act has to be washed clean, not the act itself. If you murder you will come under judgement of the shadow law and there is nothing anyone can do for you. However you are still responsible for the action in thought and deed and this will be required of you in full upon the return trip to school. If one is executed for a crime this does not own up for the responsibility that was incurred by the thought.

KARMIC ACCOUNTABILITY NEEDS TO BE TAUGHT ONCE AGAIN

People need to know that no one gets away with anything. The shadow law is only a copy of the true spiritual law. Can you see the mystery? Grace allows for the reconciliation of all error in your immediate lives or return trip. Although there is one other granting factor in this puzzle. One can be washed clean by the power of the flame of fire known Biblically as the Holy Spirit. When we acknowledge our true origin and accept the light of our Christ through the savior Jesus then we can begin to walk the spiritual walk of life. And all our past sins by virtue of complete change will burn up in the fire of the Holy Spirit. There is truly only one thing we lack and that is true change. We must all change from the pathway we have been walking and enter the light, the true WAY! True change will never occur if people continue to believe they have no responsibility for their actions. This is why I have addressed this book primarily to Christians even though it applies to everyone. Christianity has held the keys to the mysteries for 2000 years and yet they fail to use them. Instead they have been seduced in teaching a doctrine of the spirit of antichrist.

The spirit of antichrist comes from the mentality of only paying homage to the physical law and ignoring the karmic law. This causes individuals to judge others to eternal damnation while thinking they have no wrong. This in turn creates the attitude that so many have in churches today. Deep, hurtful, spiteful, thoughts running rampant towards others, but the outward show seeming to portray love and fairness. Jesus spoke of this also when he said the religious hierarchy would clean the outer cup for appearance, but inside they were filled with dead men's bones. For 30 years I witnessed the aberration of truth under

151

the auspices of appearing righteous rather than being righteous. It is not that one truly wants to be like this, but when you remain under the shadow law, under bondage within the veil of cycles you can never see where each of us play a key role in eternity. Christianity is not the only blame, we are all at fault because whether you agree or not, or are religious or not, everyone has come under the shadow Lords whether they believed in them or not.

CHANGE IS BROUGHT ABOUT THROUGH MATTER

We must understand in the spirit world we were changeless beings so we need to bring about change from within the veil. The Bible declares, that "God changes not." We had to have our reality change so it would create change within beings that could not change by themselves. Some may wonder, if we couldn't change how did we fall from paradise? Our fall occurred after we entered the shadow lands. We had already entered the veil of darkness. Our higher presence is still in its perfect state but it lacks its own identity. We are the identity in action so we can bring it back to our higher presence. If we fail to bring back our identity to our Father then we will forever be locked in the shadow lands. And our portion of the Father will forever lack its own identity separate from the eternal primal spirit. We are giving our Father the greatest gift of all, to have a distinct personality and identity of the primal spirit, while remaining one with the whole. Do you see the beauty of this? Jesus said, the Father and I are ONE! Jesus' Father gained his identity through Jesus! And it was the mind consciousness of the Father, the Christ, and the Divine SON that created the WAY through Jesus to accomplish this feat.

It was the power of the divine Son to make right what had gone wrong. This power will not work by itself. You must use this power thereby making you the third person in a trinity concept. God is not a trinity, he is all in all. But the concept of trinity was designed for the lower matter human to comprehend through three-dimensions how the plan of the Father works. The Father is each individual and is one, the Son is each individual and is one, and each of us are individuals and we are one. But within a three-dimensional plane of awareness we can only conceive of there being three: the Father, the Son and the Holy Spirit. In reality these are only concepts that teach, the Idea (Father), the Spoken Word (Son), and the Action (Holy Spirit). The Idea is our thoughts coming from our higher self. The Spoken Word is those thoughts manifested unto realities of our dimensions to comprehend. The Holy Spirit is the action that we produce using the idea through the Word. If we fail to act upon that which is given, then the (Idea-Father) and the (Word-Christ) both fail through us.

WE ARE TO BRING INTO REALITY WHAT OUR FATHER THINKS

We then become the people in which the works of the Father are performed through the Divine Son. I must repeat again, we are co-heirs of Christ and heirs of God, we the three are one! Jesus, using the mystical symbols of the Passover also taught this. The fruit of the vine, the cup represents our oneness with the Father, heirs of God. The bread broken represents each of our portions of the divine Son co-heirs with Christ. So when we eat the mystical bread it illustrates our bringing into action the cup of the vine, which are the Father's thoughts. When we act out in the lower dimensions the thoughts originating from the Father our higher 'I AM' presence, we become co-workers with the Divine Son sent forth on our Father's behalf, and we become one with the Father.

Jesus spent his entire ministry teaching of the Father and the light of Christ. Yet he never once claimed to hold all the cards to either of these two. There were times that Jesus could not even use the power of the Divine Son because of the disbelief of the people. Yet one might wonder how could the people impair the working power of God? Because we are all one! We are all the power of the Father. If one part of the body stops functioning the entire body feels the pain. Just because the hand is not the leg does that make the hand any less important

153

than the leg? If we examine this truth by realizing that we all play separate functions of one complete body we will then realize that each of our roles in this mission is predicated upon all of us succeeding. As a tree has sap that runs through all the branches giving it life we also have the spiritual sap running through the body of the Father. If the branch does not want to be part of the vine then the branch breaks off and withers and dies. Without the sap of life we cannot sustain ourselves. Each of us plays a part in the role of faith. Faith is our connection to the source and our reliance upon such source. But someone else's faith cannot sustain one that has no faith. Faith is our action that brings us into the oneness of all.

THE POWER TO HEAL COMES FROM WITHIN ONESELF NOT ANOTHER

Jesus could no more heal one who had no faith, than a vine could give sap to a broken tree branch. Our individual attachment to the oneness of all is the active, creative power that ignites the flame. When the branch has been supplied by the true source, the needed energy, then the branch can produce its own flower of beauty. This flower becomes the identity of the source, yet separate from all the other flowers. If the branch will not produce the flower using the sap of the true source, can the vine produce it for the branch? The answer is no! Neither could Jesus heal those that did not have faith. Without the action on the part of the believer it would not produce its own fruit.

Now learn another mystery! All power of heavens and earth is within the branches as it is the vine. If the branch fails to use its own power the vine can do nothing. All the vine can do is stimulate the branch's awareness of such power so in time it can produce its own results.

Often Jesus would ask the recipient of healing if they believed or not! This wasn't done for some religious experience or show. Jesus knew that the doubt of the recipient could cause failure. A stumbling block would have manifested blocking out the energy power. I will address the function of Faith in detail in a later mystery. Right now I AM only touching on it for purposes of this illustration.

ROMAN OFFICER EXEMPLIFIES TRUE FAITH

One such case comes to mind dealing with the Roman officer that came to Jesus for healing of one of his soldiers who had taken ill. Jesus asked him to bring the soldier forward to be healed and the officer replied, "Just say the WORD my Lord and it shall be done." My, oh my what a magnificent testimony of faith. This was a testament to this officer's respect of Jesus, but also a testament to the officer's own faith. In the military one does not question his commander! Military men are told to respond without question to all orders or they will be severely disciplined. This is a Gentile rule of Government brought down by the shadow Lords. It is not the way of the Father but the way of darkness. This officer gave Jesus the same respect he would have given his own commanding officer. All Jesus needed to do was give the Word, and it would be done. In the military a subordinate is to give his acting officer due allegiance as if he was father, mother and God. You were not to question them, period. When this officer went to request for healing of one of his men both the officer and the one that was ill were relying on this chain of command.

The soldier gave his faith that his officer would seek this healing, and the officer gave his faith that Jesus would acknowledge this request. When Jesus heard this man speak he stated, "I have not seen this kind of faith in all of Israel." What a statement! Jesus gave his word and the soldier was healed that very hour.

DID JESUS NEED ANOTHER'S FAITH TO HEAL? YES!

Now some will say that Jesus didn't need this kind of faith to heal someone. And I will say in return, Jesus didn't heal the soldier. It was the faith of the two men that brought about this gift. Faith is internal not external. If you are relying on someone else's faith then you will surely fail. Jesus did not want people to have faith in him, the man. He wanted them to rely on the Father. He was just an intercessor bringing this divine knowledge out in the open. He became the Divine Son incarnate to illustrate the working that each of us has access to. He pictured in the flesh what transpires from the spirit. The divine Son illustrated by Jesus is each of our personal intercessors for our higher I AM presence, the Father. When Jesus asked for our faith it wasn't so he could heal us, it was to bring us to awareness that the Father in us is the healer and the Son is our access to this Father. But if we fail to bring into action through faith, then we alone will cancel out the power. If Jesus were a one and only then our faith would have nothing to do with it. And I AM sorry to say that there are too many that believe this way.

It doesn't take a mathematician to bring two plus two together to comprehend that what the Roman officer did was beyond incredible. Something very special occurred that most have failed to understand. Just as the woman who had been ill with a blood disease for twelve years. All she had to do was touch the garment of Jesus and she was healed. It was her faith through the Son that caused this tremendous energy to surge through Jesus. Even in this instance this was not perfect faith, she still felt the need to touch Jesus to access this healing. She was still looking to someone other than the Father. However her faith was strong enough that she believed she would be healed if she could just touch Jesus. The Roman officer needed nothing other than Jesus' word. And we need nothing other than the WORD for us to have the same benefit. That is why Jesus said, "I have seen no greater faith in all the land."

Jesus never went out to draw a following to worship him; he sought followers to walk with him to come before the Father. As I stated, Jesus said to the young man, "Why call me good, there is none good but one and that is GOD!" Again we see

156

here the separation of the fleshly man Jesus with the divine Son from the Father within.

CALL NO MAN MASTER EXCEPT FOR CHRIST

I realize that there are areas in the Bible that would appear to contradict this, because Jesus' own disciples called him master. And Jesus said, "Call no man master except for Christ." Some have believed that Peter was the first to acknowledge Jesus as being with the Christ. I have a problem with this for one simple reason. Andrew was Peter's brother, and he followed the teaching of John the Baptist. Andrew learned about Jesus before Peter, and it was Andrew who told Peter that Jesus was the Christ. Why was there this discrepancy in the scriptures? When I studied the early history of Christianity I realized that there were two factions or groups that came forth from this time period claiming to be the true Church. There seems to be a strong indication in the New Testament that Peter was somehow the chief among the Apostles. There are scriptures that teach him becoming the Rock. But in reality these scriptures have been tampered with, and I will explain.

CONTROVERSY OVER CHURCH LEADERSHIP?

First of all Christ is the Rock of all ages, he is the light of ages past. He is the water of enlightenment. As the scriptures indicate Christ was the Rock that brought forth water in ancient Israel. The term used in the Greek language for Rock was Petra. When Jesus called Peter the rock it came from the Greek word petros, meaning little stone. Jesus said, "I will build my church upon the Petra, the Rock, not petros, Peter." Jesus also taught that his disciples were not to become like the Gentiles where one ruled over the other. He taught they were all equal with one another and with Jesus. Others believed in the first several centuries that since Peter was the first to see Jesus after his resurrection then that meant Peter was the chief, vicar, somewhat like a Pope today. But again, Peter wasn't the first to see Jesus after the resurrection. Mary of Magdalene was the first. The only reason the disciples came to the grave site in the first place was because the two women went back and told them about Jesus. The only reason Peter got there next was because he outran John as they both headed for the site of the tomb. It would be ridiculous to ascertain by this that Peter was next in command after Jesus exited.

The next point to realize is that Jerusalem was the center, and the church was stationed in Jerusalem as a home point. This is where all the major decisions took place in considering doctrine. However Peter wasn't the individual that headed the Jerusalem post. It was James! Peter and John worked together as they traveled with the Gospel. Another point of interest, in the decision making process when Paul came to Jerusalem to seek out information dealing with the uncircumcised it was James that made the final decree, not Peter. Another area that dispels this concept is that Jesus taught that his disciples, along with the 70 others that were called and trained, were to go out two by two. This illustrated that no one was in command.

The final problem to consider is that once the Gospel had been preached to all of Israel the function of the Israelite church ceased. The age of Israel finally came to an end with the destruction of the Temple some 40 years after Jesus walked the earth. Afterwards those among the church in Jerusalem fled into the mountainous regions and basically disappeared. However the Catholic church claimed at the time that Peter set in motion the church when he went to Rome. And supposedly they believed the true church continued throughout the history of what is called the Catholic Church and the many Protestant breakaways.

What had been forgotten is that the Church in Rome was in a Gentile land. Peter had been killed and much of the teachings of the original Apostles died with Peter. But there was one other that kept the faith alive in the Gentile world through the church, and that was Paul.

TWO CHRISTIAN GROUPS CAME OUT OF THE FIRST CENTURY. ONE SURVIVED ABOVE GROUND THE OTHER BELOW GROUND!

It is here that the separation begins. The Gnostics were the Christians that came from the regions where Paul taught. The Catholics came from the region where Peter had been murdered. This began the war within the Christian Church. The Gnostics taught a mystical religion and the Catholics taught a letter of the law, and humanistic religion. These groups fought bitterly against one another. The Gnostics believed and stated that Paul taught that everything Jesus taught was mystery embedded within the letter. The Catholics taught that mysticism was pagan and accused the Gnostics of being Sun worshippers. The Gnostics taught that humans existed in a spiritual state before the foundation of the world. The Catholics taught that we are only brought into existence within the life we are born into. Then came the big one, the battle over whether Jesus was a one and only or was he like all of us. The Gnostics taught Jesus was like each of us, preparing us for our journey back to our spiritual homeland. The Catholics taught that Jesus was a one and only and salvation only came through the church, as well as making Mary the human mother of Jesus, an Icon to worship.

I believe now that the clash of these two groups is once again coming head to head. Nearly 98% of all Christians today teach the Catholic doctrine whether they are considered Catholic or not. However there is a tremendous surge taking place where the Gnostics are coming back out of the woodwork like ants to their supper. Many Christians are realizing that something is terribly wrong with the concept they have always believed, especially as we enter the vital year 2000AD. Many are turning against the ancient paradigms that have imprisoned people in fear. I for one firmly believe that the Gnostics were the ones who carried forth the true mysteries and everything else is only illusion.

GNOSTIC GOSPEL OF PHILLIP DECLARES ONE MUST BECOME WHAT THEY SEEK

The Gnostics understood, as the Gospel of Phillip alludes in the Nag Hammadi texts, that we must become what we seek. He taught, when a man sees the light he must become the light. When a man sees the Christ he must become the Christ, and when a man sees the Father, then he is the Father. Each of us, once we have been united with the Christ, must become the Christ. This proves that we all have the same two-fold nature that Jesus had. We are the Son of Man by our physical bloodlines, and we are the Sons of God by virtue of our being the actual created spirit of the Father/Mother. Therefore Jesus like us is both the servant and the master.

JESUS BOWS BEFORE THE CHRIST IN US AS WE BOW BEFORE THE CHRIST IN HIM

This concept was illustrated when Jesus bowed down and girded himself with a towel so he could wash the feet of his disciples. This was a humble ceremony back in those days. It was unheard of for a man of Jesus' stature to bow before anyone to wash their feet. This was the job for the lowly servant. Jesus bowed before Peter and began to wash his feet, and Peter was beside himself with uncertainty. He said, "Lord I cannot allow you to wash my feet." And Jesus said, " If I do not wash your feet then you are none of mine." We may not understand the humility that was involved in washing feet. In those days people wore sandals and walked in dirt and mud all day long. When they entered someone's home it was the servant of the house responsibility to wash the guest's feet. Peter could not understand why the Lord master was bowing like a menial servant to accomplish such an act. What Peter failed to see was that Jesus was bowing before the Christ within his disciples, just as they were to bow before the Christ in Jesus. Each of us are to become one with the Divine Son so we can enter the mystical portals of divinity again.

These acts and teachings from our friend Jesus were to direct our human minds away from the veil and unto our Heavenly Father within each of us. Jesus was never meant to be a one-man show but rather a master of many masters to come!

WHAT IS THE SECOND RETURN OF CHRIST?

In approaching the subject of Christ it would be amiss for me not to discuss what many call the second return of Christ. The Bible teaches that the days would come where we would hear, Lo, here is Christ or there is Christ. He is in the desert or the secret chamber. It also said not to believe this and we were instructed not to go forth. The Bible reveals, as lightning shines from one part of the heavens to the other so also would be the coming of the Son of Man. It states every eye will witness this incredible event.

When we investigate this subject more thoroughly it becomes clear there are many inconsistencies ranging within this subject that many have overlooked in examining this picture. The Bible states, "So as the days of Noah were so also shall be the coming of the Son of Man." It also uses the same explanation in describing the days of Lot prior to Sodom and Gomorrah's destruction. Lot, the Nephew of Abraham, was warned to leave the city before its destruction. Other scriptures say that one will be taken and the other left. It speaks also of Christ being revealed in secret where some will be taken. The disciples asked, where would these be taken, where were they to go. Jesus said, "Wheresoever the carcass is there also the eagles will be gathered."

Other scriptures indicate the kingdom of God comes not by observation. Observation comes from the Greek word for "ocular," meaning to see with one's eyes. Jesus went on to reveal that the kingdom is within you. And again to make things more confusing, there are more passages that reveal that the kingdom will overtake people as a thief in the night, and people would be caught off guard by the shock of secrecy. It also teaches that Christ is to return to earth whereas other scriptures state the people would meet Christ in heaven.

APPARENT DISCREPANCIES IN THE WRITTEN LETTER

Here is our list of scenarios: (1) He is not in the secret chamber. (2) Every eye will see the return. (3) The return is likened unto Noah and Lot's days. (4) The revealing is in secret. (5) There will be a gathering of some taken to witness the revealing. (6) The 'eye' cannot behold the coming. (7) The kingdom is within you. (8) It comes as a thief in the night. (9) Christ will meet us on earth. (10) We will meet Christ in heaven.

These contradictions alone are enough to create massive confusion. Can you imagine trying to explain this to a little child? First of all, if Jesus was truly bringing this magnificent kingdom with him and every eye shall witness this event, then why does he say, the kingdom comes NOT by observation, where the human eye would not witness this event? Secondly, what would Noah and Lot's days have to do with the coming of the kingdom? There was nothing in those two stories that indicated a kingdom coming and being set up. These stories were about certain people who were protected against great disasters. Are we to conclude that the return of Christ is a disaster in the coming? Some do.

If your brain is not doing flip-flops right about now then you are not reading this close enough. It also reports where some would be taken to go to this event, whereas others would be left behind, unable to attend. (One will be taken, the other left behind) The scriptures warn against Christ being revealed in the secret chambers or the desert. So here we have Christ being revealed in secret, but he can't be revealed in secret. Then we learn that every eye will see this, but the human eye

162

can't see this. Then to top it all off, he is coming as a thief in the night.

If a teacher were to take this into a classroom filled with young eager minds and teach this subject as it really states, the students would probably have a massive stroke trying to ascertain whether they were coming or going. Do you know what the problem with this entire evaluation is? I have been giving you the written letter, and as I have stated throughout the written letter was to cause the uninitiated not to comprehend the mysteries. It was designed to throw you off, and it does just that! The Bible has to be deciphered like a Sherlock Holmes code-book!

TRUTH REALIGNED WITHIN GNOSIS OF MYSTERY

If we go back to this material using the keys to the mystery we can straighten out some of this confusion. First of all in the scripture it reveals that prior to this event there would be false Christs and false prophets. Jesus was warning against following men of the flesh. These would be individuals male or female that would parade themselves as being God's representatives and use deception to gain their own following. They would use tactics that would allure unsuspecting victims into their web of deceit. They would use the name of Jesus Christ to gain followers. They would teach that Jesus is the Christ and the only. And because Jesus was the one and only he would have to replace himself with certain ones to represent him while he is away. Thereby making that leader the Vicar of Christ, one who replaces Christ. The teaching throughout all of religion reveals that men must follow men. Thereby changing a Christian, one who is to follow the Divine Son the Christ, into Christianity, people who follow other people.

These churches set up hierarchical structures within their organization creating a protocol of systematic design. They teach that the leaders of the church are the only ones that have the answers, and if you don't attend their structured organization then you will go to hell. This became the damning call to salvation. One who believes they're actually being saved from God, the very one that is supposed to be saving them.

Jesus made it very clear, he stated, "Do not as the Gentiles do, where one rules over the other." Jesus told the disciples prior to his leaving, that the Holy Spirit, the comforter would teach them all things, even the hidden secrets and mysteries of God. Scripture later reveals that no man need teach you, for the comforter within would teach you all things. Jesus nowhere in the entire Bible stated that men would reveal the hidden mysteries of God, nor did he teach that the Bible would reveal the hidden mysteries of God. He taught that these things came from within you. Jesus did not tell his disciples, "I will leave you the Bible to teach of my ways." Whenever something of great magnitude was revealed Jesus said, "No man taught you this, only the Father above taught you this."

But it was the false prophets and false Christs that taught such damnable heresies for personal aggrandizement. When I had my first edition of this book out, one lady wrote me chiding and demeaning me for not understanding that the Bible clearly states that Jesus told all his disciples to write the Bible. To be the only truth given to mankind. She then said, "I love the Lord whether you do or not." I had to cry inside for such ignorance. This woman probably really believes this is in the Bible because someone told her that. She is probably going to live her entire life believing in this erroneous concept, but what can you do? False Christs and false prophets have been spreading damnable doctrines for 2000 years. As Jesus said, they would make you more the two-fold child of hell than even they are.

BEWARE OF FALSE CHRISTS...

A false Christ and a false prophet are those that teach you to follow other people and not the divine Son within. The entire concept of the church was built on a false premise. Jesus never meant to set up a physical organization structured where people ruled people. As I said earlier, the name church in the early New Testament, first century, meant to become an initiate, a called out one. Some may wonder why did there appear to be a physical structure? Because in the early church it was recognized that the people were not understanding the mysteries, they remained as babes in Christ. The hope was to bring these people into a community where everyone had all things in common so they would learn the mysteries and then teach others. This was part of the secrets coming from the groups called the Essenes which Jesus had been part of. The Church was to be a vehicle to teach the hidden mysteries without persecution from the outside world. Instead it took on another look altogether.

As Paul stated the problem was "They did not grow." They stagnated and remained as carnal babes in Christ. The whole purpose of the Church was to train initiates to go out to reveal the Mystery-Gospel (good news) to others. However it ended up becoming a place for worship and not for training.

Today we witness that the only ones who attempt to bring forward the Gospel are the icons of churches, the religious heads. The people on the other hand feel they have no responsibility other than giving some money, and going to church once a week. They think that will get them into heaven. Jesus never built a physical church. He started a spiritual training program for the inner awareness of the Father to enter the hearts and souls of the fallen ones. Flesh and blood cannot please the Father, nor can it inherit eternal life. But preachers, priests and ministers continue to teach that you have to abide in a physical temple to gain eternity. That is exactly what you do not want to do. For it is our physical temple, the flesh and blood biological body, that has kept us away from our eternal and internal awareness through blindness of the truth. If you continue to remain in this state you will never be enlightened. The temple in Jerusalem was destroyed a long time ago to teach that we are all veiled in a human tabernacle. What good is the church doing anybody when they rebuild the temple and lock us inside?

THE MYSTICAL THIRD EYE WILL WITNESS THE SECOND COMING, THROUGH YOU!

Now finally, what could it possibly mean that every eye will see this auspicious return, and then it states your eyes cannot see this return? When the scriptures teach that every eye will see, it is speaking of the mystical third eye. What so many do not understand is that we are spiritual beings living inside a physical body. We have the ability to see beyond the realm of flesh. Every night when you go to bed and dream you are using the mystical third eye. When I was younger I told a friend to close his eyes and tell me what he saw. He thought I was crazy. I asked him to try it and see if he saw anything. At the time I had no idea of the mysteries of God. I knew however that I could close my eyes and concentrate and see actual moving pictures of people, places and things in full color. I wondered if others could do this also. My friend attempted it but to no avail. Years went by until I read one of the Nag Hammadi texts. I believe it was one of the lost Gospels, where Jesus told one of his disciples to close his eyes and tell him what he saw. Chills went up and down my spine realizing that I had said and done the same thing without any prior knowledge of these lost fragmental scriptures. I hadn't used this inner gift for quite some time because when my friend couldn't do it I thought maybe I shouldn't be doing it either. However I have once again begun practicing this art and it is unbelievable.

This is the third eye; it is the spiritual awareness of things beyond the veil. It is as real as you and me. This is the eye that Jesus referred to when he stated every eye shall see. It is the third eye that would bear witness to this incredible event. The ancient myths told of the one-eyed Cyclops. If you recall from pictures this eye was centered between where our two human eyes would be. This is the area where our third eye is located and where you can visualize many things beyond the veil. When it stated that the kingdom comes not by observation this is clear enough. Your physical eyes will not be able to behold this event. Later I will explain why.

OUT OF BODY EXPERIENCES?

The reason comparisons were made with Noah and Lot to the return of Christ is to understand that these stories teach of men who were physically protected from physical disasters. I now firmly believe that these are all mystical arguments discussing the phenomenon of going Out of Body. One will be taken, the other left behind. It shows that the revealing would be in secret, but it also states that Christ is not in the secret places. This is because we are talking about two different dimensions. Wheresoever the carcass is, refers to our humanoid bodies. And there the eagles will be gathered. This is another mystical statement referring to the exiting of our bodies, and being as eagles or vultures would be at a feast. Now when it says not to seek Christ in the secret chamber or desert, it is revealing that he will not be found in a physical place, but a spiritual place. There are also esoteric references behind these embedded clues that deal with earthquakes, floods, earth shifts, pole shifts, ice cap melts etc... But I want to center on the mystical references to going Out of Body. This is a subject I will deal with in detail towards the end of the book.

We must comprehend that we are spiritual beings living in a matter universe. We have hidden glories and powers that evade our use because of the veil. In retrospect we can plainly see that the teaching of Jesus never placed any hierarchical form of government over his church. The brotherhood of Christ was to serve humanity, not to rule. It was man by the fallen consciousness that the Bible terms Satan, which placed this bondage upon one another. When the scriptures in Revelation said that Christ would come and rule with a rod of iron these were misinterpretations of the Greek words. They actually referred to a shepherd leading his sheep in love. The term rod comes from the Greek word meaning a shepherd's staff. A shepherd does not beat his sheep, he lovingly leads them.

In the spiritual kingdom of God, which everyone accesses through their own divine being and the mystical third eye, we are to honor one another as we are all from the same spiritual family. The motto of the brotherhood is service, service, and service, and of course absolute, undying love! False Christs are those from whatever race, creed, color or religion that desire your obedience to them instead of the Christ within. True men and women of the Great Father/Mother spirit are those from whatever race, creed, color or religion that teach of the light of the Great Spirit within. Which in reality is your I AM presence, your very tree of life, the great Omnipotent Father/Mother spirit.

Jesus said, "You will know them by their fruits..." Divisions will always be created as long as there is class warfare where people rule other people, and the wealthy dominate the weak. The freedom that everyone searches for is within the kingdom of God buried deeply within our veil. Earnestly seek it and it will shine forth like lightning from one part of the heavens to the other, and your mystical third eye will indeed see this great event.

MYSTERY REVEALED!

Galatians 4:19 "My little children, for who I labor in birth again, UNTIL CHRIST BE FORMED IN YOU."

The Apostle Paul uses some dynamic scriptures in teaching of these wonderful mysteries. Did you recognize two of the mysteries in the above verse, labor in birth again and Christ being formed in you?

Romans 16:25 "Now to him that is able to establish you according to my gospel, and the preaching of Jesus Christ, ACCORDING TO THE REVELATION OF THE MYSTERY WHICH WAS KEPT SECRET SINCE THE WORLD BEGAN."

Colossians 1:26 "THE MYSTERY THAT HAS BEEN HIDDEN FROM THE AGES AND FROM GENERATIONS, but now has been revealed unto his saints."

I Corinthians 2:7 "WE SPEAK THE WISDOM OF GOD IN A MYSTERY, THE HIDDEN WISDOM WHICH GOD ORDAINED BEFORE THE AGES UNTO OUR GLORY."

Colossians 1:27 "To them God willed to make known what are the riches of the glory, of this MYSTERY among the Gentiles, which is. "C H R I S T I N Y O U." The hope and glory!"

Paul understood that one of the most profound mysteries is that the Christ is within us. This is our only hope of glory. This is our personal salvation! This is our grace! This is our forgiveness of sins! We really do have a PERSONAL SAVIOR, one whom abides within you as the light consciousness of the mind of the Father.

Jesus is our Christ and shall always be, but we are also partakers of the same spiritual body, if indeed we eat of this flesh and drink of this blood! This is the mystical reference that Jesus is like all of us, and that we must do what he did to succeed. It is also our portion of the inheritance, the divine Son. Then truly the bread of life that came into the world through Jesus will also abide in us.

The body of Christ was mystically broken for each of us to take our part of the Divine Son, the unity of the Father, to eat of and live. To actually believe that Jesus kept the divine Son to himself would be to deny the very Christ that was inside Jesus.

Jesus said, "My Father gives you the true bread of life..." When Jesus became united with the divine Son of his I AM presence, he then became the manifestation of the bread of life for the whole world. But Jesus' mission was to break that bread and divide among those that were ready for initiation, and give to each of the enlightened ones as they passed their tests. It was eventually to be given to all of mankind to finally overcome.

Jesus fulfilled in his temple what is required of all of us. He went on to reveal within John Chapter six, that the bread of God was not something physical that you actually ate, but a mystical revelation of something much greater. He said, "The bread of life is the Word of God." And the Word is the Divine

Son. It was to be shared equally between all those that entered the light of their true heritage.

So at Passover Jesus broke the bread representing the divine Son and passed it around so that the divine Son would enter within the temple of man. And the fruit of the cup was passed also and it represented our unity with the Father through the spirit. This revealed that eventually the children of the Father would unite again as the supreme deities of the Father/Mother Spirit. And one day the mystery would eventually unveil itself within each one separately as they are ready. And then they would return to their Tree of Life, the heavenly presence of the great I AM.

So goes the mystery of our Christ.

MYSTERY FIVE
The Mystery of Death

The subject of death has been one of the most averted. Most do not like conversing about death, and in truth, who would? It is a morbid subject that would best be left alone. I have experienced the pain of losing loved ones, especially the death of both my parents. I know the sting of death, and coping with the loss of loved ones is a dramatic battle that everyone will in some way face before the time comes for them to also pass on to this uncertainty. As we delve into this dark subject we must comprehend some of this mystery from our own perspective. We have lived our lives believing in the finality of death. Although we learn to handle this misfortune we realize how difficult it is to experience the loss of communication and the sharing of experiences with those that have passed on.

Often we wish certain individuals were back in our life to help us with instruction in time of need. We seek compassion from those that knew us well and understood our plight in life. Memories begin to fail over the years as we eagerly try to recall events.

I have wrestled many times with this enemy called death. I have lost friends by accidents, others by suicide and still others by that enemy called old age. It is incredible to ascertain how fragile our existence on earth really is. I became so withdrawn and heart-sickened by the constant loss of friends and family over the years that I began to hold back my love for others. The fear of losing anyone else and having to experience this agonizing mental torture was more than I wanted to deal with, to the point that death really became the enemy that the Bible speaks of.

Over the years I continued to withdraw from this subject. I did not want to talk about it, and I actually engineered a callous attitude due to my misunderstanding. This in part was responsible for the terror that was created in my mind. Oh, don't get me wrong, I did believe in an afterlife. I was raised in a Christian world having the belief that there would be a resurrection at a future date where all those that died would surely rise again. This of course gave me a hope that many do not have; yet it did not lessen the pain. And of course it never removed the doubts either. There always remained the fear of the unknown. Let's be honest, how many ever witnessed someone rise from their grave? Who is living today that can give testimony to such an event?

DID TWELVE MEN WITNESS A MAN RISE FROM THE DEAD?

This was the story that was passed down to us from 2000 years ago about a man named Jesus Christ. There were a mystical number of 12 Apostles that were specially chosen and trained to witness this demonstrable event so that it could be passed down by word of mouth. This small entourage was with Jesus before he died and afterwards.

This miraculous event leaves much room for doubt because no one in existence today can vouch for it, thereby leaving enough question to create the fear and uncertainty that we all have to deal with. We are left with a document that has been edited and reinterpreted many times by differing mindsets, which have postulated their own ideas over the years. This manuscript of a compilation of hundreds of translations may or may not be completely accurate, thereby leaving us with the task of proving its validity. Whatever the source it leaves one to ponder the possibility if there really is life after death? We can be brave and believe with certainty that this book of books is absolutely correct, and all one must do is believe with faith that it is true. This does not however change the facts that we have absolutely no viable proof that it is accurate when dealing with a subject such as death and an afterlife. Let's be honest, why did Jesus need people to witness this event if all it takes is faith? Why was witnessing this event important? Because without proof no one can be expected to really believe.

WHY DID JESUS FEEL IT NECESSARY TO GIVE TESTIMONY OF HIS DEATH?

There is also the plaguing doubt that encompasses all Christians, that we were always told Jesus was special and different than we are. So many might believe that this event was only meant for Jesus the Son of God, and not for us. Again, whatever you believe is immaterial because without proof you really don't know, do you? There are those that believe Jesus never really died in the crucifixion, and that another died that day in his stead. Even some of the lost fragments of the Nag Hammadi texts show Jesus speaking with one of his disciples during the crucifixion and he claimed that another named Simon was being put to death, not really Jesus. I for one believe that the death of Jesus was absolutely real in order to prove the mystery. Yet I also have no problem believing that Jesus could have spoken to one of the disciples during this crucifixion. WHY? Because Jesus was a divine being as we all are who abide in the flesh. The spirit of Jesus wasn't killed, just his mortal body. He could have left his body and transformed in front of his disciple and spoke to him during the crucifixion without any problem whatsoever, and through history the discussion could have been misinterpreted. Either way you look at this is up to you, but Jesus' own body perished so that he could teach the mystery of the true resurrection from the veil.

I know there are going to be those that say, "Well you just have to believe and that is all there is to it!" My response to this is that when one matures they recognize that what they thought was accurate as a youth is no longer a part of their indoctrination. If changes can occur this easily in this temporary existence then how can one stake their entire life on a concept of eternal truisms, knowing full well they might find out later they were incorrect. And that their understanding was based on misrepresentation and wrong information. Ever since I was a young boy I wondered why there were so many differing religious beliefs. A Catholic might disagree with a Protestant! Protestants may disagree with Moslems! And Moslems may disagree with Hindus, and Hindus might disagree with Jews, but are they all right, or are they all wrong? Or maybe they all have a piece to the puzzle. They all may be right in the over-all picture as a segment to the entire thesis. It could be that everyone has a piece to this puzzle, but it only becomes truths when they admit we are all part of a bigger picture. And limited views are just that, a limited reality of the whole concept!

WHAT IF YOU CAN KNOW FOR SURE THAT YOU REALLY DON'T DIE?

What is the possibility that the gnosis of an afterlife does not have to be an uncertainty? What if one could know absolutely that not only is there an afterlife, but death is only a transition to another dimension and that one never really dies. They actually enter another plane of awareness. And perhaps what occurred with Jesus 2000 years ago had nothing to do with him personally per-se, but was to instruct that death was just a shift in awareness. And that his immediate resurrection was to prove that death is an illusion. What if the afterlife that Jesus was speaking about when he said, "If you believe on me you shall never see death," is really instantaneous? What if we really don't die, as we have always understood death?

THE SERPENT IN THE GARDEN MAY HAVE NOT LIED AFTER ALL!

In the account from the allegorical Garden of Eden the Serpent told Eve to go ahead and eat of the forbidden fruit. Eve replied, "That every tree of the Garden we may eat, but of the tree in the

174

midst of the Garden we may not eat of it lest we die." The Serpent immediately responded, "You shall not surely die, for God knows that the day that you eat therefore, you shall become like him, to know good and evil!"

My entire life I had been instructed that the Serpent lied to Eve that day in the Garden and that's all there was to it. Do not question it and do not look for any other answers. Come on! We all die, don't we? It was obvious that what the Serpent stated was incredibly stupid. And today it is even a greater flaw for one to believe this! Just walk over to the nearest cemetery to refute this bogus comment.

I had accepted that the story given in Genesis was true, and the Serpent was the devil incarnate sent to destroy the helpless humans on their quest for eternal life. If anyone would have come to me and questioned this account I would have been astonished, and frankly would have wondered if they were also affiliated with this great deception of Satan. It wasn't until years later that I went back to this account and read something that literally threw me for a loop. I was completely dumbfounded!

When the Serpent revealed to Eve that eating of this forbidden fruit would make them like God and they would know the difference between good and evil, I was shocked to comprehend that the Serpent was telling the truth, at least on this account. Because in Genesis 3:22 God himself stated, "And the Lord God said, BEHOLD, man has now become one of us, to know good and evil..."

Now unless my thinking has been altered in any way, this is what the Serpent told Eve, Right? But haven't we always been told that the Serpent lied to Eve? Why was God confirming this? God personally said, "Man has now become like one of us..." We seem to have a problem here! If the Serpent didn't lie about becoming God, are we sure he lied about not really dying? Obviously becoming God would have to be more than just attaining knowledge, a great transformation would need to take place. If you continue with this epic story in the Garden, it becomes apparent what God stated! If he did not block the way back into the Garden when he thrust Adam and Eve out, they could get back in and take of the tree of life, and live forever. But the question remains "How can mere mortal man live forever." And wasn't this what the Serpent told Eve, that they would not surely die? Why did God send Angels to guard against the reentry into the Garden? Could it be that the Serpent was telling the truth all along?

God told Adam and Eve they would die after eating of this forbidden tree. Then God forced them out of the Garden so they would not live forever. What is going on here? After years of research I began to comprehend the mystical reference of the Garden of Eden and what was truly transpiring in this gnosis. It became obvious that this story was indeed an allegory that depicted metaphoric events that had transpired long before the story of the Biblical Adam and Eve. These events were actually constructed within the material world of flesh and blood beings to enlighten them of what had transpired from a spiritual Garden of Eden, not a physical one.

The depiction of the Serpent was to enlighten one of their pre-mortal pasts, and to instruct how the human race had fallen into darkness via a spiritual world into a physical world. As a born spirit one can never die, it is impossible, and this is what the serpent was telling Eve. However if the table is turned and you are cast out of this spiritual plane to adopt another awareness, which we call flesh and blood, you can most certainly suffer the agony of death. And yet as Jesus said, one will never see death. Remember that God stated that if they ate of the tree of life they would live forever. What really occurred was that while living in the Garden one would never see death, and eating of the forbidden fruit was a description of how one could be made aware of this reality while under captivity. And then the captors would be brought to light as the Gods of both good and evil.

The Garden of Eden was a story of how the human race was once divine beings that were kidnapped because of a lack of

Gnosis. Their captors were higher evolved beings that ruled as gods over mere man. But they would be recognized if the humans understood who their captors were. So we were led out of paradise to follow our captors into a world of delusion and illusion. Our fig leafs of material flesh and blood bodies became our coverings over our divine nature, so we would forget our spiritual past and rely upon the Lords of good and evil. Then as spirit divine beings we entered a reality that would experience the sensation that we call death. However Jesus came to quell this deception, and tell us that we don't really die, just as the serpent stated. Some may find great offence to this argument, wondering how dare I compare Jesus with the Serpent. However, I am only comparing as the Bible compared the two. Remember when Moses was seeking the healing of the Israelites that were attacked by a flying creature and were dying because of its bite. Moses placed a Serpent on a staff and had the people come before this serpent for healing. Later in the New Testament it was revealed that the Serpent represented Jesus. The Bible reveals, "To become wise as a Serpent and harmless as a dove." The Serpent is a symbol for wisdom and gnosis, not necessarily for evil as we have always been led to believe.

Living forever was not a lie, it was a truth. So the Lords of good and evil had to design a way to take our reality from us so that their law would be fulfilled, because while living in these garments of fig leafs we would certainly experience death. This occurred when the appearance of eternal life was removed and the spirit-born children of God tasted the sensation of death.

As the spirit-born children of the Father we had been brought down into the lower life forms, and these new forms would become our new reality. We were subjugated to this lower form of mass to the point it eventually appeared as real. Our flesh and blood then became more real than spirit. And if we could be encased within this tomb of flesh for a very long period of time we could eventually forget our pre-mortal past altogether. All memory of that greater awareness would be erased by virtue of continually reliving another reality.

The Tree of Life is our personal portion of this great expansive divinity as our "I AM" presence. It was our free gift given to us before the foundation of this world. We were at that time placed in the family tree of the great divine and were children of the highest supreme council of divinity. The family tree of life was a genealogical tree known Biblically as the Book of Life. When we lost access by following the shadow Lords we became bonded and enslaved in another reality and dimension. We became separated from our own "I AM" presence as a willful decision to follow our captors. We then got lost in the great unknown. Our projected soul spirit was then separated from the eternal "I AM" and our consciousness underwent a great change, also eliminating memories of our true reality. We then began to experience pain, tears and death, and this became our new reality. The shadow Lords would then rule from both sides of the fence, here in the fleshly plane and on the other side in the spirit plane. However we would still be cut off from our highest plane of awareness.

OUR PRESENT REALITY BECOMES OUR CONSCIOUS AWARENESS!

It is not difficult to comprehend that if our true reality has been altered then our present reality would become our true conscious awareness. When the shadow Lord said, "We shall surely die..." it became true when we lost our first estate and conscious awareness. So now within our new reality even if we live many lives it would always appear to each of us that the life we are living at present is the only life, and death is all we can look forward to in this future. The truth about reincarnation is simply the fact that we can't really die. We can only be absorbed into another reality. Yet every time we return to this environment we will still be in bondage to this reality until we break away from our captors and do what Jesus did to return to the Father. What is so apropos about this gnosis is watching people argue as they contend we are only human and that's it, just mere flesh and blood. This is because their reality has suffered such a change that they can only see in darkness of the veil and not the light of the Father within! If the light from within would be revealed, then they would forever acknowledge what Jesus and the Serpent said: "You shall never see death."

GOD IS THE FATHER OF ABRAHAM, ISAAC AND JACOB; AND GOD IS THE GOD OF THE LIVING NOT THE DEAD!

When Jesus was asked about the possibility of an afterlife he continually repeated the accepted phrase of his day. "God is the Father of Abraham, Isaac and Jacob. He is the God of the living and not the dead." When I first read this I found this statement extremely profound. How could God be the Father of these Patriarchs, and also be the Father of the living and not the dead? I questioned this because when Jesus stated this, these three men had long been dead and buried. How could Jesus make a blanket statement like this? Abraham, Isaac and Jacob were not dead because as Jesus said one can never see death. But until you become aware of this truth you will die in whatever lifetime you exist in. That is why he stated you will never taste death. Many have translated this erroneously that we are all headed for eternal death and without Jesus you will die forever. What they fail to comprehend is that we are already living in an eternal death and until we awaken to the true mysteries we will forever live our days in illusion and delusion.

Notice the anger of the religious hierarchy of the day when Jesus brought some of this incredible gnosis to them.

John 8:51-56 "Verily, verily I say unto you. If a man keep my saying he shall never see death. Then said the people unto him, now we know that you have a devil. Abraham is dead, and the prophets; and you say, if a man keep my saying he shall never taste death. Are you greater than our Father Abraham, WHICH IS DEAD? And the prophets are dead? Who do you think you are?" Jesus answered them, "If I honor myself, my honor is nothing; it is my Father that honors me; of whom you say that he is your God. Yet you have not known him. But I know him... Your Father Abraham rejoiced to see my day, AND HE SAW IT. And was glad."

Jesus pulled no punches in his explanation. He made it extremely clear to those that had ears to hear. Abraham was alive and well after his known death in the veil. This also backs up other verses showing Abraham alive and living in another dimension as the story of Lazarus and the rich man relates.

LAZARUS AND THE RICH MAN!

Lazarus was a poor sickly beggar. He would often lie waiting at the gate of the rich man's home to see if he could be fed with the leftovers off the rich man's table. Lazarus was in a very bad way, and the dogs would even come and lick his sores.

It came to pass that both Lazarus and the rich man died in the veil. Immediately upon leaving the veil Lazarus' soul-projected spirit was escorted by two angels into the realm where Abraham was living. However, the rich man did not have it so fortunate. When he left the veil he went into the belief system of torment by fire. From this horrible place the rich man called out to his Father Abraham. He asked for relief of the great pain he was agonizing. He beseeched for the cool finger of Lazarus to wet the fires of his torment.

It is such a shame that many cannot see the metaphoric content of these scriptures was not to be taken literally. Yet they attempt to relate them in an ordinary way by the letter. It was so obvious what the rich man was saying when he asked for the cool of Lazarus' finger to wet the fires of torment. He was asking for forgiveness of how he treated him while living on the earth plane. The fire was a metaphor for a burning conscience.

Too many try to explain this as a spiteful God taking his vengeance out on ignorant humans for their failure to do the right thing. But notice, the rich man did not ask God for forgiveness. He was seeking for Lazarus to forgive him. The rich man understood he was suffering partly because of what he did to Lazarus, but how would he know? It is because after one dies they have a life review, and in this review everyone sees the good and evil they performed while in the flesh. The rich man saw how he ignored Lazarus when he was begging for some scrap of food and was very ill. He saw how he ignored him while he lived in substance and had much to offer. This pained the rich man greatly to see how he handled a brother.

The rich man also asked Abraham if he would warn those of his own household that they needed to change their thinking. He became aware that his religious beliefs were wrong, and now wanted to warn the rest of his family so they would change before they died. So he asked Abraham if he would make an appearance before his family. He thought if they could only witness Abraham whom they believed was dead, alive again then they would believe and repent from their error filled ways. However Abraham stated that he didn't believe the rich man's family would respond to see their Father alive and well again. He said they failed to believe Moses, so surely they would reject him.

So what was the rich man's real concern here? Was it his suffering? That was part of it! But the issue that needs addressing was that the rich man had false values while living on earth. He learned that when one dies they really don't die, but enter another dimension to learn lessons of how they handled themselves during their physical lifetime. He realized that the judgement was an ongoing judgement that existed during training in the earthly plane. He understood that Earth is where we grow and learn from our mistakes. He was able to witness his life and saw where he failed in a very important matter. And he realized that our beliefs, no matter how confident we are in them, could be wrong!

Also the torment of fire was created out of his belief system and it actually represents a two-fold occurrence after one dies. Remember that Lazarus was escorted out of his dimension by two angels whereas the rich man had no assistance.

HELLISH PLACES? CREATIONS OF THE MIND!

It has become apparent ever since the days of Enoch that one can enter a place of fire and burning and experience agonizing pain. But these places are not real in the sense that many believe. They are actually created out of the mind. There are places of torment that are like hell that have been created by false concepts and belief systems while living on earth. Usually faulty religious views create these hellish places. This parable of the rich man and Lazarus was not to be taken as a reality but more as a concept of truth. It was a metaphor teaching about the afterlife. So the fire the rich man was enduring was a metaphor of what can take place in duality on the other side, both mentally and through illusion! But they are illusions of the mind, and I will address this later on!

Those men like Abraham, Moses, Elijah, Samuel, Lazarus and Enoch were very much alive and even reincarnated at times after their account written in the Biblical history. The Bible teaches these concepts, and relates most emphatically that death is just a transition or a change. A return to the reality we all came from. However because of our separation from our Father, the "I AM" presence, we cannot grasp our true reality even when we are between the cycles. That is why we keep returning to learn more lessons. We continually fail to reach the divine gnosis of salvation and eternal life, so we return to this hellish world to keep taking exams.

There are those that are waiting between lives. There are those that are experiencing traumatic events because of faulty belief systems and are actually trapped in non-realities created by the mind. But all of us are searching for the true Holy Grail; our divine establishments back with the Father.

The Father was not responsible for the fire that tormented the rich man; the fire of his faulty understanding was tormenting him. Even Abraham called the rich man SON denoting that he was also part of the great "I AM". Whenever an individual exists within the realm of the belief system engendered by false understanding, these trials are only for a time of purification until an individual is ready to proceed to the next level of training, or reincarnated back on a 3 dimensional plane like Earth. Paul spoke somewhat mystically of these events when he declared that your works could be destroyed by fire but you yourself could still be saved. The works are the faulty egos and belief systems we create while on the earth plane. It is these egos that are being destroyed by non-real events, which teach the observer about a better reality. That is why it is so dangerous to create a false belief system in this world, because if you do not control the ego you will suffer the ignominy of your own reality. Jesus spoke of this when he said, "Judge not that you be not judged..." If you condemn others to a hell fire believing this is our Father in Heaven's will then you may have to experience the pain of your judgement. You will have created this hell in your mental realms, and now it must be played out. All will reap what they sow. If you believe our Father has a hell to punish and avenge, and you judge others to this hell of torment, then you will experience this plague of judgement by your own making, until you can be cleansed by the fire of illusion of this judgement and iniquity.

Abraham understood the law of cause and effect. That is why he couldn't intervene for the rich man's sake even though he was pleading for help. He could not remove that which the rich man created for himself, anymore than Jesus could remove us from something we create for ourselves. They can point the way, they can teach us how, but they can't do it for us. The rich man because of his lack of mercy while living on the earth plane created the world of his afterlife that he was suffering in the mind. The old saying goes, "Whatsoever goes around must come around!"

THE BIBLE VERIFIES AN IMMEDIATE AFTERLIFE!

After researching hundreds of verses in the Bible that deal with the afterlife it became obvious why most do not comprehend the mystery of these events. They do not understand the mystical interpretation that is embedded in the words; they see them only as literal events and cannot comprehend the mystery. They see from the blinded side of the veil of human flesh and it becomes impossible for them to recognize that which they understand not. Because, their reality teaches differently!

As discussed earlier, Adam and Eve did not die the same day they took of the forbidden tree, but something did occur that created a change in their awareness and they lost the mystical gnosis of whom they truly were, thereby creating a death of illusion. Entering another reality unlike the one they were created in brought about their death.

Physical death occurs only through the temporal law of cycles, and it can occur often. However when one is not enlightened, then death is real, and is permanent in the mind. If you live thousands of life times but are never aware of these past lives or this gnosis, then you are living in an eternal death. The Bible speaks of eternal death called the second death. Our first death was brought about by our separation from the Tree of Life. Our second death occurs every time one is unable to comprehend this gnosis and end up losing their identity after death. Some may say, but if the second death is a death that can last forever then how can you ever be redeemed from it. This is where the light of the divine Son and our reuniting with our Father comes into play. Jesus is like all of us. He was an eternal being of divinity, but he gave that up to enter a temporal existence. He was still an eternal being! And because of this, if he was unable to return where he came from, he would still live eternally. But in death of the veil through the cycles and not life in the spirit. Although we pass onto the other side of the veil, we never really return into our Father's realm. That must be internally sought.

There are those that believe we can be reabsorbed into the Father and be as though we never existed and this is the second death. I believe that happens all the time in a sense.

Because every time one dies and are unable to retain the gnosis of that period and goes on to exist in another temporal existence, then they have been absorbed back into their Father. They do not recognize who they were. They are as though they never were. Each lifetime we live we create an ego that defines our personality and the way we are as a person. And although we carry the roots of that personality from previous lives, we do not remember. Yet if this reality does not realign within the Law of One, our eternal Father, then we will lose that which we created from this lifetime, at least within our own memory. However all that we do that is good and is building upon our true divine self is always saved upon our higher presence. Until we rejoin that higher state of magnificence we will not remember what we have accomplished; again a state of death! And all we do that is not in alignment with our Higher Selves, as cycles return in their orbits, we will return to deal with that error that we committed. We may not realize why we are enduring such infliction or for what purpose, because we failed to retain the identity that brought these things into our illusion.

An easy example would be to parallel this with school. Let's say we are in 12th grade but we fail the final exam. Before we can enter another level of training, such as college, we have to take that class over again, and learn those things that we failed. It doesn't matter what you passed, because that knowledge is now a part of you and you will have that knowledge for later use. The primary reason you take the class over is to learn where you failed. If you never get out of the 12th grade, then you are eternally bound at that level and you can never comprehend what the next level of training has for you, because you have failed to pass the required tests. The in-between lives can be paralleled like going home after school and doing your homework. You can go out and get a job but unless you have specific training your expertise will only be based on what you have accomplished thus far in your life. You cannot go to the next level of training; you have to go back to school where you are required to take the same class over and over again until you pass the test. You could stay at home and not go back to school, and maybe over a longer process of time you could eventually pass to the next level by experiencing events that will help you learn another way. This however will take a longer period of time. It would be the difference between reading a book versus experiencing what is in the book first hand. And I truly believe that gnosis is internally gained through live experience, not through external means. At least most of the time!

ONE DOES NOT HAVE TO RETURN TO THIS PLANE OF AWARENESS!

This is the same with being between lives. One does not have to return to this plane of awareness. You could remain between lives and learn there, but the process is much slower because the demands to grow are not as heated as experiencing through trial and error. When we do not complete a test while living in this biological container, then it is important that one return here to finish that exam, because this is where the exam was given in the first place.

Some may wonder, wouldn't a person on the other side finally realize they don't die and wouldn't that remove them from the error of death? No, just because you become aware on the other side of who you are from an eternal perspective, it does not mean you really understand the ancient truths of why you are. You only grasp what you have learned up until that time period. As soon as you return to the earth plane or whatever training ground you are sent to by your choice, then you will be creating another ego complete with a new personality. Or should I say one that you have brought with you from prior existences. And after you perish from that existence you will bring to the other side what you learned in that particular lifetime. Until you are reunited with your higher conscience you can never see the entire picture. We are like a broken journal of events trying to weave through the unknowns to find our true reality. Look at yourself as a picture that is broken into pieces of a puzzle. Now take this lifetime and recognize it as only one piece of that puzzle. Realize that when you die in the veil you will transfer to the other plane or dimension. There you will see the piece of the puzzle that you created in this lifetime. That single piece is still connected to all the other pieces of the puzzle, but your perception of the entire puzzle will only reflect that one piece.

Until the light of Christ the divine Son enters you, you cannot see the entire puzzle. So each lifetime gives you an opportunity to see another piece of the puzzle, but your awareness again will only realign to that one single piece, even forgetting the other pieces you have already seen. Some believe that on the other side you can view past lives. And this I believe is true, but it still will not give you the needed awareness to advance to other levels. You must begin here at school to advance to other levels. It is like viewing pictures of events through home movies that we were part of many years ago. You might be able to recall some of the events that occurred, but overall you cannot really relate to it anymore because it was so long ago. Those events made you who you are today. Your being able to view them again might bring awareness to some hidden memories, but the effects are not the same as when you actually endured the process. Remember that living events take one second at a time; events remembered speed up at an incredible rate.

We have the ability now to see our past lives as we become more aware, but a past life cannot be changed no matter how much you view it unless there is a turning point. More on this in the next mystery. It is the present life that was created from the past lives that can be changed or modified. Again, you must advance past 12th grade before you can enter college. Your knowledge of 5th or 7th grade may be fine to help you see what you have become to this point, but those events will not be altered. Only your experiences now can be altered. Thereby bringing you new realities for your future endeavors. All the events you have experienced have produced the real you good or bad, whether you remember them or not! So we are continually trying to advance to higher levels of gnosis so we can eventually return to our true divine reality and leave the lesser dimensions forever.

If we continue to remain stagnant and do not advance, then we are surely in eternal death in continual temporary lives.

LOOKING AT IT FROM THE VEIL, DEATH APPEARS PERMANENT!

Those that remain in the veil of deception may believe that death is real and permanent. However those that die only change realities and are still very much alert and aware. They are living in another plane of awareness waiting their time of return. Physical death is just changing garments. Spiritual death is our inability to become aware of this simple fact.

This is why the people of Jesus' day were angered with his saying, you will never see death if you believed what he taught. It is because their reality was only flesh and blood, and in this reality, flesh and blood perishes. And when one dies such as Abraham, he was still dead. The death that Jesus said you would never see is spiritual death. He was teaching that one may die in the flesh, yet if you understood the truth you would understand that you-the soul projected spirit really is not perishing, the real you is in transition. If you failed to understand this while living in the biological, then you would enter death with doom and gloom and a morbid sense of being. He spoke of this by stating even though you die; you have not really died.

However to retain your true identity, you must first learn what the mystery of death is, and that is why you must learn the mysteries of the Kingdom of our Father. And this is what the Gnostics attempted to teach 2000 years ago. Because of disbelief of those who lived in the wrong reality, the Gnostics were killed and forced underground and much of their gnosis has only been saved through word of mouth until the recovery of the Nag Hammadi texts.

For years I read accounts of people who died and passed through what they described as a tunnel of light. Many of these who experienced what is called the "near death experience", stated they spoke with beings of light. They spoke of a divine love that came from this awareness, a greater love than they ever experienced in the earth plane. I used to believe when I heard these stories that either this was some wild hyped imagination, or they were experiencing some strange hallucination, or even may have been involved in some sort of demonic activity, even possession! At that time I could not accept that people were going into a heavenly realm and speaking with personages such as deceased family members and Biblical heroes such as, Moses, Abraham, and yes-even Jesus!

THERE ARE MILLIONS OF EYEWITNESSES TO THE AFTERLIFE, EVEN CHILDREN!

What changed my stubborn mind was when I read hundreds of these stories all verifying the same basic account. I asked the logical question, "If we can convict a person of a crime by only one witness in our court of law, then why do we ignore thousands upon thousands of eyewitness accounts in this area?" I read children's stories about these same accounts. Children that had near death experiences spoke with deceased siblings that died prior to their birth, and were never informed of this by their parents. Stories such as these are all too familiar to those that have researched this phenomenon.

One has to ask some serious questions. There are too many of these children's stories that cannot be refuted. And for those that believe this is all demonism, then take heed to yourselves, for if evil has this much power then woe be unto anyone ever being saved.

Jesus instructed us to forbid not the little children... He taught, "Except we become like unto a little child, in no way shall you enter the kingdom of heaven." What became obvious to me was that when children who were recently on the other side came back they were able to recall events that most of us lose via the process of years and false indoctrination. Little children have come from the other side to be reincarnated again. These little souls carry with them the most untainted gnosis from their spirit home between lives.

Many of them recalled events because they just left that realm. Yet we as adults, as the years tick away, become so saturated in the flesh and the belief systems on this plane of awareness, that we lose our memory of what had taken place. In one book there was a story that was amazing and had the most auspicious words that a child had spoken to their newborn baby brother. From the other room the mother overheard her five year old speaking to the newborn, and asking if the baby would tell her more about GOD, because she was starting to forget. If that doesn't amaze you then apparently nothing will!

When little children confront their parents with these typical stories, parents usually laugh them off as nothing more than childish imagination. I am sure most of you have heard the stories of children that speak of their invisible friends. Maybe some of you can relate to this by virtue of your own experiences. Nevertheless at the time these events took place, it was a reality for the child. Parents are the ones who have trouble believing, so they pervert their children's thinking by establishing belief systems that will eventually do great harm, and in many cases convince the child they are not really seeing what they claim. Thereby making the world from there on a hypocritical adventure.

The other day I was speaking with a female friend who has several children. One of her children was a nineteen-month-old son. She was doing her laundry in the basement; and her son was at the top of the steps. When she finished and went back upstairs she watched her son look back down the steps and said while waving his hand, "Bye, Bye!" Who was this child speaking to? Who was down those steps? I have no problem believing that children see their guides/angelic protectors all the time when they are young. These events occur much more than people think. The problem is that at present the two main paradigms of thought are: the child is imagining things, or it is a spiritual demonic activity. Both of these ideologies are damning.

CHILDREN HAVE INCREDIBLE SPIRITUAL EXPERIENCES ALL THE TIME!

The sad fact is that the parents are the ones who are failing to learn these important lessons from their children. We have given too much credit to abstract imagination or evil entities, and not nearly enough to good old spiritual reality. We spend our time filling their minds with Rabbits that lay eggs or a bearded white haired man who travels the earth in one night delivering presents. But no way will we allow our child to speak about their invisible friends. I believe little children often times have incredible experiences of the spirit world, because they are still in a purer state. As children enter adulthood they learn the distorted views of the paradigm veil, and those child-like experiences become no more than a fanciful imagination.

Jesus didn't tell us to become like little children because they have great imaginations or the devil is always at their doorstep. It was not the child's fleshly attributes that Jesus was concerning himself, but the spiritual attributes those children possess.

There are thousands upon thousands of these stories in which people learn some of the mystical secrets of the kingdom. They speak of their near death experiences, or their out of body experiences. A few years ago there were well over eight-million reported cases of these events in the U.S. alone. That number may be doubled by now, not taking into account how many have been afraid to reveal their own personal experiences for fear of ridicule and job pressure. *Eight-million witnesses?* What does it take to change paradigms in this world? Nearly all of them have reported the tunnel, the bright light, beings of light,

191

angels, holy men, saints, and deceased relatives and on and on...

AUTHORS REVEAL THEIR OWN STUNNING EXPERIENCES!

Many authors have reported their own hair-raising experiences such as Dannion Brinkley, Kimberly Clark Sharp, Bettie J. Eadie, Dr. Raymond Moody, Brad Steiger, the list goes on and on. Their stories speak of a wonderful master plan that eliminates all these fear-based ideologies. These are everyday people just like you and me. However they have experienced something that changes the rules, so-to-speak. They speak of illuminating experiences that go against all that we have previously believed based on the faulty knowledge that has been passed down over the centuries. These authors and many more like them speak of multi-dimensional worlds and spirit planes of awareness.

They have written about life reviews, prophetic knowledge, and newly accessed divine psychic attributes, such as healing and mental telepathy and so on! They related how they spoke with relatives that had passed on, who told they were living in a peaceful place and were happy and filled with an indescribable love. Their encounters with other spiritual beings of light were revealed in the most auspicious way. They speak of the geometry of divinity that is revealed by radiant colors and the beautiful radiance of illuminating light that shines greater than our sun!

These people really have seen the light, so-to-speak. Those of the religious community that speak of seeing the light are only witnessing the shadow of the light based on others' experiences and not their own. They have the candle but they do not see the true flame, they only envision it. But these on the other hand have seen more than just the light; they have seen the incredible design for all humanity and those that exist within the veil. They may not all retain the same information because we can only learn according to our evolved growth, but they all witness the basic plan and it is one of joy, love and peace.

Everyone comprehends the mysteries according to their own evolved mystical growth in accordance with karma of cause and effect. But all who have these experiences realize we are the children of the light, and we are the Undiscovered Mystery of Christ, which have been in existence since before the foundations of this known world.

What many do not comprehend is that each of us has acquired our individual talents through past lives. God doesn't arbitrarily hand out talents to whom he sees fit, just as he doesn't decide to love or hate on no more than a heavenly whim. The Bible explains that God gives us our talents according to our every ability, but again, this is mystical. These talents are acquired through the cycles of grace, and yes, in a sense it would be as though our Father was giving them to us, because it is our Father who lives in us and does the good works through us! People are not born with greater talents than others because a God decided to be nice to one and not to the other. This kind of thinking is ludicrous and creates divisions and class warfare.

WE ARE HERE TO LEARN TO BECOME, NOT JUST BE!

One of the basic absolutes in the universal cosmic law is free choice! The Father/Mother of all divine spirits established the law of free choice so that each of us would 'BECOME!' This entails personal growth and character. If we did not have complete free choice we could not become a separate and unique spirit. We would only 'BE' a robot, without personal identity.

EVERYTHING THAT I AM SHOWING YOU IS WORTH NOTHING EXCEPT IT BE REVEALED IN YOU!

How each of us learns will depend on our specific growth process up to that point of our training and comprehension. One does not just come upon these mysteries by accident, because if these mysteries do not become eternal truths you will never accept or understand them. I went through a long arduous journey to attain what I know at present. It wasn't just handed to me on a silver platter. Neither did I acquire this gnosis through only one lifetime. It was a building process that led me to where I am at present. But the learning never stops! I had to be trained to accept and understand the mysteries so I could be ready to ascertain new levels of gnosis and awareness. My relaying this information to you will not do you or anyone else any good, unless your timetable is set to where you can personally comprehend this gnosis. Nothing I say to you will do any good. It will only pass through the outer aspects of your ego and soon perish. Simply stated, Gnosis must come internally or you will not accept it. It would be like trying to feed steak to an infant, or sending a first grader to college. The body and the mind are not prepared to handle this, so it will reject it. However, the good news is, eventually everyone will comprehend. And unlike some religious ideologies that teach you had better get it now or else, this one will always be patient, waiting continually on your success for your future. As King David once decreed, "God's mercy extends from one side of the heavens to the other..." Can you even imagine the vastness of our universe? Then how can you limit the mercy of our Father to one life? Our Father/Mother divine is forever patient, never limited by the false values and wrong paradigms that man has created for his lack of spiritual awareness and truth.

One thing is certain, the more I learn about these hidden mysteries the more I realize how little I really ever knew. Yet unlike religion and science that decrees to have all truth, real expansive truth is utterly realizing our lack thereof. Our Father has all truth and we are just a piece of the myriad of parts to the entire puzzle. I am still learning day by day. What I understand today is only a small piece of the grand design! While living in the veil we are very limited and must do our very best to understand or comprehend what we can.

If anyone ever claims they have all truth or even suggests that they are not in need of more truth, they expose themselves, and in them lies faulty reasoning exposing their ignorance. The Apostle Paul stated that he only knew in part...as looking through a glass that is darkened. Paul was a mystical writer, and many of the Gnostics believed him to be their true source for the mysteries. Yet Paul only knew in part! Paul learned a unique way of presenting the mysteries in coded fashion, but at the same time creating the belief that he only required the knowledge of the letter. I will address many of these mysteries later in this book.

Each mystery works within the individual's own law of "Geometry of Divinity." You will only receive that portion that you have been prepared for through your life's experience. Each person will eventually learn all the hidden mysteries, but only our personal higher presence, the Father can know how long this will take for each. We are all at different levels of growth. We are all trying to achieve that same point of reality, but accessing this individual reality comes only by personal growth, laying up for yourselves treasures in heaven...

When my mind opened to understand some of the mysteries, I then learned a great deal by others' experiences of the near death and out of body realm. However, unless you experience these spiritual truths from an inner awareness called gnosis you will never realize the tremendous import and value they play within your own reality. Learning these mystical truths for oneself is the absolute in total inward growth.

DOES IT REALLY TAKE PERSONAL EXPERIENCES TO COMPREHEND GNOSIS?

This brings me to a very interesting point; does it really take personal experiences to unravel these mysteries? Is this the only true way we will really find out who we are? Do we have to live life in ignorance just to prove that at death we have failed again, just to return to the everlasting cycles of the veil?

What did Jesus really mean when he said he was the WAY? What is the WAY? Is it that simple just to speak the name Jesus and all your troubles will be taken care of? Will all gnosis of internal awareness just be handed to you, or are you the living channel to experience that which one eventually evolves unto?

For one to learn the necessary elements of eternal awareness they need to change their entire view of physical reality. We must become adept in placing this veil of illusion and ignorance down. And use the incredible FORCE that reigns supreme within us. It means to reject the temptations that pander only to the flesh. It means to overcome the will of the world with the will of our Father. It means to practice the art of loving, not preaching it. We must learn to set examples, not order others around. We must become what we seek. Jesus did not teach us these qualities so that the world would continue in the direction it always had. He led by example so we would imitate it, not just talk about it.

JESUS USED THE POWER OF THE FATHER TO REUNITE WITH HIM!

This power is not a force that acts on its own. It operates as one uses it. You make your own realities happen. Jesus decreed that he could lay down his own life, and take it back up again! There is no second party in this deal. Once you learn the mystical secrets of the Kingdom of your Father, then you can tap into that same power for your own use. Neither Jesus nor the Father can do it for you, but they will set you on the right track so you can discover the hidden secret from within yourself.

All matter is energy vibrating at different levels. Spirits who walk through material objects are as real as we are. Those of other dimensions are vibrating at different intervals enabling them to pass through slower vibratory objects. What makes us different than spirits from the other side is that we as a spirit live within a veil of mass that slowly vibrates at the ratio consistent with the matter world. When we leave these material bodies we do not change who we really are, we just leave the physical apparatus that was used for a three-dimensional world. We leave our virtual reality and return to the higher vibrational dimensions. Then we become aware of that which seemed invisible while living in the mass of material clay. Matter in itself is not solid as it appears to be, but vibrates at a certain speed that makes it appear solid to those that are vibrating at the same speed.

If that matter were to vibrate faster it would slowly disappear. Watch the spokes of a bicycle wheel as they turn slowly. You can see the rotation of the spokes. When the rotation picks up speed you will recognize a change in the nature of the spokes. It will even appear as if it was going backwards. The faster it goes the harder it becomes to make out the appearance of the spokes, until eventually it will appear to fade away.

EVERYTHING BEGINS WITH ENERGY!

Matter is only illusion, that is why it decays. It is nothing more than an appearance of something that operates based on the speed of the vibration of the molecules and atoms. Everything begins with energy. All energy can produce an appearance of an illusion. As an example, you are able to see mirages in the desert. These are illusions that appear real but are not, and over time begin to fade. As we function at a certain biological rate we operate at a certain speed that makes everything on the three-dimensional plane appear to be real, because we are existing within bodies that are congruent with that rate. If you leave the biological vessel then you have abandoned that which gave you reality of that dimension. Thereby making the material dimensions seem unreal, because you are now in another dimension that will appear real to you.

When Jesus gave up the ghost as the Bible said, it simply meant that his physical body expired and the real projected soul spirit/ghost was loosed from that domain. This is why he

197

stated he could take back his own life. How could he do that if he was just flesh and blood? He was able to raise his own vibrational rate and could actually disappear. He could cause his mortal body to disappear or reappear. In this case his mortal body had ceased to function, but his spiritual body was always there. By using this force of the power of one you can literally change your dimensions instantaneously. Jesus was able to revive that physical body and change its vibration rate until he caused it to completely disappear into the spirit world. This was done to prove that through the power of the Father, you control life and death. *"I AM THE RESURRECTION AND THE LIFE!"*

One of the truths Einstein discovered is that energy just exists. It cannot die, it just materializes through something else. We the true spirit being are nothing more than energy, and although the clothing of vessels we place on our selves may perish we will go on existing because we are spirit energy like our Father. When your flesh and blood body stops functioning you the soul spirit moves elsewhere. There are many who when placed in traumatic situations, such as an operation, have actually stepped out of their body to watch the operation from the exterior side. Ronald Reagan, our 40th President of the United States, spoke of such an incident after John Hinkley shot him in 1981. He described leaving his body during the operation, and described exact events that took place while he was physically unaware. These are not strange occurrences without any logical answers. These are events that happen every day all across the planet earth. Most are afraid to discuss these events. Even Reagan's family had a hard time understanding what had taken place. Their only response was one of a religious oration crediting God with such an auspicious event. I do not believe they ever really thought he left his body. They examined the issue and decreed it to be a religious experience, whatever that means. But I am sure if the truth were known, President Reagan has a much different point of view about the experience, because he experienced it personally- i.e. internal awareness. Gnostic!

Often times when the mortal body is under tremendous stress and trauma our soul-projected spirit will leave it during this turmoil. There are stories that go back thousands of years that speak of torture victims who described their torment from outside their physical bodies. They actually witnessed these monstrosities to their mortal body while they watched from the outside feeling no pain whatsoever.

THE REAL YOU IS A POWERFUL SPIRIT BEING OF THE KINGDOM'S CREATION!

To ultimately realize what I am trying to say you must understand that the real you is not the flesh and blood body, you are what is inside this body. Your body is nothing more than a biological garment given to you for your schooling apparatus. The real you is a powerful spirit being of the kingdom's creation, but while under Maya of illusion we do not remember how to control from within. We allow events on the outside to be our controllers. We lost the ability to heal and create because of this shortcoming!

Spirit cannot die. That is why we can only experience the sensation of death while living in decaying matter, which can die. All power on heaven and earth is within each of us at all times. We have always had the gift to return to the Father, but we must learn how to find the narrow road that leads back to our eternal Tree of Life. Jesus found that road within himself, and that is exactly where it lies for us also. As the hourglass of this temporal existence fades away, most will once again fail to attain the great jewel, the crown of eternity. The truth remains that lifetime after lifetime people continue to die and are reborn never realizing that the crown of hope has always been within them.

Many have wondered how long this process will take, not realizing the beauty of the plan. That is why we live in cycles of the material world with a continuous refresher from time to time into the middle plane or spiritual plane of awareness. It is because time is only a reality that exists within the matter plane. That is why time is in cycles, because time may appear to last forever when in reality it only operates within a set perimeter sectioned off from the spiritual plane as if it was rotating continuously in circles. Thereby what we call the circle of life. What may be a million years in the cycles will be as nothing from the spiritual plane of awareness.

Take a ball and place it on the floor in front of you. Visualize a line going around the ball that would represent time. Now make that time to be one trillion years. Now envision you had lived on that ball at one section of this trillion year timetable. Between lives you are back in the spirit world looking at the entire scope of time allotted by this ball's timetable. From outside the ball you can see the entire trillion years instantaneously, but while stationed on the ball you could only grasp the short allotted segment of that particular area. Also see yourself above the earth where you can view the entire Continent of North America. Now envision yourself exactly centered between New York and Los Angeles. At the moment you look down upon this plane of awareness you are witnessing 3 hours of time and 3000 miles of space instantaneously. Notice how time can become extremely trivial to your point of view? You could say the same about astronauts. They can see one entire side of the planet earth so they are visualizing 12 hours of time zones instantly. And yet when you are located somewhere on this globe you are visualizing time one second at a time. See the difference? Time is a construct from the orbital path of the cycles in continuous motion. Time is not linear, it is orbital! This is why if you are stuck within the constructs of time it is eternal because it keeps looping. We have to break out of the loop!

BALL PLANE OF AWARENESS THROUGH TIME!

What you have accomplished by doing this experience is you have witnessed a long period of time instantly without being in bondage to it. So your perspective of time is greatly reduced by the fact that time has no power over you. Now imagine that in your spirit world there was no time, that time is only applicable to that ball. Picture yourself entering that ball at a section where you will live for 70 years. Once that 70 years has expired, you leave the ball plane of awareness and return to your spiritual observation post. Although 70 years transpired, no time had elapsed in the spirit plane, because time is only calculable by the cycles of the ball. It would appear as if you never left the spirit plane of awareness, but you have gained gnosis via the 70 years you were subjected to the ball plane through time.

It doesn't matter how many lifetimes it takes because in retrospect everyone's success will occur as if it happened instantaneously. It is nice to know that there is a spiritual recorder that remembers all these events lifetime after lifetime, and records them in what is Biblically known as the Book of Remembrance. You may never know while in training how many lives you have lived unless you tap into the power that will access this gnosis. Edgar Cayce was one of the first of the 20th century to learn about the spiritual recording device called the Akashic records. It is possible for anyone to have these events brought back to their memory. Hypnotic regression therapy is one way, but the easiest way to recall these events is directly through Out of Body experiences, which I will discuss more thoroughly shortly.

CONSCIOUSNESS SHIFTS BRING ABOUT GREAT CHANGE!

Another important aspect to this gnosis is to understand how much change occurs during a consciousness shift. We all experience these shifts every night. When the consciousness shifts, strange things can take place, especially when we enter another dimension. It takes great training and awareness to recall events from other planes of awareness.

One night while dreaming I was given an interesting piece of information. Someone in this dream told me where somebody I had never met personally was employed. I recognized I was gaining insight that I could not possibly know from a dream plane of awareness. The information turned out to be correct, but trying to keep the awareness of this information was very difficult. This is what I mean by a consciousness shift. When we dream we enter other conscious planes of awareness, especially if you are lucid dreaming. This is the type of dream where you become consciously aware while in the dream. I have to laugh when people reject the idea of reincarnation based primarily on the fact that if you can't remember, then it can't be so. When you realize how easy it is to lose information that is given in a dream, then why is it so hard to believe that one can forget a past life! Even in this plane of awareness it is very easy to forget things that happen just a short time ago.

When we enter this physical plane of awareness it is very easy to lose information from the other side. We are not as steady as we should be, and our minds are too noisy. We need to quiet ourselves so we can retain that which is given us from the spiritual plane of awareness. It is there, but we must seek it and be prepared.

GNOSIS FROM THE SPIRITUAL PLANE COMES AT GREAT SPEEDS!

Information from the spiritual plane is coming at speeds that far exceed our physical brain's ability to lock into it. We are very slow beings when locked into this shell. While we are on the other side we can pick up this information at the speeds that it is operating, and it will make total sense to us. But when we reenter the earthen vessel, our brain becomes the operating device to sort out the material to process it. However, at that point the brain slows down the information so that it loses control of the speed, and begins to blot out the necessary elements while transferring it to our consciousness. So our soul-projected spirit that was able to ascertain the necessary elements has reentered the physical mass, and the human brain then slows the speed to the point that we cannot catch up with it.

How many times have you been in a situation where you need answers quickly, and you know you have them, but you can't bring them to the forefront of your mind? This is because the brain is working too slow in conjunction with your consciousness. Think of this as a computer, if a computer can only handle in memory 6 gigabytes of information and you try to cram in 7 gigs you will overload the computer's capability. And when you try to bring that information out you will lose quite a bit of the necessary elements.

So it shouldn't seem strange that we forget things from the other side so easily. If we can forget a dream, we can certainly forget a past life. So when the brain loses the ability to transform the signal to our awareness then the information enters the sub-conscious. Also remember, a past life was part of another biological body and its components. While living in this new mass neither our body nor brain has any recall of our past life without the soul-projected spirit. Only your soul-projected spirit can truly recall the events, and then it can place the new information in your new biological pattern awareness. But this takes training. The information never leaves you, it is just placed into another realm of awareness until you can access it later. As we live our lives everything is kept in perfect order so that nothing is ever lost except eventually darkness.

THE BOOK OF REMEMBRANCE / AKASHIC RECORDS CONTAINS ALL EVENTS THROUGH TIME AND SPACE!

The Akashic records that Edgar Cayce spoke of is a divine spirit book that records all vibrations from all dimensions that are locked into cycles, from every level of time and space. Everything you think is instantly recorded into this divine memory guide. That is why Jesus warned us to control our thoughts. Our thoughts are energies that become realities. Those who have had near death experiences speak of life reviews. These reviews are all recorded into the majestic *Book of Remembrance,* and everything we think or do is locked into a thread of electronic energy. Dannion Brinkley not only described what it felt like to review his life, he also claimed to have the feelings of those he harmed.

WE ARE CONTINUALLY SEEKING TO RETURN TO OUR SPIRITUAL FOUNTAIN OF YOUTH AS ONE OF THE ILLUMINED ONES!

As we continue down this road to learned gnosis it is necessary to fathom why the character building process is so important. In the book of James it states that, "Faith without works is dead!" So returning to the heart flame of our Father will take diligent effort. It is true that our tree of life is a free gift and this is where so many become confused. It is free because we already belong to the tree of life. But our identity we have chosen to purchase through the lower worlds of good and evil is very costly. We are continually seeking to return to our eternal fountain of spiritual youth, as one of the offspring of the illumined ones. When we finally return to our Father's bosom we will be carrying a separate and distinct individuality and the true expansive love fitting only for the children of light. We will ultimately leave the darkness behind forever, and the shadow-land will become a thing of the mortal distant past. Yet understand the mystery, eternal life is always with us. However it depends on where you spend it, either in the illusion of the shadow, which is death, or in the light freedom of the Father.

The subject of faith, which I will address in detail in a later chapter, is one of the key highlights of both James and Paul. Faith as defined in the Bible is the substance of things hoped for and the evidence of things not seen. But faith in itself is not complete! You must have more than hope. You must come to know, and this requires effort. One must experience their belief as a reality so that belief will finally and ultimately become a knowing. Most stop at faith alone, they believe that is all that is necessary to achieve their goal. But the mystical decree of the Bible is really teaching that your growth must first begin with simple belief. But it cannot end there; you must build upon that belief until your faith becomes a truth, not just a concept. If all you have is hope for something, then your reality is uncertain, the foundation is rocky. Once your faith has been tried and tested and has become part of your knowing, then you no longer need to hope for it. Once faith is fulfilled there is no need for hope! Faith was never meant to remain a hope. It was meant to build on so one could venture into the hidden mysteries. Most in religious circles have learned the art of hoping, and some even learn how to believe. Yet when it comes to really knowing, that is where the line is drawn in the sand!

WITHOUT REAL PROOF THROUGH FAITH THE UNCERTAINTY OF AN AFTERLIFE WILL ALWAYS BE THERE!

This is what James really meant when he said faith without works is dead. As an example, one could hope for a miracle, one could even believe in that miracle. But only the person who has experienced the miracle has truly witnessed faith by works, and it is much more then just belief. Another example is a person who has had a near death experience versus a person who has a belief in an afterlife. Which one of these people will have the strongest faith concerning an afterlife? The answer is quite simple; it is the one who experienced the other side. In account after account those that had out of body and near death experiences have nearly lost their fear of death, because they have witnessed the other side. Yet those that just believe will still have an overriding fear of death, an uncertainty, enough doubt to always make them wonder.

When you experience the miracle then you have truly witnessed faith in action. Now it can be understood what James meant when he said, "You show me your faith without works, and I will show you mine with works…" meaning with results.

Can you imagine what kind of following Jesus would have received if he did not perform the works of faith before the people? What if Jesus promised healing for the sick and every time he laid hands upon them they died. What if he never walked on water but actually sank, and then declared to his disciples, "Well, you just have to have faith." Understand though, your faith should not be made strong because of someone else performing miracles. I am only using this as an analogy of how people would have reacted if Jesus never accomplished these things. Certainly Jesus did not need to do these things, but he was filled with love and mercy and wanted to share with those that believed in his mission. Jesus was a very unique man in the sense of his training and abilities, and was able to tap into the great power many of us still lack through ignorance.

One of the main illustrations of faith was when Jesus said one must first have the faith of a mustard seed... Why would he use this example? Simply because a mustard seed is very small, it represents the basics of faith and belief. But a mustard seed also grows; in fact this particular seed continues to grow into a much larger plant. So the illustration is to understand faith is a learning process that continues to grow. It does not remain stagnant or dead.

It was so obvious that the entire work of Jesus was a work of establishing proof. Can you imagine what would have happened if he didn't return from the grave like he promised. Well I can, there would be no Christian religion upon the entire earth. Belief alone is dead; you have to have proof to make it an eternal, and internal awareness to be included in new gnosis gained. Even doubting Thomas was allowed to have his proof. Why didn't Jesus tell Thomas, "Well, my friend, God only expects you to believe and that is all there is to it!" No, he allowed Thomas to gain his needed proof. Why? Because proof is necessary! However proof should be internal not external! If it is not internal then one would believe only Jesus had this ability and would fail to attain their own glory!

PROOF IS A REQUIREMENT!

Do we need proof as our testimony of faith? Or are we to live our entire life hoping and believing but never really knowing for sure? Should we live our life based on what others think and believe? Are we to be led from one religion to another, one church to another, constantly trying to piece together others' experiences? Or could it be that you live in total secularism where science is your only hope, having only a scientific theory based on other people's perspectives. Science and religion are the same things. They both have scholars who try to lead others by their own findings, whether you personally know it to be true or not. How long must we live in total ignorance?

Wouldn't it finally be nice to really know something for sure instead of walking around with confusion? One of the key elements about human nature that I have learned is that when someone truly does not know for sure, they are the first to try to shove their beliefs down your throat. Those that really know for sure have a quiet confidence and they do not feel the burning need to force feed the truth to someone else. They realize everyone will know in due time.

How many would truly like to know that one does not really die when their material biological bodies perish? How would you like to prove this for yourself? What if you could know for sure what I am saying is true?

WHY DID THE RELIGIOUS HIERARCHY HAVE JESUS KILLED?

Why did the most powerful religious hierarchy in the world at that time have Jesus killed? Why did this religious hierarchy team up with the most powerful Government in the world, the Roman Empire, to eradicate this man of love? It was because Jesus was teaching the mysteries of the Kingdom of his Father. Mysteries these people never heard taught, except by mystical groups that they branded heretics and pagans such as the Essenes and Gnostics. They continuously attacked Jesus claiming he was a devil, a drunkard and womanizer. They accused him of almost every despicable act you can conceive. But weren't these religious men and women faithful followers to their holy books and scrolls? Weren't they God fearing people?

The answer is yes, but only in the flesh! They did not want to hear about things pertaining to the spirit. They attributed any talk outside the accepted norm as devil worship. Doesn't this sound familiar?

If I am wrong about what I am saying, then why would Jesus have ever been crucified? Some teach that the Romans had Jesus killed, not the religious hierarchy, but if this were true then even more of the Old Testament Prophecies would have been false. The Old Testament prophesied that the builders would reject the chief Cornerstone. The builders were the tribes of Israel; it was especially a name that Solomon the King of Israel was known by. The Bible instructed that Israel killed the prophets. It stated that the Gentiles would have accepted the warnings of the prophets, such as with Jonah and the city of Ninevah. But Israel had the prophets killed, and also many of the Apostles killed and even Jesus. Now granted they were working closely with the Romans to pull off this conspiracy. And you can bet these type of things still occur today. Religion has much more power and control than people would give it credit.

I ask all Christians to begin to rethink their stance. Bringing accusations against those that are teaching the metaphysical and the mystical is bipartisan with that same mentality that wanted Jesus put to death. If Jesus taught what most Christians believe today he would have been run out of town, and the people would have never accepted what he had to say.

I have never rejected being Christian, although I have come to realize that there is a great difference between Christianity and one who is simply a Christian.

THE TERM "CREATION" HAS BEEN UTTERLY MISTRANSLATED IN THE BIBLE!

I believe the divine spirit through the light manifestation created all basic principles for life in the spiritual plane of light.

It was a divine policy to allow free choice within all aspects of creation. Free choice means allowance for evolution! The word creation has been mistranslated in the Bible. Many think that creation is a word that means to snap your finger and like magic, voila, there it is! That is not logical. The truth is, creation is evolution. Try to think about this in another way! You are a parent that has a child, that child in turn has children and on and on and on. You were the progenitor of this long family line, but you had absolutely nothing to do with your children's offspring coming into this world. They evolved through the process of birth through their parents and so on. But being their progenitor you would be known as the creator of this long line, because without you it would have not existed. Evolution is the creation of a process of events that began with the Father/Mother divine spirits. Nevertheless, the Father does not have to intervene at every given place to create something. He has set evolution in motion as a glory to his creation ability.

WHY IS IT WE CAN ACCEPT EARTH BOUND BIOLOGICAL EVOLUTION BUT FAIL TO BELIEVE IN UNIVERSAL SPIRIT EVOLUTION?

The Hubble space telescope has viewed distant galaxies where it actually caught the beginning formation of new star systems. So there is a constant state of evolution that takes place at all times. When the moth turns into a beautiful butterfly God did not have to be there on the spot to cause this to happen. And throughout long periods of time and through metamorphic change things occur that can alter the pattern of almost anything. Ants multiply and can build large anthills that will literally change the format of an entire landscape. Did God create the change? Why is it that we allow for evolution through almost all events of biological life but we fail to understand that it is also being used throughout the cosmos?

HEBREW WORD FOR CREATION IS BARA, THE PROCESS OF EVENTS - EVOLUTION!

The actual word for creation in the Bible comes from the Hebrew word, "BARA." It means to cut down, like wood, and select, feed, as a formative process of events. It was never meant to be instant creation! I am sure the Father could create anything instantly that he desired, and could create all universes by fiat, but that would never serve the purpose. Our divine progenitors love uniqueness and originality. They want to see life and forms evolve, not just be! That is why the spirit divine did not instantly give us our own identity. We were to become an individual with unique characteristics and personality. This is done through a process of evolutionary events. If you were the Father/Mother, would you not want to do this the same way? These are simple truths wrapped in question form! To me this makes for a much more expansive God than one who just snaps his fingers and voila, there it is. Not that it can't be done that way, it just serves very little purpose.

So evolution does not take away from the creating ability of our divine parents through the Son Christ, neither does it eliminate God altogether! Evolution is the power of creation wrought about by our divine family.

THE STING OF DEATH, OUR INABILITY TO COPE!

As we return to the subject of death we should now have a greater awareness of our divine family. When the Bible speaks of the sting of death it is referring to our inability to cope with what appears to be a loss of a loved one. Our uncertainty is harder to deal with than the reality. However, if a loved one told us they were being sent on a mission and they wouldn't be able to contact us for 20 years. You would certainly miss them, but you would not feel the sting of death. The old saying goes, out of sight out of mind. With death something else occurs, and that something is uncertainty. Uncertainty is the sting of death! I remember when I was away from my father for some 3-4 years. I didn't see him, neither did we speak. Afterwards I moved back into his area and spent quite a bit of time with him. A few short years later he passed on. About 3-4 years later I contemplated about this thing called death. It was very difficult! I realized that when I was not around for several years that I missed my Father, but I didn't feel the sting that I felt after he died, because I always knew he was still living.

Yet after he passed on I wondered why I felt this sunken feeling in my heart? Some may say, because when you were away from him you knew you could see him again. When he died that was final. Do you see the illogic in this statement? It is called uncertainty. Now if I were to say, wait a minute, don't you believe you will see your loved one again? A person may say, well of course. The truth is, not really. Because if one really believes they would see each other again and that the party is still alive and functioning, then why would they feel the sting? Yes they would still miss them, but the sting would be gone. THE STING IS UNCERTAINTY.

So the sting of death is our inability to understand what happens when we die. We peer inside the turmoil of death with gloom and despair. And of course, there is that other agonizing pain that grips us at death and this is the fear that religions give us. Are we going to heaven or are we going to hell?

Our vibration rate of this biological garment gives us the illusion that the matter world is real, but it is not. It is like playing a virtual reality game that appears very real to you. After you remove the game garments then you realize you were only interacting within a created visualized consciousness.

When a loved one dies they are removed from the virtual reality playing field and return to the more real environment. Yet as long as we are still in game playing mode, so-to-speak, we still observe and see our virtual reality as the real thing. When we pass on to the other side it is likely that family members who had passed on earlier will possibly meet us. At that moment we will understand that the virtual test is over and we have returned home. Our life and death reality will inevitable remain the same as long as we keep viewing it from this side of reality. We will see beyond this gaming mechanism that creates the illusory reality after we take off these biological garments.

So death becomes only an experience that is sensed from this side of the playing field, but it is not real and will be uncovered as soon as you pass on! Everywhere there are spirit entities around us. Some of them are outright wicked beings and some of them are loving and caring beings. If you could flip a switch that would raise your biological vibration rate you might be surprised who is looking over your shoulder at this present moment.

Once you begin to experience the higher realities of this truth then your fear and uncertainty of death will change. I was one person that feared death all the time. I hated the thought of having to leave this reality for any reason. I was absolutely and totally mystified about what death really meant, no matter what I was taught or thought I believed. I am no longer afraid of death. In fact as the days continue I become less and less fearful. It is the lower dimensional death that keeps us captive. Simply stated it is our ignorance of the realities of truth that create the fear of death in us.

The Apostle Paul made it extremely clear when he stated that Jesus defeated this enemy called death after he rose again. Jesus said if you could only understand the true mission of Christ and partake of this reality of the light, then you would never have to experience this lower dimensional fear of death. It would be like packing for a trip and journeying onward. Once you truly understand that you really don't die, that you just change places or dimensions, you will begin to engage your mind with a new perspective and a new reality.

Many of those that have had near death experiences have lost their fear of death. They now realize that death is only a change, a transition into the spirit world they came out of. Try warning these people of the uncertainty of death and they will just lovingly laugh at your misfortune of not knowing.

Millions have witnessed beyond the veil; they have seen it and have been there! As Paul stated, not all will sleep but all will change. This implies that not everyone will have their biological body die, which represents the mystical sleep in the Bible. Some will actually leave their garments to peer into this spirit world while their biological bodies still function. Yet it states, all shall change! Whether by death of the biological, or near death experiences, or out of body experiences, all shall change and realize that death is just a passing.

I HAVE PERSONALLY SEEN BEYOND THE VEIL!

I am personally aware that no one really dies. They just enter another reality as the Bible and many other ancient manuscripts have taught, because I have seen beyond the veil myself. It is thrilling! It is a world of newness. Yet I have not died to see beyond the veil. Just like Paul said, "Not all will sleep..." But I have seen beyond the fleshly veil that millions have become aware of also!

Some may wonder how this would be possible? When you thoroughly understand that we are a consciousness of our soul spirit and we inhabit this life form called the biological, then one can ascertain the truth about their own reality, and realize that if you can enter these biological bodies then you can also leave them. Our part in this fleshly temple is a spiritual part. Our human brain is not the device that does the thinking. Our brain is a tool of this lower vibration rate to bring realities of the spiritual into this fleshly plane. It registers memories and experiences of our lifetime that we exist in at the moment. The soul conscious is the real man and women inside us. The OLD MAN that the Bible speaks of is the realization or our limited reality, believing we are only flesh and blood. The NEW MAN is the recognized reality that we are spiritual beings that reside inside this vessel. It is the NEW Man's consciousness that allows the OLD MAN to function. We are spiritual in nature living inside a physical domain. The spiritual is the real us, not the biological. The Biological is just a living organism of matter to sustain the illusion of the lower matter world.

When the biological dies the spiritual counterpart exits. Then the spiritual aspect is all that remains and continues to function. Its new awareness will now become congruent with the vibration rate of the dimension it has entered. When the biological brain ceases to function, it stops sending information to the lower vibration rate we pick up while living in the biological vessel. Therefore the conscious awareness moves into another level to receive and send information as it regains its awareness that was terminated by the death of the biological message sending process. When one leaves their body through death, or near death experiences, or out of body experiences, they are actually entering another real plane of awareness and existence that is called the astral plane.

When you leave your body by whatever means, you enter another level of reality, or the first level of awareness that exists upon many different planes, such as, the mental, emotional, memory etc... However, the first level of awareness may literally be the surrounding you just exited in the physical, giving you the awareness of the physical surroundings you just left. But your new surroundings will appear somewhat faded and out of sync because you are approaching these same surroundings with another rate of vibration.

You may actually witness loved ones grieving for your demise if you exited your body through the biological death state. Some have witnessed the transition when their biological ceased to function on an operating table where a doctor was performing surgery. You may even witness the accident you were in! However all these scenarios have one thing in common, only a higher evolved individual will be able to see your presence, because you will be vibrating beyond the capability of the three-dimensional to pick up your awareness.

You will go unnoticed giving the feeling to your loved ones that you are gone, whereby you might be standing right next to them. Whatever brought about your physical demise; you will be able to see from another dimension that parallels your own that you just exited. Many have stated they felt no change within themselves and wondered why no one was paying any attention to them. Those that are still vibrating at the biological level would not acknowledge them nor speak to them, which to the unlearned can become very frustrating. Now where you go from this point depends on your karma and your belief system. One thing to always understand is that everything is free choice. That is why it is important that you learn the internal gnosis before you die, because you have a major choice in what you will do and where to go next. However if you do not have the gnosis through proper training then you will just go down the same path you have been going down for many eons.

Many are assisted out of this realm by angels or guides that lead through a tunnel that many describe, which I call the wormhole vortex, or the transition belt between dimensions. They will direct you to an area I call the rest. It is a place of evaluation between lives. Not everyone enters this rest, depending on his or her belief system. Some become trapped in other dimensions such as the lower astral dimension. Many of these occurrences are actually created out of your very own belief system. If you believe in a raging hell after death, sadly you may project yourself there because that is what your internal awareness prescribes. I will deal with this subject in a more detail in the next mystery.

MANY BODIES ARE GIVEN ACCORDING TO YOUR DIMENSION!

Some have wondered what they will look like when they get over to the other side? Again, your belief system will direct this also. There are those that have reported seeing loved ones who have passed over, and they spoke of how young a grandmother looked. They may also appear very vibrant and healthy; whereas when they died they may have been old and in ill

215

health. I have personally seen both my mother and Father on the other side years after their passing. My Father passed on at about age 64, when I saw him on the other side he appeared much younger. Understand another mystery, as a soul conscience is projected from a higher awareness, you are no more than a dot of light. You can take on bodies that will be congruent to the dimension you are in by your own thoughts within these realms. In the flesh we are given vessels that are created by a three-dimensional birthing process. However in other dimensions you access bodies much differently. And one way to access a body is to process its form directly out of your mental and memory system. You will project your new form according to what pleases you. Remember you might have had ailments and loss of limbs in the biological, but that is all gone now. You can have whatever body you choose, and that usually means a healthy, vibrant and whole body. There are those that revert to a past life and take that body instead of the one they just discarded from this life, because it was more pleasing to them and they identified with it better.

Some may wonder why would you keep the basic design that you had when in the flesh? What if you were not happy with that body? That is entirely up to you, you may choose whatever body pleases you for your form. Remember the real you is the projected light dot of consciousness. One thing is for sure, in many other dimensions you can change your appearance readily at will, so it is your choice. Whatever dimensions you go to, you will need the body which vibrates consistently with that dimension. An example would be that a physical body could not function in the astral plane, because of your rate of vibration, versus that of the astral plane rate of vibration. Right now there are dimensions around all of us taking up the same space, but you cannot see them nor are many even aware of them. That is because our awareness level only accepts that which is vibrating at a congruent rate to this three-dimensional plane of awareness. Some have however heard voices almost as if people were sitting around speaking to one another. They have heard these things within their homes. The voices are unintelligible and they have no clue where they are coming from. I believe this is a dimensional overlap. They are hearing people in other dimensions!

There are entire books about the many dimensions and realms you could enter. I do not have the time or space to detail these functions. If I were to illustrate the real us in simple terms it would probably blow you away mentally. I will just explain that we are all multi-dimensional beings. This simply means that as a dot of light projected from a single source, we can divide and multiply our reality and awareness through many dimensions and forms all at the same time. We are spirit beings! Our reality in this world can only perceive three-dimensional aspects to a single reality. However we can divide in many different aspects in many differing realities. We can live in multiple universes and dimensions, and yes, even multiple existences in the same reality. This may be very hard for many to swallow when dealing with this dimension. I am telling you that we are multi-dimensional beings, because we are not flesh, but SPIRIT! Throughout this entire book I have been revealing to you three-dimensional separations from one self, the Father, the Son, and the fallen projected spirit. I also mentioned we have separated from our other half. Each of us is the Adam and Eve. We are only singular in our awareness on these planes.

If you are going to transcend the physical, then you must understand the spiritual. If you perceive the spiritual as you perceive the physical, then you will not gain the necessary tools for enlightenment. That is why I have spoken of our higher-self and higher bodies. We are not limited to the conscious awareness of any earthly or material plane lifetime. That is only one aspect of what we are. You have pooled upon the heavenly realm treasures in heaven over many lifetimes, realities and dimensions. And those qualities are your real identity. But when you come back into training, you do not use or even know the many abilities and qualities you actually have, because they are not necessarily needed for this one aspect of reality. You may be working on one single point of reality in this one lifetime, and it might only pertain to 1% of the entire you.

That is why so many feel they are useless and don't belong, when in truth they are not using their complete attributes.

However other aspects of you may be working on other points of reality in different dimensions. As one who has walked into other dimensions in my life I understand this reality.

In a three-dimensional world we see ourselves as a single entity. We envision our mental, emotional, memory and even our physical body as one single body with many characteristics. Few understand that these are all different bodies. If anyone of these bodies fail, the entire system fails, but each has separate working qualities. You can be on track mentally but emotionally you could be out of sync. Three of your other bodies could be working perfectly, but if your physical body is decaying the rest will also be impaired, while living in this awareness.

The Christ body as the intercessor stands as our link to our highest phases of spiritual life. It is the same link that brings the unlimited power of our Father, our highest presence into the lower phases or bodies of our divine nature. This power is the ignition switch that catapults our ability to do those things which are pleasing to that highest realm. Again as Jesus said, "The works that I do the Father does through me, and if you have seen me then you have seen the Father." This, my friends is an absolute!

TIME TO DISCLOSE MY PERSONAL EXPERIENCES TRAVELING BEYOND THE VEIL!

I will share with you now some personal experiences I have been blessed with, that enabled me to literally leave the veil of this fleshly vessel and enter other dimensions. It is called out of body experiences, dimensional shifts, or time travel. This is where you can consciously or subconsciously leave your body. You can witness past lives, and even travel through time: past, present, or future. The Apostle Paul mentioned this ability when he discussed meeting the Christ which taught him through trances or out of body.

I know the reality of going out of body! For a guy who was raised in a Christian philosophy that taught there wasn't even any immortal soul; to make this leap of faith was extremely incredible. When you go out of body consciously for the very first time, your entire religious concept or paradigm of thought screeches to a sudden halt.

Going out of body is exhilarating! It is another reality filled with new dimensions of hope and glory. I have written down some of my very first experiences as they occurred. Some of these experiences may not seem like much to the more advanced OBE individual. But to the novice I surely was, they revealed a different reality than I had ever been led to believe with my five senses in a three-dimensional plane of awareness. These stories tell of worlds that exist within worlds, and beautiful places of both the mind and spirit. They also show frightening aspects of the spirit world, and even evil entities that prey on the unlearned novice. So going out of body is not a game, it is a lesson. It is something to be learned as you evolve to higher levels of inner awareness.

I have had many OBE's! I have traveled to other dimensions, planets, and parallel universes. You name it; I have been there. It is like having the ability to press a button and enter Rod Serling's Twilight Zone. Yet this is not a movie, dreams or a brain disorder that modern day medicine claims. These are real experiences that can be proven with the more experienced traveler. Many OBE travelers usually go no further than the astral plane of awareness. However some have traveled beyond this lower realm and entered the higher vibrations where beings of light can be seen and communicated with. There have also been a few who have traveled to the highest of all, the "I AM" presence and have returned to speak of the unknown in the best way they can.

What you are about to read is true! The reason I chose some of the first experiences is because I want to show how I also had to battle with these activities like anyone else educated in the Christian or fear based reality. I want to show that these experiences are not demonic, neither should they be frowned upon, but are beautiful avenues to enter the world of the Father's presence. It is my humble opinion that this is one of the only ways to really grasp your true nature of being spirit beings, outside of dying in this flesh or having near death experiences.

WELCOME TO THE WORLD OF YOUR MULTI-DIMENSIONAL SELVES!

One of the many ways one can induce an OBE is through the Dream State. I learned that I was able to induce OBE's from the lucid Awareness State of mind. Simply meaning, when you are dreaming and become aware that you are dreaming while in the dream! This is known as lucid awareness! You can train yourself to become lucid by preparing your mind every night to watch for clues that will identify that you are dreaming. I have used several methods, but I have found the one that works best for me is to program my mind just prior to falling asleep that I will become aware while dreaming. The closer you get to falling asleep the better your chance of success will become. Try to shut down all your thoughts and keep concentrated on only one aspect and that is your conscious awareness while you're dreaming! Usually you will enter a dream only minutes after falling into a sleep mode, so if you can keep your mind alert until you actually fall asleep, then you should be able to recognize that you are dreaming when it occurs! I want to state that I have traveled dimensions and time from a waking state also, so those that think these things only happen when one is asleep are sadly mistaken and creating doubt in the process.

When you become aware inside a dream you have access to abilities through commands that you never knew existed. The reason this occurs is because your physical mind-brain has now fallen asleep and another consciousness takes over, which really is your projected-soul spirit! That is why it is so hard for many to remember their dreams, because they are coming from another reality and dimension. And when you wake up your physical brain sets back in gear, and it usually does not have the ability to retain what was learned on another level of awareness. You can train your brain to recall events but it takes effort. It is like rewriting a program for your computer so that it will pick up more information. Your brain needs to be rewritten! These commands also exist within your waking consciousness, but the garbage that has filtered into your mind displaces this reality with the three-dimensional reality. Simply stated, you can change your physical reality also by using this power, however this takes training.

FIVE PERSONAL DREAM STATE AWARENESS LEVELS!

#1

There are many dream-states of awareness. I have personally experienced five that I will identify. The first is a regular dream, which everyone is accustomed to having. It is where times, people, places and events tend to overlap into an incomplete scenario jumping from one scene to another. These dreams usually have no real consistent content and usually pertain to imagery and symbols that are difficult to pick up or understand. However there is usually a message coming from higher aspects of yourself. Most people who dream have this type of dream.

#2

The second dream reality that I have experienced many times is the lucid dream reality. This is when you are aware you are dreaming and can actually control the events of your dream, like flying or entering different places just by command. The difference between the dream world and other consciousness changes is that dreams usually come equipped with images rather than a literal aspect. Example: one might dream about animals instead of humans yet knowing they are representative of the human. This is an image to reveal something within your life. Each animal has a characteristic and if you are dreaming of a particular animal that is representative of a particular person. My advise is learn about the behavior patterns and characteristics of that animal and you might be shown a revelation about the person.

#3

The third type of dream I have had is what I call the Meta-World, meaning the metaphysical world. I love these dreams! Most have never experienced this state of being enough to become aware of them. A Meta-world dream is when another aspect of your soul is in contact with other souls either from this plane of reality or another for the purpose of gaining information. Yes, that is right, you can come in contact with other people in this plane of awareness and learn and discuss information as if you were speaking to them in your three-dimensional plane of awareness. However usually both parties do not recall the event when they wake up. This plane of awareness is just like your physical reality; your five senses can actually work in these states of awareness. Anytime you begin to feel your five senses in a dream, stop, there is information being sent to you by someone else. You need to become aware. I love to ask questions in this awareness to learn information I could not possibly know, and then confirm it later. This reality is also broken into two parts. The second aspect is when someone else is contacting you without you approaching them, and you are evolved enough to respond to the contact. I have literally had conversations with people I haven't talked with in 20 years or more, and I learn things that could result from no other means. If you dream about a person you know, tell them of your dream no matter how absurd it seemed. You will be shocked how many times they will reveal something that proves the dream was teaching you a reality.

#4

The next dream reality is the OBE reality which is both conscious and subconscious. Meaning you are either totally aware that it has taken place, or you do not remember or cannot be sure if it was real. In this state of awareness you actually project outside your physical body and can travel anywhere you are evolved enough to enter.

#5

The final Dream State--and I by no means claim that these are the only five, but these are the ones I have inner-awareness of-- is dimensional travel and/or time travel. Going from one plane of existence into another that is very similar to this one but with slight changes. I have actually slipped dimensions from a waking state, however that has only occurred once. Yet it was absolutely amazing. I have seen myself in similar circumstances in other worlds, but there were always slight changes. And even attitudes were different.

As I reveal my personal OBE experiences, I want to discuss that being raised a Christian with all the fears that come with it made it very difficult to enter this new paradigm of gnosis. I was raised with the belief that these activities fell under the heading of demonic activity and playing around with wicked spirits. It was never my intention when I began these conscious OBE's to displease God the Father. I, as any other Christian would have done, prayed and asked Christ and the Father to prevent me from entering this world of gnosis if it displeased them. I did not want to do wrong! I would never willingly set myself up for deception. So I prayed and asked if it was proper and good in the sight of God to experience these activities. I then became bolder. Not only did I ask for the permission to accomplish these tests, I asked that they provide a way to accomplish it through me.

What I experienced the very first time I requested this was something I was never mentally prepared for. What I learned instantly changed my view on Christianity and religion and God in seconds.

THE VERY FIRST CONSCIOUS EXPERIENCE!

The first night I attempted this I had programmed myself to awaken in the dream as the Lucid State of awareness. I had two dreams. It was obvious that a higher power was definitely intervening to accomplish these events. My first dream was about going back to elementary school. I had very little recall in this dream, and I did not become Lucid. Yet I woke up immediately and realized I had missed a great opportunity. I was a little upset, but I tried again. As soon as my head hit the pillow I began to dream. This time I went back to school again but it was High school not elementary. When I began to understand the gnosis behind these dreams I realized I was being taught that religion was like being at elementary school, but I was still asleep unable to see the mysteries. Now I was led into a higher education of the mysteries. I entered High School.

In this dream I entered the doors of a school with other friends. I at the time had been out of school for nearly 20 years. So it was very odd that I was walking into a high school to learn again. As we walked into this class it became more and more obvious that something was not right. I then noticed over at the end of the room, there was a stove for cooking. Now unless I was in a home economics class something was out of whack here. I then sat down and jokingly said, "What is going on here? Are we going to cook meals in this class?" As soon as I said that my mind opened consciously and I realized I was dreaming. Like floodgates opening, I became totally conscious. I woke up in my dream without ever leaving the dream. The oddity of going back to school and seeing some strange things like the stove became what I call dream triggers. These are elements that are out of place from the physical world that will help you become lucid.

This is where commands come into play. Once you enter lucid awareness you can make commands that will instantly be adhered to, because as I have said, we are spirit beings first,

224

physical beings second. When you enter the spiritual world even through a dream, you have access to spiritual capabilities. Immediately I made the command to leave my body! I stated out loud within this classroom, "I am out of body now!" Instantly I began to float upward out of the chair I was sitting in and slowly to the back of the class. I even waved goodbye to the others in this classroom that were watching me float upwards. As I floated to the top of the room, I then made one more command, "To my home now!" After I made this request I began to slowly turn in mid air and then I blacked out. Changing conscious awareness levels and entering new dimensions can cause a blacking out or phasing. You are not really losing consciousness, you are just changing it. And through this change many times a person appears to black out. You are not losing control; but everything in your vision seems to darken as if you are blind. If you do not have mental control you will probably wake up and miss your chance to go OBE when you enter this change.

As soon as I turned and blacked out I felt the sensation of floating down. I still could not see for a span of about 5 seconds. Immediately my vision opened and I saw I was floating in the room where I was sleeping. I floated down and slowly touched the surface of the carpet. My vision was very localized though. I was only able to see a small area of carpet no greater than one foot by one foot. I then made a command to have, "Clarity now!" Immediately I saw the entire room. That is when I realized I was no longer in the Lucid dreaming state, but had advanced to the OBE state. It was then I decided to do something that really should not be done until after your first few tries. I went to my body, which was still in the same position I left it when I fell asleep. This time I was looking at it from outside my body, not inside it. At that very moment, instantly my entire religious philosophy changed. I was not dead, this was not an NDE. My brain was not sparking and firing millions of neurons all at once as some scientists claim of near death experiences. I was healthy and I was not on drugs or any other substance. I was simply outside my physical body.

I now knew once and for all we are spiritual beings that just reside in a fleshly tabernacle. In the many books I read about this subject, I learned that when entering the other dimensions not everything will appear as you believe it to be. Again there are reasons for this that I will discuss later. This was true for my first time out. I recognized that everything in my house seemed to be normal except there was a table missing. And the appearance of my body had slight changes to its features. First of all, I saw the eyes were completely soulless. There is a good reason for that; its soul was outside the body. I was standing next to my physical vessel. Secondly, the appearance of my body was slightly different in that it looked like me 20 years ago. That was quite a shock. At that moment I realized that when you think or look upon your body you are going to be pulled back into it again. So with one final conclusion to this remarkable discovery I patted my body on the shoulder and said, "Well done John!" I then immediately was sucked back into it and became alert on the other side, now inside my physical body. Sometimes reentering your body you may go inside backwards or upside down. This may sound more frightening than it really is. I have had this occur and sometimes you get stuck in wrong and you can actually see outside from the back of your head instead of your eyes, strange indeed.

My body was tingling from head to toe. It was the feeling when your foot goes to sleep and then comes back to life; with feelings of tingling needles all throughout your foot. This was similar but not quite the same.

I had disconnected from the physical body and then reconnected. This brought this feeling, because my physical brain was picking up the sensation of the spiritual counterpart, which controls the workings of my body awareness.

My first attempt was an absolute success! I was thrilled and yet stunned by what I had visualized. Witnessing my very own body from the outside was a momentous event. It changed my entire view of religion and science. No one will ever be able to take that experience away from me, no matter what they say. Because until you experience this event you will never understand what I am trying to relate.

I can truly say that this first experience will go down in my record book as one of the most powerful events to have ever occurred in my life. I recalled how men and women were accused by the religions and government of their day as being witches and warlocks because they had these experiences and spoke of them outright. These poor souls were hung or burned at a stake because they were perceived as evil and in league with the devil. I marvel how shallow humanity can become within their veil of deception and illusion! Why people are so frightened of the wonders of our Father and our own design is beyond belief. Why do people want to worship a God they are scared to death of, thinking he will destroy them at every corner? Why have people been so deceived?

MY SECOND ATTEMPT!

After my first success at leaving the body I decided to try again, but this time to attempt to travel to different places. I wanted to use more controls that I had read about by the more experienced travelers, so I could have an exciting journey beyond the veil. Once again I attempted to enter the OBE state from a lucid dream. I was unable to become lucid but I did dream. I woke up immediately after the dream around 6am in the morning, and realized I was unable to become conscious within the dream itself. So I closed my eyes again, and as I was drifting off to sleep I mentally repeated, "I am out of Body. The dream is my trigger to become aware." I continued to repeat this until I fell fast asleep. I was not prepared for what transpired next. Since I was a little boy I have awakened in the middle of the night in sheer terror because of a phenomenon that created a cataleptic state of feeling paralyzed. Many have described this event as the feeling that you have lost control of your body. There would also be an eerie feeling that someone was in the room with me, and they were taking me over, almost in the sense of demonic possession.

CATALEPTIC!

When I was younger I believed this was demonism. It scared me to death, and I was afraid to speak of this around my family, because they might perceive me as being demon influenced. This is the kind of abnormality one has to live through when they fear everything and anything around the corner. I was programmed to believe that everything outside what our church taught or believed was of the devil; therefore you must stay away from these undesirable events. Well I didn't choose for this activity to occur, and I assure you I did not want to experiment with it. Yet it would occur many times as the years went on. And every single time it occurred it brought deep fear with it. The struggle and the fear scares you so badly that you fight it and struggle against it until you break free. You can't move, you can't even cry out. You are completely without control of your body, yet at the same time you are definitely feeling a strange presence in your midst.

No one likes to lose control, and this is exactly what takes place when this cataleptic freeze asserts its presence. You feel like you could be whisked away into no man's land or even into death. And while this is taking place you fear you could be taken over by some evil spirit that wants to harm you. Those who have experienced this understand exactly what I am speaking of. It wasn't until I learned what was happening that the fear began to subside. Now don't get me wrong, it is still a fearful thing when it occurs, because it happens so suddenly and without warning. Now I am able to regain enough conscious awareness to understand what has developed. To individuals that are attempting to induce an OBE this event is sought for. Those who understand what is happening want this strange occurrence, because it is the beginning of leaving their body even from a waking state.

So in my 2nd attempt to go OBE I had to endure this cataleptic state, but I was so frightened again, I broke free from the sensation and then realized what I had done. When this event occurs you are not to fight against it at all. There is no fear in what is happening. You are experiencing a very natural phenomenon that if responded to could separate you from your physical body. What is taking place is that your projected soul consciousness, that part of you that inhabits the body, has already separated from the physical, but not completely. It hasn't left the parameters of the body. You are waking up at the very moment of separation, and your biological brain is alert enough to recognize it has lost control of the body. This brings forth the fear. Have you ever been awakened so suddenly by a sound that when you jumped up out of bed, you felt paralyzed and could barely walk? This in a sense is the same sensation, except you can't move. This is nothing more than your projected soul spirit has disconnected from the biological while the material body rejuvenates in its sleep. What is occurring is that you have awakened in both dimensions at the same time. Except the spiritual counterpart has already entered the next dimension at the same time your brain becomes alert to realize it is not in control. You cannot move because the controlling devices are already outside the body. You have lost control and this is what brings the immediate fear.

You still feel as though you are in your body but can't move! Now the strange presence you feel in the room with you is your very own soul projected spirit presence. Yes, you are feeling yourself from two different awareness levels. The fear that you have and the feeling this entity is evil is because you are not able to ascertain the conscious shifts from the physical brain. And the event comes across very weird to the novice. I must reiterate something here; if you fear evil entities even in this state you could draw them to you, but more on this later. Our brain can only perceive a three-dimensional world. Now all of the sudden it has perception of a fourth dimension and it cannot handle that!

This occurrence that happens to millions of people is absolute proof that without our spirit and soul, we could not have life conscious controlled awareness. All matter life would cease to exist if it did not have a spiritual counterpart. When your body goes to sleep it has to wake up or it will die. Because the counterpart, the real you often leaves the body at night, but only a few are trained and aware enough to become conscious during this activity. We are spirit beings first!!!

I became internally aware that these activities are normal for all of us, but most stifle them because of their petty fears and hang-ups. My entire thesis throughout this book decrees that real Gnosticism is an internal awareness. And I fully believe that all truth above and below is within us, but we must learn how to tap into it so we can partake of it. I personally believe that OBE's are one of the greatest teachers of this gnosis. Fear is one of the deadliest traits in the human nature. We must learn to overcome our fears. Fear holds a strong individual captive. Fear binds the soul! We can learn to overcome fear by going out of body. We will learn lessons there that may not be available anywhere else. As the Bible suggests, "The spirit of our Father is not fear but peace and truth."

When you become aware that you are a powerful divine being and that nothing can harm the real you, then only fear can take that away from you. Fear is the enemy of our Father. Fear is nothing more than illusion based on the false reality of a temporal existence located in the time and space realm of the shadow. Now learn another very powerful mystery; learning not to fear is the highest evolution of our growth awareness in this realm. Once you conquer your fears then you will have mastered the force, sound familiar?

As you comprehend this secret then the fear that has controlled you will have to depart, thereby decreeing as the Bible teaches, "Flee from Satan and he will flee from you." I have personally witnessed people that believe the Bible is the Word of God, and say they love Jesus, but they are so fearful about everything. Their lives are under total control of fear. And yet they do not realize or comprehend that fear is their real God not the Father. The very term Satan is the spirit of fear. Satan is nothing more than an adversary to the light of the Father and his Divine Son. And no, Satan does not have to be a single entity. It can be anything or anyone that has the spirit of fear. Jesus said, "Get behind me Satan." Anyone or anything can become Satan the Devil if you allow it. We are the creators of Satan by our fears and the creators of light by our love and faith.

The reason I have set such a lengthy foundation in my second attempt in going OBE is because I wanted to share with you what I also had to learn to overcome. I know what I am talking about in this subject because I have personally lived through it. I had all the fears! After I failed to use the cataleptic state to help me exit the body totally, I broke through it and went back to sleep. However moments later I began to dream, and this time I became Lucid!

Immediately I commanded, "Out of body now." And just like the first experience I began to float upwards still inside the dream. I then blacked out as before and slowly descended to the room where I was sleeping. Again I landed on my hands and knees and could only see a small area, so I commanded, "Clarity now - full conscious awareness!" I then stood up and decided to exit the house. I had well trained myself prior to entering the OBE not to look or even think about my body, because when you do this you will be sucked back into it. We are always connected with our body even though we have disconnected to leave it. There always remains a contact that the Bible refers to as the *silver cord.* It always keeps us as close as a thought away. So don't ever be afraid that you could lose your body or fail to return. If you ever need to return to your body just think on it and zoom, you will be there faster than lightning. There have been some obstacles to returning to the body, but they are usually induced by fear. Sometimes a friend on the other side may need to give a helping hand in the event you begin to struggle. We are still babes in so many ways!

After I stood up I commanded, "To my front door now." As fast as you can say it you can travel it. In less than a milli-second I was standing staring at our living room door. After acknowledging the excitement brought about by that quick movement by command I decided I had some traveling to embark on. One thing I want to add here is that I am describing OBE experiences that were my first consciously aware activities in this realm. The truth is I had been having OBEs all my life but I never knew what they were. I always categorized them as a dream beyond a dream, something very strange and unique. I had the ability to fly through solid objects at will and had done so for years during these OBE events. But until I realized what they were I never had the controls. I didn't realize that there are no limitations in OBE's, by space and time, or other dimensions. I only used them to involve myself in petty activities. It is like having a secret weapon that can do anything you want, but you only use it for the most menial tasks because you failed to understand its grander design.

So when I stood next to my door I knew I could fly through it as if it wasn't even there, and that is exactly what I did. I flew through the door and ran out on the sidewalk yelling and shouting in excitement of what I was doing in a total conscious state of mind. I then simply commanded, "Leap to the roof of my home now," and I actually rose to the top of my home and landed. I looked around our area and everything seemed in order. It was still somewhat dark but I could see everything as clear as a bell!

It was then that I made the request to fly to Paris, France. I slowly lifted off my home and started flying. I began picking up speed; it was so fast everything became a blur. I continued to pick up even more speed and was flying at what best can be described as hyperspace dimensional travel. If you have ever seen the movie Stargate, how it appeared when they traveled through one of the gates, it was similar but not quite the same as what I was witnessing. The sensation was startling but I felt no G-force or heavy impact against myself. I was thinking while this was happening, I guess I am flying all the way to France. When one is OBE you are able to do basically anything you can comprehend. I knew you could instantly go from one place to another. I also knew you could fly there at a much slower pace than instantaneous. Yet I was somewhat confused because I knew I was flying at such great speeds that I would have passed France in a split second. I continued to travel at this breakneck pace. I wondered where I was going!

Somewhere during this flight I began to black out, and I quickly said, NO! I then made commands to stay alert and aware consciously. I thought I was being sucked back into my body. What indeed transpired was something I was not aware could happen. I felt the sensation of being pulled back into my body and then I woke up. I sat there mesmerized by the little journey I had taken, but was somewhat disappointed that it couldn't have been a longer trip. I also was upset that I never made it to France. However as I sat there I realized the speed at which I was traveling was exceedingly fast. Nothing in our physical ability could travel at those speeds.

After this little escapade I decided to get up, yet I noticed it was still early. When I looked around our house it didn't hit me right away, but something was not right. I looked into our living room and I saw a white chair setting in the middle of the room. However, we don't own a white chair. This was very startling indeed. I also noticed that the room I was in was about 10 to 15 feet wider than our home. I then knew something was wrong. I realized that I didn't come back to my body or my home. I was somewhere else!

The problem with this entire scenario is that it appeared to be my home in one sense, but it also had some strange things about its surroundings. I guess one might say that this was a strange dream or possibly a nightmare. The problem with this theory is that I was wide-awake. The situation made me realize that this was not really home, but I had no way to know when and where this event was taking place. When you wake up and you are in another world so-to-speak what is one to think or do? I believed that I was whisked away into a dimension other than my own, but it had similarities. In my belief system at the time I began to shutter with the worry that I was being plagued by demons. Everything in this place became very weird. The furniture was moving on its own. I walked back into the bedroom where my wife was still asleep, however, her body was now bouncing up and down and vibrating as if I was watching a sequel to the exorcist. I became very frightened thinking that my attempting to go out of body lured demonic activity. I was at a loss to think of what to do to change this experience. I did not know if I was ever going to get back to my real home.

Being startled I knew I had to awaken my wife in hopes that what was occurring to her would stop. To my surprise she did awaken, and because she was very groggy she was unable to ascertain what was happening. I explained that I thought I might have invited demonic activity, because I was playing around with OBE experiments. I was sorry and scared, and I yelled out, "Oh, my God, please forgive me." We then went into the other room where the furniture was continuing its dance. Then I saw a goat, which I first thought was my dog, walk into the room with a dog collar wrapped around its neck. This had all the settings of a weird mystical movie about ghosts and such. Standing in the living room I then said, "Listen, I do not know who you are, but get out of this place and stop bothering us." Nothing transpired after this feeble attempt. I then said as a good Christian would, "In the name of Jesus Christ, get out of here!" Again I had no luck. I was shocked and dismayed when the activity continued, because I believed that if you use Christ's name, evil spirits had to depart. Nothing was responding to anything I said or did. As I stood there in sheer terror I began to think about what I was learning in this metaphysical process. I knew God was helping me accomplish these things. It didn't make any sense why all of a sudden these activities would bring on evil spirits if this was something God approved of. I then remembered that we are spirit beings also, and the only thing that can be possessed by these entities is our biological body. Being a spirit we have as much or more power as these evil entities have, and only our fear gives them the energy to do anything.

It was like a light turned brightly on in my head. I actually started laughing, and my wife was wondering if I was going crazy. I said, "Listen. This is ridiculous. Their power is only given to them when we fear. They have no authority or power over anyone. It is people's fear that gives them the ability to possess and of course, frighten them senseless." I then looked at the moving furniture and realized how stupid this whole thing was. I thought how ridiculous that we would be frightened over something this silly. I then stated with clarity and precision, "I don't know who or what you are, and frankly I don't care. But now you must realize that I have no fear of you, and you are trespassing in my domain. I have equal and more power than you, and I demand you leave, because you have no right here and never will have."

Instantly as I spoke these words I blacked out again, and found myself back in bed where I had started. I realized what had occurred was a test to learn to battle these unfounded fears. I was thrilled that I had passed this first test of many to come. I then completely realized that our fear was our enemy, not roaming spiritual entities on the other side.

Since this experience my entire outlook on demonic activity has changed immensely. I no longer have fears about these entities that roam the lower astral realms. This was such a relief, and I realized from this point on that OBEs would become the new teacher in my life. This second conscious experience was truly a magnificent gift from my Father!

One thing I would like to add to resolve any potential confusion about this OBE. When I awakened in a different realm I really believed I was awake just like waking up from sleep as I have done over ten-thousand times before. It was not a dream, as one would normally perceive it. It felt as though I had arisen from sleep and entered my normal awareness, but in this case with some strange occurrences.

There are those in the Christian/religious world who will still identify this activity as demonic. I feel very sorry for them. Their fears are going to bring about their ruin. What I learned from these experiences and later ones is that our thoughts are energies that produce actions. I have been attacked multiple times by powers greater than you can imagine, and I realized every single time that they have no power over me. Yes, they get angry and very upset. They even attempted to force me to obey and worship them as Gods, yet I refused and they had no power over me. At times they can even penetrate the brain and actually make it feel as though they are squeezing your mind tight, but through it all if you remain fearless they have no power.

When entering the regions or dimensions that are beyond the three-dimensional plane of awareness, you see how quickly our thoughts can create. Each of our thoughts are being translated literally. If you do not control your spiritual mind then your spiritual mind will begin to control you. If you have fears then those fears will begin to manifest and produce that which you are frightened of.

Now maybe it can become clearer what Jesus meant when he taught how our thoughts were more damning than our actions. He said even if you think the thought you have already in your heart broken the law. Our thoughts, while living in the biological container produce the same phenomenon, but at a much slower rate because of our dimensional awareness. When you leave your body then your thoughts are translated into immediate action. If you fear demonic activity or ghostly apparitions or even monsters, then while you are out of body you will produce this activity instantly, because your thoughts are real! I will delve more into this in the next mystery of Spirits!

I decided to write these first two experiences I had with OBE's because I felt they would lay a ground work for what I am trying to reveal. I have had to deal with the same fears that many of you are dealing with now. I have walked this road and I know what I am speaking of. So I am relating this information as first person personal so you can relate to it helping increase your chances of gaining an opening for personal intuitive internal awareness, GNOSIS!

One of my later experiences was the first opportunity to finally leave my body from a waking state following the cataleptic experience I have spoken about. This is when one wakes up feeling paralyzed. I finally broke through my fears and used the activity to leave my body.

ONE WINTER MORNING PROVIDED A WONDERFUL OBE EXPERIENCE!

It was a winter morning when I first was able to consciously use the cataleptic state to leave my body, however I thought it failed! I woke up about 5AM and I was in this paralyzed state. My first reaction of course was to fight it, because it occurs so suddenly that one can hardly be prepared for it. But this day I accepted what was occurring and told myself not to fear. I then relaxed as I was still paralyzed and simply requested, "I am now leaving my body." But nothing happened! I said again, "I am now floating to the ceiling." Again nothing happened. I was shocked because something definitely should have taken place. I failed to realize the significance of what happened next until after the entire experience was over. I remember reading that you can seek divine help to assist in leaving your body. So I lifted my arm upwards and asked if someone would help me out of my body?

Again, nothing seemingly occurred! After a while the feeling of being frozen or paralyzed subsided. At this time I was upset that I couldn't leave my body from this state of awareness. So I turned over preparing to go to sleep. But instead of sleeping I gazed at the lit kerosene heater, and felt as though something was wrong. It seemed to be giving off too much heat. I then got up and walked over to the heater and began to suffocate in the heat. It was very hot and stuffy. I could not understand what was causing this unless there was something wrong with the heater itself.

I opened the front door for about 30 seconds to allow some heat to escape because it was still too cold outside to turn the heater off. I then shut the door and went back to bed. I rolled back over into a comfortable position, and as before gave one last gaze over to the heater before I fell back asleep. However there was another problem. When I looked at the heater it was turned off. I said, "Wait a minute! I did not turn that heater off." I wondered if it blew out because I had the door open. But I knew that wasn't the case because when I left it, it was still lit. I didn't know what to think. So I got back up and went over to the heater to see if there was something wrong. To my shock, it not only was off but had been off for some time, because it was already cold around the heater elements. I didn't know what to make of this. So I decided to leave it off in case there was something seriously wrong. I could fix it in the morning. I headed back to bed when I decided to take one more look at the front door. I was stunned; the door was open. Again I said, "WAIT! I closed that door, how could it be open?" At this time it became clear that some funny stuff was going on and I didn't have a clue why. So I shut the door and walked back toward my bedroom, taking one last assured glance towards the door. What I saw threw me for a loop. The door I looked back at was not our living room door.

I don't know whose door it was, but it wasn't our door. Our front door is made of partially metal with glass panes down the middle. This door was mahogany or some type of oak wood. It was very beautiful as doors go, but it wasn't our door! I looked quickly around the room to see if everything else was in order, and sure enough it was. All the furniture was correct, and the room setting and size was also correct. Everything was in order except we had another door where it shouldn't have been. What was going through my mind really didn't make any sense but I was thinking that I must have left my body after all. Yet I thought, how was that possible? I was never asleep. Whenever I left my body before I could never touch physical objects because my hand would go through them. Here I was touching objects and even feeling temperatures etc... How could this be?

One thing I would like to add before I proceed is that when I requested help to leave my body it didn't dawn on me till after this experience ended that I was paralyzed. How could I have lifted my arm up the way I did? And secondly my arm was buried under the covers. Yet I lifted my arm and saw it and there were no covers blocking its way. I later realized that the arm I lifted was my soul arm. Now that is an experience! When you can see your astral body, or see through your eyes when they are closed, it is an amazing experience. That is what happened to me this night. I was already OBE and never realized it. All three times I had been in another dimension, and yet I felt wide-awake and no different than normal.

Getting back to the scenario of events I wasted no time after realizing that I was OBE. I simply flew right through the door with a single leap and then flew up on the roof of our home. As I stood there gleaming with excitement, I chose to fly to Nevada. A friend of mine was in Vegas on vacation, and I wanted to see if I could find him while OBE.

I simply commanded, "I am flying to Nevada now." Immediately I floated slowly upward and started to fly out over our neighborhood and then began flying west. The speed at first was very slow and then started picking up rather quickly. I was flying across the United States without being in an airplane. I could see the land and terrain as it zipped by me. I could see housing developments, and city lights off in the distance. Everything you could see from a plane I could see except a lot better, because I was flying only about three to four hundred feet off the ground. I was so amazed by what was occurring that I had to stop and land. I simply said, "Stop now." At first nothing happened, I then repeated the command much bolder and the speed automatically began to withdraw and I slowly floated to Earth. I was all by myself standing somewhere only God knows. It was a large green open area that appeared to be somewhere in the Midwest. It was slightly hilly, but no mountains. I stood there looking around with my mouth draping on my chin. I wondered what it would be like to get this knowledge out to everybody. This was better than any ride at an amusement park. This experience will always go down as one of my favorite things I have done in this life, whether physical or spiritual.

With excitement I declared that I must continue onward. I then just thought about flying again and I began to soar high in the sky like a bird. I must have flown for some time when I recognized that the terrain below was taking on the southwest appearance with desert. I then wanted to know where I was, because I didn't have a clue. I had been flying towards the west and I knew basically where I was but not exactly. It is different when you are in total control as an airline pilot. They have gauges and instruments that tell them where they are. But when you are flying like this you have nothing but instinct to guide you. As I became concerned about where I was I commanded, "Where am I?" Nothing happened after this request. I then repeated it and slowly started to fly over a housing development. I could see the fences of the backyards and how this development was laid out. I was flying very low, probably about telephone pole high now. I could see the houses and apartments. I could see which ones had lights on and which ones didn't. I then flew over these houses and into a more desolate area when I saw what appeared to be a diner. I then flew towards the diner and landed.

It seemed very early in the morning; the diner was open but it catered to mostly truck drivers. I decided to walk in and see what was happening. The waitresses dressed in white with blue aprons were serving their customers and it seemed as though they all knew each other, as if they were regular customers. The restaurant was arranged with a horseshoe type counter that extended around in the front of the restaurant and then the horseshoe straightened up towards the back of the restaurant where tables were set. I wanted to know where I was, but I thought that asking a question like that might sound stupid. So I walked to the back of the diner where I saw a young lady who seemed quite sad sitting by herself. I wondered if she would tell me where I was without too much embarrassment. I figured she was alone and everyone else was in the front of the diner so they didn't have to know. As I got close enough to ask her this question I realized that something wasn't right. I had come close enough to her that my presence should have startled her. I then walked around her table trying to get her to notice me. She wasn't moving at all nor did she appear to even sense my presence. It was then that I realized, even though everything appeared normal from my point of view, I was at a different vibration rate than they were. I was actually a ghost in their presence. Now try that one on for size? All these years I was afraid of Ghosts or demons, and now here I was nothing more than a ghostly apparition around these people that could not see me?

It was strange to think that we can also become a ghost or spirit apparition around other humans, and realize this probably happens all the time. Have you ever thought that some of these ghosts or the demons everyone is afraid of are actually OBE travelers? How funny!

I then realized that if I was going to find out where I was I needed to do my own investigation. I listened to the conversations to try to pick up where I was, but nothing was really revealed. The truck drivers definitely had another topic on their minds, mainly the waitresses. I heard one of them say as he was leaving to get back to Philadelphia. I knew we were not close to Philadelphia. I lived and worked in Philly for several years and I know what that area looks like, but these were truck drivers that probably traveled all over the country. I went back outside and noticed that there were two newspaper boxes. I felt I could look at the paper through the box and see what city they originated from. Well, that was a lot easier said than done. When I peered through the glass I couldn't make out the print! The print was too complicated to read. I found out later after reading other works on this subject that at times the astral eyes are unable to pick up physical print if it is too small. I could not pick up the print at all! I did see the main heading

241

across the top of the paper on one of them. It said, "DEALER." This paper appeared to be one of those small local town papers, so I don't have any clue where that would have been. Some have suggested that Cleveland's paper is called the Plain Dealer, but I was not near Cleveland. That was obvious by the surroundings of the diner. It was in a desert area. And this paper I saw was only a small paper possibly from a very small town or one of those local thrift-mart type papers.

At this very moment I began to black out, and the next thing I remembered was waking up and getting out of bed to shave. As I walked to the bathroom I mediated on how absolutely exciting this OBE journey that I had just taken was. As I was shaving I looked into the mirror and saw that I was clean shaven. Then it hit me, "Wait a second, I don't shave. I sport a beard. Why am I in here shaving when I have a beard?" Again I began to black out and the next thing I recalled was waking up again for the second time. This was so odd, I thought I had awakened and even began to shave before it hit me that I was still OBE!

This was really a strange experience. However, this time I knew I was awake as my wife was already up fixing some tea and breakfast. So I went out into the kitchen to tell her of this fantastic voyage into other dimensions and how great flying across the country was. I was talking to her and she didn't respond. I thought, how rude! So I asked her, "What do you think of what I have said?" There was no response! I became a little perturbed. Then it dawned on me again that I was still out of body. That is when I said, "Oh God, this is incredible!" I then heard my wife say something. She turned to look at me sleeping in the other room and said, "I wonder if he is out of body now."

This is hard to explain, but at that very moment I became frightened. I thought she might try to wake me and see my soulless eyes as I remembered seeing the first time I saw my body from the other side. I believed if she had seen me like that she might perceive that I had died. Instantly I went slamming back into my body so hard I must have bounced two feet in the air, and while I returned I was yelling out, "I'm ok, I'm ok!" But it became apparent that all that was for naught. She never came back into the room. She turned and went into another room. This time as I woke up again I sat there and wondered if I was really awake this time or still OBE. It appeared that this time I had now returned to this reality. I then walked over to my wife to learn the next most incredible thing. I asked her what she said to me when I was sleeping? She said that she had said nothing to me. I said, "Didn't you say something to me just a couple of minutes ago?" She said NO! I said, "Were you just in the kitchen making tea and breakfast?" She was kind of taken back by that comment wondering how I knew unless I was awake. She said, "Yes, I was in the Kitchen doing those things.

I realized that she couldn't see me, but I could see her. She said, "But I didn't say anything to you." There was a slight pause as I tried to gather my thoughts. I asked her, "Did you turn and look towards me in the other room?"

OUT OF BODY BRINGS OUT THE GIFT OF MENTAL TELEPATHY

To my greatest shock she then said, "I did turn to look at you while you were sleeping, but I never said anything. However I did think about something. I wondered whether you were out of body or not." It was then that I first realized you could hear peoples' thoughts from the astral and other dimensions. What a startling piece of information! I could hear her thoughts as if she spoke the words as clear as a bell. What a thrill!

Without going into too much detail I have now had many OBE's, dimensional shifts, and even time travel and witnessed past lives. I have been to other planets and met others just like us from different worlds who know about us, but we do not know about them. I have also learned some of the reasons why this is so. I have even witnessed myself in other dimensions living in at least 6-7 different worlds. And I know there are more! I know that to the unlearned this sounds like science fiction. And I would have to agree that I could never prove it to you. You can only gain this awareness from within yourself. But at least I can lay a foundation in what to expect. I felt it was necessary to share these personal experiences so you could at least visualize the necessary components of conscious out of body travel. When you become consciously aware and in control while OBE, there is no greater avenue in my humble opinion to teach of the mysteries beyond the veil.

In your soul body, or the out of body reality, things that seemed real to you in the flesh begin to appear as nothing more than an illusion. It begins to fade away with an ethereal appearance. The physical matter world appears to us on this level as being the real world; it has form and seemingly solid substance. When you view spirits from the three-dimensional world they appear to you as a ghostly presence, ethereal. But when you are in the same dimension of vibration through the OBE state, then spirits look normal, but matter takes on the same appearance of the ethereal. It begins to slowly fade away as an illusion. It is all a matter of different vibration rates.

When you think a thought in the fleshly apparatus of the brain it will only be a matter of time that your spiritual presence begins to form that thought into real energies that will exist. You can then pattern that thought into your reality of this dimension. Energy of thought is creation! It is accomplished because when you think a thought and dwell on that thought long enough you are creating the pattern of light energy of that thought in the fourth dimension or higher. If you began to slow that patterns' vibration rate down you could then bring that energy into form into our three-dimensional world. Thoughts that you think when you are in the other dimensions are automatically carried out unless you put a stop to them. But in this realm, thoughts take sometimes years to develop where they will come to fruition.

Going out of body is not a game! It is a spiritual tool teaching spiritual mind control. If you fear evil you are the one giving it energy to be created. Evil is only an illusion of fear-based entities. That is why Love can so easily destroy it, because it doesn't really exist. It only appears to exist because people or spirits that are using their energies wrongly are bringing it out of the astral dimensions. When love is missing, evil will appear as real as anything else. When an individual uses their energy to take another life, then evil becomes real to the one that was affected. It is still only an illusion, because the entity that was killed is still alive in another dimension. However the illusion remains real to a loved one, especially when they are only accessing their reality in this dimension.

If your heart is seeking good experiences through love, then your experiences will be filled with joyous events that lead to peace, long suffering, goodness, kindness, gentleness, temperance etc... The Bible states, "To the pure all is pure." If a person wields evil thoughts then evil will become a reality to them. When love is your counterbalance, then you will have defeated the illusion of evil and fear.

RELY CHIEFLY ON INTERNAL GNOSIS!

We are always being guided along the way, like a parent nurturing their newborn child. Our Father/Mother divine does not want us roaming around in the spirit world without controls and balances to overcome the possible negative experiences that can and do occur. Others that have already experienced realities in these other dimensions can assist by weaning you off the matter world, the unreal dimension, into the spiritual world, the true dimension. But never forget you are chiefly responsible for your own evolvement. If anyone tries to take that responsibility away from you then you must reject them. All gnosis is within you! Rely on internal gnosis rather than anything or anyone else!

As Jesus told Nicodemus, "Except you be born again you can not see the kingdom of God." I have desired to share with you all through this book that these statements Jesus made were a mystery to be decoded. And I am showing you certain steps that will enable you to realize this Gnosis from your own experiences. As you enter beyond the veil you realize what Jesus meant by these mystical statements. You can better understand what it means to enter the Kingdom of God and why one needs to be born again. Jesus spoke of it being like the wind where one is unable to see it, but they know it is there. Spirit is all around us, yet at our level of vibration we are unable to view most things of the spirit world. Being born again is when one sheds the veil, the flesh, and enters the spirit world. When you die you will have an out of body experience whether you believe in them or not. However, where you go will depend largely on the fruits you have produced in this particular lifetime. The fruit becomes your belief system!

Now understand another mystery and read closely. You are a divine being of free choice, where you go after death is your choice. It is not to be regulated by anyone else except you allow it. I want you to keep reading this statement. I have shown possibilities of where one goes after death. I have spoken a little about the light and the tunnel and I will continue to do so. But you must realize once and for all, no matter where you go you have taken the same path thousands of times before and you keep ending up back here. If you can break the code internally, it will finally put a stop to your recreating the same scenario time after time!

FOLLOWING OTHERS IS A FORMULA FOR DOOM!

There is no law that says you must go to the tunnel. And remember this, just because someone may be there that seems to have love beyond anything you can imagine, and they come across as an angel of light, it doesn't mean you are to follow them. Paul said that the spirit of Satan can come as an angel of light or a ministering spirit. We have been locked in the portal of shadow and we have to break out. And following anything other than the divine Son the Christ is a formula for doom!

But on the other hand it would be better to enter the tunnel than to become lost in the realms of imagination, which I will speak on next chapter. There are discarnate entities that roam the astral regions. And some that have never been embodied in the physical. There are some that have perished in the flesh and entered these regions of a world made up of their own imagination. And if your belief system was one of hell and demons then prepare yourself for a mental war. Some have even experienced this sensation of the mind as hell where they believe God is punishing and tormenting them. But it is all an illusion, built by their own faulty reasoning, an illusion that could be dispelled instantly by love!

It is important to understand that the spirit world will not make right what you have done wrong in the flesh. The spiritual imprints upon a higher body beyond the flesh and until one overcomes it will be there with you. If you die a good spiritual entity then you are such an entity after death also. But if you die a wicked person then you bring that flaw of character with you. Revelation 22:11 states, "If you die a sinner then behold you are a sinner." This entire concept that Jesus' blood will instantly make the sinner righteous is a doctrine sown in error and lack of gnosis. You are what you are because of what you have thought and created, not because of what someone else did. If you have flawed character then part of you is flawed. If you were filled with this error then for Jesus or anyone else to remove this from you would be tantamount in removing you! What is left of an evil person when evil is removed? Righteousness? Of course NOT! Righteousness is an act not a name. Being righteous is something you must become, not something that is handed down to you! An evil person must fill the void that was occupied by that evil with something good. Doing what is right will replace what has been done wrong. But doing nothing will replace nothing! Granted there are many who are teachers and masters on the other side of the veil who can and will assist, but it is still free will.

So what you learn in this lower school world you will take with you past the veil. If evil was produced then it becomes your karma of reaping what you sow, and now will have to be rectified by your return to the cycles of matter. Now some may ask, don't we have free choice? What if I don't want to pay for what I have done wrong? Well, gnosis is a sneaky virtue, because if you do not have it, you cannot ascertain your right of free choice after death. You will only follow. One that has gnosis will attempt to overcome that which is evil and replace it with good. One that is internally aware will not lead their life doing evil acts thinking they can bypass the karmic law. Usually those that do wrong have no idea of the karmic law. That is why they continue to do what is wrong. You will remain kidnapped if you continue to do what you have always done. Be assured of this one thing!

Evil will never attach itself to your heavenly body where treasures are stored. Only good works enter that realm. Evil must be rectified on its return orbit in the space-time continuum. If you continue to lack gnosis you will forever fail to enter the heavenly body that has stored your good works. You will never know what you have been creating for yourself, because you will still be locked in the shadow.

I have to laugh and cry at the same time when I am accused of saying there is no good or evil, so one can do whatever they want. Have you read what I am saying? Everyone has free choice to choose what is good and what is evil. The shadow Lords handed this down eons ago. But we as a divine being has free choice by law, beyond what the shadows have taught. I am not teaching that evil has no bearing one way or the other. I am saying that if you commit transgressions against the spiritual or physical laws of nature you will remain trapped. Your lack of Gnosis is the true evil. Everything else is an illusion! I am not the one stating all your evil is removed by what someone else did. I state that you have to deal with your own evil, and Jesus showed us the way. He didn't do it for us. Now who is the one teaching that there is no sin? Think about this for a second!

SO WHAT DOES IT REALLY MEAN TO BE BORN AGAIN?

So what did Jesus mean when he said born again? We have heard Christians espouse the concept that they are born again. What is being born again? The Greek words that this terminology comes from in the Bible actually means being born from above. However being born again and being born from above imply the same usage and intent in these scriptures. The ultimate meaning of being born again is becoming aware of your true reality. It is that which is beyond the veil of shadow. But why does it say born again or born from above? Nicodemus understood in this ancient language what Jesus was referring to. So many try to read into the scriptures things that are not there. If they stuck with the contextual pattern they would indeed understand the meaning of these words. Nicodemus asked Jesus, how can a man be born again? Will he enter back into his mother's womb and be born? At this point it becomes quite obvious that Nicodemus understood Jesus to mean one must be born again in the body. But Jesus told Nicodemus that the birth he was speaking of was a spiritual birth, one that could not be seen. Where so many have lacked the gnosis in these verses is that they failed to comprehend its true meaning. If Jesus was talking about being born again, and Nicodemus was incorrect in believing it was a physical rebirth from their mother's womb, then how is one born a second time spiritually? What did Jesus really mean, "Except you be born again from above?" Could it be that Jesus knew we were all born spirit children of the divine Father, and because of our fall into the shadow we have forgotten this? Thereby decreeing one must reenter the divine to witness our true heritage?

TO BE REBORN A SPIRIT MEANS YOU ARE ALREADY SPIRIT!

Notice how Jesus put this in words, "Except you be born again you cannot SEE the kingdom of God." Why use the word SEE? Because that is the key! We are unable to see our true heritage while veiled in the shadow. Jesus was implying until we shed this veil we could not see who we really are! Nicodemus understood what Jesus meant, but he could not understand how this was possible. That is why he said, "How can these things be?" If we as humans have to be reborn as spirits then that implies we were already born spirit. You can't be reborn if it hasn't happened the first time!

So we must come out of the veil to give testimony to our rightful origin, but if we lack gnosis then we will not return to our rightful domain. We will most likely remain locked in the shadows. Being born again in the spirit is really only a play on words to illustrate our multiple births in the flesh. Energy always exists, you have not disappeared, you have just relocated. Our symbolic disappearance came when we entered maya of illusion. Being born again is the lifting of the veil. When you remove the veil you can see the kingdom or the dimensions of spirit!

Jesus also made it clear that the Kingdom of God is within us. The kingdom will not come by physical observation but by spiritual observation from within, meaning past the biological garments. This brings me back to the statement, "You are what you are when you die." Experiencing beyond the veil through near-death or out of body experiences is so important because you are gaining vital Gnosis about your true inner self while still observing and living in the veil. You can pass the ultimate tests now and grow to the evolved stage of eternal reality. You can leave the shadow world now, forever.

The matter world can help spirit beings change. When we live in the flesh we have the best opportunities to change our spiritual inner nature. However if you continue to die and fall prey to the karmic wheel of debt then you will continue to come back, until it finally dawns on you that this is not the place you belong. This is not your world! Jesus said, I am not of this world, neither should you be. He said, "If you love this world then the love of the Father is not in you." This does not mean the Father does not love you. It means you as the fallen son do not have his love in you, from your point of view. For if you did you would be like the Father and this world would not be your world either! We are all star-children from distant dimensions. We are locked in a portal of mystery because of our lack of gnosis.

As flesh and blood beings we are corrupt. Corruption will never inherit incorruption. The perfection of gnosis that we seek cannot come within our flesh. But the flesh can be used to help perfect our fallen spirit. Paul taught, "In a moment, in a twinkling of an eye, we shall all be changed, and the corruption must give way to the incorruption, and mortality must bring on immortality." Religion has offered theories on what this means, but once you know the mystery it is perfectly obvious what Paul is saying. Corruption, our flesh and blood, must give way for incorruption, our spirit born reality. Mortality, our life in the shadow, must put on immortality, the light of our true nature.

Paul went on to address this issue by stating that as a seed is being planted it must die before it will grow and produce fruit. Many do not realize that when one plants a seed in the garden, that seed first dies before it begins to grow. This mystical reference is to our flesh and blood vessels. Our physical bodies must give way for us to recognize the true spiritual fruit of heaven, our higher selves. The seed being planted is our flesh and blood bodies, but the real being is inside the seed when it dies. And that is where the fruit borne comes from. Once the seed has perished, or as the Bible teaches, the OLD MAN has been buried. Then the NEW MAN of the spirit can bring forth the true fruit of change. Our corruption, being the veils, will give way to incorruption, the soul-projected spirit leaving these veils. Then our mortal will be swallowed up by immortality.

Our good works, are set up in our spiritual bank account in the metaphorical heaven, where moths and dust i.e. carnal things, cannot corrupt. This is our spiritual building pool for our return to a truer identity. When you do well in the flesh then it is attributed unto your Father's spirit, which really performs the good works in us. All good works are really our Father living and abiding within us as our higher dimensional selves. It is not us, the lower dimensional son that does the good works. It is our Father in us through the Divine SON, our Higher selves, that perform this miracle.

If your works are evil, meaning of the "energy veil" of darkness, it is because you have blocked the flow of the Father/Mother spirit divine through the SON. And the energy veil (EVIL), is an illusion placed into the karmic wheel of rebirth (repetitious cycles, hell). And we will continue to be buried in the shadow unable to see the true kingdom of heaven.

How are we judged then? The Father does not judge anyone, only the son. And each of us is that son being united with the divine SON projected away from our true presence. After we die we will see what we performed, and the judgement will be our decision wrought by what we did. Some have taught Jesus is the judge, but Jesus said in his own words, "I have not come to judge the world but to save it." You can't have it both ways. A Father loves his children; he does not condemn them. You can't have a father who loves and condemns, for one will counteract the other.

The law of karma is our judge. When we breach a law we have to be accountable for that debt on a return trip. It is as simple as touching a hot stove; the law is already embedded within the punishment. If you touch the hot stove you will be burned. No one is going to burn you for you. You have done it to yourself based on the decision you made to touch a hot stove. As long as you are within the shadow you had better learn the karmic law of reaping what you sow, otherwise you will forever be doomed within the cycles of illusion never knowing where you came from. That is why Jesus said, "Judge not that you be not judged, for whatsoever judgement you judge you shall in return be judged." This is the law. Our Father is not a vengeful deity residing in some unknown place in heaven waiting to come and destroy all humans who disobey. Could you imagine if your physical parents told you they would bless you if you obey them completely or they will destroy you if you disobey? Can you imagine what life would be like with this kind of parent? You could never trust them, because you would always know within your heart that this person threatened to kill you if you slipped up. You may obey out of fear, but you could never love them.

This is the type of God most religions fear, but it is not the true Father/Mother divine. These are the shadow Lords of good and evil. As a parent you realize that your kids are going to screw up, but do you kill them, or even entertain that thought? If you are a normal parent these thoughts don't enter your mind and if they did you quickly get rid of them. Your attitude as a parent is usually one of, "Well, they will have to learn the hard way." You hope they adhere to your instruction, but you don't threaten to destroy them. If we as flawed humans can be so longsuffering, why is it we cannot see the true Father even greater than this? A Father would never destroy his child no matter how evil he became. He would always be looking for ways to help them overcome, and grieve continually until the child learns.

Here in the lower world parents are limited to what they can do for their children. But the Father is not limited by anything, neither by time or space. There are churches that teach this damnable heresy and a evil spirited lie that the Father is sending his Son back to destroy all those that do not comply with their wishes. And the sad fact of this evil doctrine is that most of humanity has no clue what the Father's true wishes are, because they have been so confused by all these religions.

GNOSTICS ARE A PEOPLE WHO REVEAL THE TRUE FATHER/MOTHER DIVINE!

The Gnostics are a people who teach and believe the true love of the Father. They despise what the shadow activity has brought forth. And they reject persecution and destruction of any kind! Our Father/Mother divine will never strike the match to torch their fallen children; neither will Jesus our beloved friend and brother do such a horrible deed. But those who teach these things will strike their own match and suffer the terror of their lack of gnosis again and again forever until they see the light of their true divine heritage.

We must allow the light to form in us to recognize the eternal light that was also in Jesus. And this light begins to shine forth when you become aware of your internal being. When you finally acknowledge that you are the divine children from the

253

most holy divine Father/ Mother spirit from before the foundations of this world.

The Apostle John made it very clear and precise in his wording, "Once Christ be formed in you, then you will know that you were not born of flesh and blood, neither by the will of men, but you WERE (*PAST TENSE*) BORN OF GOD THE FATHER." John 1:13

When you understand deep inside you that you are not biological but divine, then the second return of our savoir will be made manifest within your temple of the veil, where your eyes will behold his same glory within you. You will then raise from the lower dimensional OLD MAN unto the higher vibratory rate of the NEW MAN, which is the holy Christ, the Divine Son incarnate. And the hope of your ascension will begin in preparation for the harvest.

NOW we are already the SONS of god! I John 3:2! Death will no longer have authority over us! For the Son of our Father has claimed victory through Jesus, and through YOU! John 5:16-47

O death where is thy sting?

O Grave where is thy victory?

MYSTERY SIX
The Mystery of the Spirits

Once you understand the mystical secret of death then you can comprehend why so many have had their lives changed overnight by near death experiences or out of body experiences. The reason it is so very important to access this knowledge now before we exit the biological three-dimensional world is because it is given to us by our Father enabling us to break free from the bondage of the shadow! We are here in school to grow! If we come here and continue to play on the playground of life, we are not accessing the knowledge that will ultimately deliver us from this bondage, i.e. the karmic wheel.

In each of our lives there are unique circumstances that position one's life for the best setting to gain gnosis and growth. These special grouping of events are correlated to take us away from the ignorance that leads the entirety of the human race. These events if acted on, could literally change the direction of your life. Even before I learned the mysteries, I believed in this concept. Whenever I reacted upon witnessing these events, something positive was usually assured to happen, at least in a directional change, if nothing else!

When the ancient nation of Israel under the leadership of Moses departed from Egypt, the hierarchy of the shadow Lords designed Holy days that taught the written letter or the physical law. The land of Egypt represented in part our bondage in the flesh, as Israel was in bondage to Egypt. When Israel left Egypt and fled into the wilderness, this was a type of schooling to teach the Israelites. A mystical message was encoded that no one had the ability to ascertain then, because of their lack of evolved growth. It taught of our training in the biological matter world. When Israel dwelt in booths for 40 years this was a mystical number, representing coming out of tribulation. It reveals the spiritual concept of coming out of bondage. The time spent in the booths or portable houses revealed how we spend our time in portable houses of the flesh. The Promised Land of milk and honey taught of a resting between lives after one had dwelt in the wilderness. After leaving the temporary dwellings one could rest and be rejuvenated and strengthened for additional journeys in the wilderness. So the land of milk and honey spiritually represented returning to the spirit world from the physical world of bondage.

The historical references concerning ancient Israel are our clue to understand the shadow law, which is a reflection of the true law. Our Father is not racist and would not set up a physical nation over other nations as being special. But the shadow Lords operated under the laws of good and evil. And they set up these nationalistic borders of both race and creed. However we can learn from what transpired through these shadow laws to help us identify our true reality.

YOUR BELIEF WILL DIRECT YOUR FUTURE!

The book of Hebrews in the New Testament speaks of this time in ancient Israel where one's disbelief can keep them out of the rest. I think the rest is obviously the place many have witnessed beyond the tunnel of light. As Israel was instructed to obey the law of the seventh day Sabbath, this revealed the rest from the six-day workweek, or the rest between lives where we spent our time in bondage.

The seventh day in the Hebrew culture represents a time of fulfillment, a completion. It showed that even God rested on the seventh day from all his labors. Each week operates as a cycle. When one week ends a new week begins. But the

256

seventh day was known as the break day, or rest day. It was the day that separates one cycle from another cycle. It gave knowledge of a needed rest between the workweek. Later during the council of Nicae in 325AD under the leadership of Constantine the Great, Emperor of the East Roman power, they changed this day of rest from Saturday to Sunday. And from this day forward the Christians' rest day became the metaphorical 8th day or 1st day. And the Israelites, known now as the Jewish race, celebrate the 7th day. There are many that get hung up on these days, not realizing that there is a greater gnosis within the letter. It was to reveal to us what happens after our mortal death. Again as I have stated often, many take the written letter and try to seal it in concrete not realizing this knowledge was to teach us something that belongs beyond the veil. Instead they bring others into bondage to celebrate the physical day without ever knowing its truer meaning.

As the book of Hebrews continued, it spoke of the Israelites who left Egypt and were unable to enter the rest because of their disbelief. Now some may be asking themselves, Why would the shadow Lords, who do not appear to really love this human race, want to find a way to teach the shadow of the true? What motive could they have to desire this gnosis be revealed when they have hid it from us? Notice though, they never reveal the gnosis. That is something you must find on your own. And much of what the shadow reveals is still not our desired goal. Going into the rest and entering a place between lives to remain until you are born again into this flesh is not something to be desired. Read closely, we have been kidnapped! The shadows Lords are not the Father. They are beings like you and me who have been around for a very long time and have evolved. However, many of them lack the trueness of the one spirit, because they have also fallen and have failed to return to their Father. They have remained cut off from the Father because they continually deny the light of the divine Son, the Christ. However, there are those Elohim that have been rising higher and higher in consciousness and are remembering whom indeed they are. They have attempted to help the human race evolve. Because of this there has been a struggle for power between the gods so-to-speak.

WHY WAS JESUS REALLY PUT TO DEATH?

Who do you really think had Jesus killed? Remember the people of Jesus' day were followers of the shadow Lords. They did not realize the God of their holy book was Ialdabaoth. They believed he was the true and only God. Jesus came to reveal the true Father in all, and they did not like him teaching something contrary to what they had learned, so thus they had him killed. So the gnosis of dying and rebirth, and entering between lives is not the Father's will but the shadow Lord's will. The Father sent his only divine Son to pay ransom for this kidnapping that had taken place eons ago. We are abiding by the will of the shadow Lords on both sides of the fence, here in the material world and in the spirit plane of awareness. Ask yourself one question: if the true God was the God of the Israelites as was told Moses, then what need would there be for a Messiah to save these people? Whom would they need to be saved from? If the great omnipotent God was walking and talking with Israel then why did they need a savior? What was wrong with their God saving them? It is simply because Ialdabaoth is not the true God. He is one who claimed he was the true God, but he lied! The people were trapped into worshipping alien Gods, the Elohim/Nephilm had only their interests to think of.

Our job is to regain the gnosis of our heritage so we can willfully return to our reality with our Father and bypass the stages of captivity which consume the lower bodies, both flesh and spirit. We have to unite with the divine Son so we can leave this bondage and enter our true domain. The reason the Bible speaks of the rest is because most were unable at that time to leave this realm and return to the Father. So it became the lesser of two evils. It is better to enter the rest than to be locked into a mind realm of thought that is controlling your existence through fear. Just as it is much better to be living in a large house than on a park bench, but in both we are still captive! This is the true issue!

WHAT EXACTLY ARE THESE SPIRITS THAT ROAM THE ASTRAL PLANES?

This is why I have decided to add this chapter on the mystery of spirits! Who are they and where do they come from? There are those that have gone beyond the veil after physical death and have remained trapped in dimensions having no idea where they are or even where they came from. They are locked in a deeper portal of deception and shadow than when they existed on the three-dimensional plane of awareness. Some are very frustrated and unhappy. Many of them are continuously occupied by created new worlds with their own illusions. They become worn out, and their imaginations run wild without control. They become bitter and angry spirits. Some are like little children playing stupid childish pranks. Some are locked into scenes that keep recreating the same scenario of events over and over again. There are some disembodied spirits that once lived as human, and after death entered a realm similar to the dimension they left. But they replay the same events they were in when they left this earth plane. And they are sometimes stuck there for hundreds of our years. They do not realize this much time has passed because they are standing outside of time, as we know it.

Some may wonder, if the veil and cycles keep us trapped in bondage of ignorance, then why are we still trapped after we leave the veil? Again, we are still kidnapped by our lack of Gnosis. These people who enter these worlds that I am describing, do not have to go there, but their lack of Gnosis has brought them there. Try imagining that there was 12 levels, and within those levels are hundreds, maybe thousands of dimensions. Now imagine that you draw a line at the 5th level, and everything below that level whether physical or spiritual is being controlled by one force. And everything above that level is being controlled by another force. We are stuck in levels of the mind and spirit. And until we bypass a certain level we are under the control of others because we lack certain gnosis. This doesn't mean you couldn't break away any time you felt like it. But you are unaware, so you willfully stay under the control of others who are aware of your ignorance and use that for their own cause.

ENSLAVED ANIMALS KNOW NOT THAT THEY'RE IN PRISON!

Take a zoo for example, you bring an animal into the confines of a zoo and leave them there for years, feeding them, taking care of them, watching over them, and protecting them. The animal will become complacent and depend upon you for all their needs. That is what happened to us when we were willfully kidnapped by the shadow Lords. They became the operators of the zoo. We are the animals enslaved! Now the animal could break away at any time and head back to their home, but they have no idea that they have another home someplace else. Many of them have become content to stay right where they are. Those animals that behave the best usually get the better rewards, like food, places to sleep, cleaner barns etc... But unruly animals also live in the zoo. However, the animals that behave badly are not given the same rewards, and many of them actually have things taken away from them. Some of these are also stuck in smaller cages. The good animals have a better sense about what is occurring whereas the bad animals are more embittered and not as aware of how things work. But still both groups are living in the same zoo. Now outside this zoo is a world of wonder. A place where animals can find anything and everything they want. They could be free and happy! But until they understand this, they will forever be locked inside the walls of this prison.

Our prison just happens to extend outside the physical boundaries. It enters the spirit world, but again our slavery can only manifest as long as we stay ignorant, lacking true divine gnosis. Once we become aware of the knowledge of good and evil and realize we have been enslaved and are able at will to leave this slavery, then we can finally bypass the shadow Lords and their domain of rule! We will have finally left the zoo! Some take offence at me calling this place a type of prison. You can call it a school if you want. The term prison does not always mean a place for hardened criminals; it can also be a place where reformation takes place. I am just trying to relay needed information using known examples of our belief system. The truth is, we are all in need to get back to the Father/Mother Divine.   When one looks at the people on this earth, it is obvious that we are a far cry from where we should be.

TERROR IN THE ASTRAL PLANES IS AN ILLUSION OF THE MIND!

Now getting back to some of the other situations that can occur after death. There are those that have entered even worse places than I have described. Some of the places are real hell, all created by the mental body of your lower realm. Some are in fiery places burning and crying and screaming for help, as described in the book of Enoch. Others have gone to icy, cold damp places that are desolate and empty. Whatever terror your mind could produce, you could experience it as if it were real. Again though, it is all only an illusion! There are others who have never embodied in the physical plane, who roam the astral regions wanting and sometimes succeeding in bringing harm to others still embodied on the physical plane. Some of these wicked entities have even possessed humans in the material world. They were able to take over the spirit's body and control it, when the soul-projected spirit who normally operated that body gave way. Because of fear and intimidation the spirit either remains frozen within the body unable to do anything, while the other entity has taken control, or they have left the body and returned to the astral regions.

CAN A PERSON BE POSSESSED BY A SPIRIT?

Now the question arises, "What about possession?" Can one really be possessed and is it something to fear? The answer is "yes", one can be possessed, and "no" it is nothing to fear. You see, fear is the main cause that results in possession. Your body cannot be taken away or used by anyone else except you willfully give it up. And I personally believe that possession is also part of karmic debt. If your karma of reaping what you sow brings this upon you then it will occur unless necessary changes have taken place to wipe clean this debt. Why would one's karma ever bring this upon one? Because, hold tight your hat, you could have possessed another in a previous life while you were disembodied! This of course is only one possibility!

Spirits are no different than the real you except you are hidden within the veil. We are all spirits, but we abide in a physical temple. Yes, many of those so-called demons and wicked spirits, and yes, even good angels and loving beings are individuals that may have lived in this earth plane of awareness many times over. Some of them may even be your deceased relatives. Some of them may even be you, but more on this later! I remember a story where an individual went into an elementary school filled with young children, with a bomb strapped on him. This bomb detonated and not one child was injured. Many of the children described what they could best understand as angels that told them what to do just prior and during the explosion. Some of the children saw their deceased grandparents operating in the appearance of angels. They were there helping them through this ordeal.

When you understand who these spirits are on the other side it helps you identify with them and understand that spirits are no different than humans, except they abide in a different dimension. Just like humans, some are good and some are bad. Some have love and some are spiteful.

SPIRITS CAN BE TRAPPED AND THEY'RE NOT REALLY TRYING TO HARM YOU. THEY JUST DON'T KNOW!

And just as humans, if a spirit has entered your house you have the right to ask them to leave. If they become stubborn, order them out. Remember you are as powerful as they are, except you are in a different dimension. Some spirits are very powerful and difficult to remove. If this be the case then either stand up to them with the light of Christ or ask someone to come that will be able to remove them. If the spirit is too powerful for you, don't play games with them. Get out of your house and seek help, just as you would if a robber or thief broke into your home. It is best to leave the premises so you or your family do not get hurt. Most spirits however that are trapped in this illusion do not realize what has happened. Some of them suffered a tragic instant death and are not really sure where they are. You can help them by explaining that they no longer are bound to this earth realm. That they have entered another dimension and it is best to go towards the light so they can be freed from this bondage.

There are some spirits out there that can really cause terrible havoc if not placed down. They can be dangerous! Read carefully: these spirits seem to be drawn to those that exhibit irrational fears! They prey on fear; it gives them their energy to exist within illusion. They have been preconditioned to live in these circumstances through their own mind. Their false mental creations are energized by fear. You have heard of the old saying, "misery loves company." This is truer in the spirit realm than the flesh.

These spirits can roam deep within the astral mind-creation realm. Some of these are very close to our dimension; they exist just on the other side of this dimension. They will even see themselves at times belonging to this physical realm by attaching themselves to a person, place or thing. Some have occupied houses where they once lived and become part of the new family that now lives there. Some can be very friendly. Others might be troublemakers. And still others are downright rude and evil. However, most of them just need to be told to exit the premises and go on with their learning in a better dimension. They just don't comprehend this because like most humans while living in the flesh they were given faulty information about an afterlife, so they become stuck between worlds, so-to-speak. Some of them do not even realize they have died. Learned individuals have instructed these spirits who exist in a type of purgatory to exit this dimension and seek the light and rise towards it.

Once a spirit is able to rise towards this light they will realize they have died in the flesh and need to continue with their learning and training. It is best that all seek for the highest realm! Until you are properly trained though you will go where you are prepared for.

There is a love that exists within the light that is able to destroy the negative creations of the illusions. Now don't get me wrong, it does not take away the karma that was created in the shadow Lands. As long as you are in the cycles you will most likely return to this world or some other world that exists for training. Many entering this light will at least be given a rest and preparation to return to work again. I want to emphasize though, we need to be seeking the ultimate, and not be seeking to return to this plane. Until you are ready though you will have to continue to return to school!

There are some who are able to enter the spirit realm through out of body experiences that can help trapped souls be released from their predicament. You can't do it for them but you can assist and explain to them what has happened, and then they can choose whether to depart from the circumstances they created or not! The Bible speaks of love being able to cover a multitude of sins. Yes, how we live our lives in the flesh will control what will happen on the other side. And sin is lacking gnosis in its truest form. It means to miss the mark, unable to see or do what was right. We then build years and years of false illusions caused by these sins or lack of gnosis. But when one is able to enter your predicament and assist you, then it is as a multitude of sins were covered by the courageous act of someone displaying love. When we understand that these spirit entities on the other side are not necessarily demons, that in fact they may be your Uncle Joe or

Aunt Alice, then maybe we can have a better understanding of how to deal with these circumstances.

ALL SPIRITS ARE OUR DIVINE BROTHERS AND SISTERS OF OUR FATHER!

All spirits whether on this side or that side, are our brothers and sisters of the Father. So we should not fear them; we should stretch forth our hand to help them. If they are incorrigible then just like humans there is not a whole lot you can do for them. But don't assume they are all evil, because they are no more lost than you are! These beings are no different than us except they are not in the veil at the moment. If we stand in judgement over them then behold; prepare to take their place when you pass over. Think about this!

The term we use today called, "demon" came out of the ancient world even before Jesus walked this earth. It came from an older word called "Daemon", which meant to have or possess a negative spirit, or attitude. This was the primary terminology that was understood in the time period of Jesus. You do not have to be on the other side of the veil to become demonic. Demonism or devils were strictly categorized as the result of having a negative spirit against that which is positive or of the light, hence the difference between light and darkness. One could just as easily be portrayed as a devil on this side of the veil. Demonism is a spiritual attitude that does not correlate with love, as where Jesus called Peter, Satan, and also called the Pharisees the children of Satan.

We are all spirit beings! When humans commit crimes against other humans that is as much a demon spirited action as an attempt made by a spirit on the other side. We are the ones we are all afraid of. The only difference is some of us are on this side of the veil and some on that side. It should be just as frightening to walk down a dark street of a dangerous neighborhood as to have evil spirits in your realm. Because both carry the exact same spiritual make-up, in that when you walk through the dangerous neighborhood you do not necessarily see any danger. You just feel its presence.

Religions teach to be fearful of the spirit world. That they on the other side will possess and take you over. They warn how we have to be prepared against these evil beings. And yet I state, another human could attack you at anytime! There are crimes committed every day on our streets. People are mugged, robbed, raped and even murdered. But the religious groups fail to understand that our concerns first and foremost should be preparing ourselves in the here and now. We should be setting examples for a better society instead of teaching fear of those things you can't see. We should be helping those we can see. Then when people pass over they will bring with them a more evolved spirit of righteousness rather than a deep seeded fear of what awaits them on the other side. Now granted, there are entities that are extremely evil on the other side who have never been in a physical body. Some call them elementals, but their power does not exist without our giving them its illusion through our fears.

Some will no doubt state, but possessions are real and we must fear that. And I say no! Your fear is what gives power to the enemy of the light to enter your realm to possess you. However, possession in not something that is limited to the spirit world. We live in a society where you cannot go anywhere without someone trying to possess you. Whether it be your friend, family, husband, wife, job, Church, Priest/minister, Government, you name it. We are always being bombarded with someone wanting to take over our thinking, our lives and our direction. This is possession in the flesh by other humans. And what usually is the formula for humans to attempt to possess other humans? You got it; it is FEAR! When a person is made to feel useless, helpless and hopeless then they are prime candidates for possession of some type. It brings me to ponder the reality mentioned in the Bible about the Son of Perdition, the man of sin. People today have heard about the so-called anti-Christ and false prophet. Religious groups constantly speak of this "man of sin" that is supposedly going to rule the world. But what is it really? What is the man of sin? It is global possession! I want you to think about this and try to understand. If fear is the catalyst for possession, then fear would become the catalyst to bring such an ideology on the world scene to try to possess everyone's lives.

IF WE SOLVE OUR PROBLEMS HERE AND NOW THEN THEY WON'T CARRY OVER!

We must solve our problems now in the flesh and quit passing off evil as if it only pertains to the spirit world. We can no longer pass this off unto some unknown spirit dimension using religious rhetoric, "Well God only knows." We, on this side of the veil have to get our act together, because we will bring this with us to the other side when we die. Do not let religious ideology convince you that it all changes, because it does not. You are what you are whether you are on this side or that. The character that you possess is always with you even though the ego is not there on the other side of the veil!

If we ignore how people treat other people then why become concerned how spirits may treat us in the flesh. If we would start passing these mysteries to those living in the veil, then we would not have as many problems in the spirit realm.

Yet I am saddened to reveal that the religions and Governments of this world want to keep the spirit world separate in both ideology and reality from the physical plane of awareness. Why is it that the two most powerful entities that possess humans, the ones we have been led to trust in, are the ones that try very hard to keep us from learning the truth about who we really are?

Wasn't it religion and government during Jesus' day that came together to stop his message? Why do religions and governments create world wars? It is obvious even by Jesus' own words that religion working with government have been the true warlords of this earth; it isn't the average person. Lifetime after lifetime the world continues to retrogress, because the same activity presents itself continuously. Who is running the show? Are they the same ones that deceived us in paradise? Are they the ones the Gnostics said try to usurp God's authority as their own? Or who the Sumerians called the Gods from the stars, the Nephilm? The serpent in the Garden tried to warn us that our captors were leading us astray. He told us we were also Gods and the gods confirmed this!

THE SERPENT CAN BE BOTH FRIEND AND ENEMY!

The reason the serpent is both our friend and enemy is because it relates a truth until now unknown. The serpent is our inner gnosis. It is our inner wisdom. It is our compliance to free will. Become wise as a serpent, harmless as a dove. But with free will comes two choices. Not every choice is the best choice, but under law it is what has been given to us. The Serpent in the Biblical Garden was the friend of the right choice, but we have not always made the right choices. Some Gnostics believe that Serpents are always good. They became aware of the grand deception that the serpent in the Bible was trying to help us, not harm us. But serpents are not always good; there are deadly serpents as well as friendly serpents. But both represent our choices!

Having choices can sometimes become complicated, because if you are not presented with the proper information the right choice appears obscure. Then we are faced with making wrong choices based on what has been presented. That is how one controls another! Humans are easily led to make wrong choices because they are bombarded with faulty information about the truth. The average man or woman is not trying to run the world their way. They try to make ends meet and help their family and children, as well as have some sort of identity on this crazed planet. Most are not conceiving of creating thermonuclear devises that will eradicate large portions of life. So getting back to my previous point, it is obvious that someone else is running the show and wants to continue to create illusions so we will follow the same path we have always followed. It has been said that the media represent the fourth estate, literal powers in its own right. It is because it has power over what people believe. We then make decisions primarily based on what we hear. If what we hear is a lie then obviously our decisions will be faulty.

When a nation goes to war, we don't just one day wake up and hear about it. No not at all, the Government tries very hard using the power of the media to actually convince us that violence is the best method. Everyone realizes if we were attacked we would want to defend ourselves. If a guy came at me with a knife, I would not stand there and let him kill me. This is obvious. But I am also not going to promote a logic that tries to convince others that I need to kill this guy before he makes an attempt on my life. Governments go out of their way to convince the population that if we strike first then we will avert a possible action against us. This is Serpent logic from the evil point of view. This reveals a plan to create an illusion to keep all the facts away from people so the decisions that are made will be based on false information. It will appear as if the people made the decision, but those that were creating the deception knew all along this road was primed with illusion.

Why is it that we call an attack on our nation terrorism, but when we attack another nation, that is just good policy? We are not running the show here. Someone else is in control and has been for a very long time, and we are the gullible sheep who keep following toward our slaughter. We are not making right serpent choices. We are being led down paths that will keep us forever in deception through the veil!

Getting back to the spirit world, I want to interject here that some have had terrifying experiences in places of the mind realm. These can be helped by soul-travelers. Soul-travelers can leave the veil consciously, such as OBE. I have read of OBE travelers that have actually helped those trapped in their own mind realm to leave the illusion behind. They can at least lead them to a better place, such as through the light in the tunnel. In one book a soul-traveler actually entered a colonial period setting where he witnessed three individuals still reliving an event over and over again.

These three were serving as peasant slaves at a party or dance. They were unaware that they had served this same event for possibly several hundred of our years. They continued in this illusion over and over again never realizing their predicament. It is amazing how one can actually enter the events created by someone else's mind. But when you comprehend the mysteries it becomes apparent that all events are really illusions until we break away from the prison we abide in. This world is nothing but an illusion, but it appears very real, doesn't it?

This particular story that I am relating about soul traveling taught how a soul traveler entered the world of the three individuals' illusion of the mind, and he was able to help them out of their situation. At first they were fearful of this soul traveler. They were afraid to leave as he requested. He confirmed that there was nothing to fear and that they needed to leave this place of illusion and enter what I call the place of rest, the light through the tunnel. He actually entered their mind-created-world and assisted them out of there.

One of the blessings of having a body is that you can return to it after spirit travel. If you didn't have your body you could be stuck in those dimensions of illusion. I assure you it is extremely easy to get lost in these realms where time and space does not exist. You would have nothing to identify with. But the longer you remain there you begin to see it as your new reality, never realizing that there is something amiss.

JUMPING DIMENSIONS CAN'T CREATE A TIME PARADOX!

I have personally learned this by jumping into other dimensions without preparation or notice. I actually awakened one day in another dimension. It was the most revealing episode I ever witnessed. It went beyond going out of body; it was like waking up in another world.

I believed I awakened in this reality. I had no idea I was in another dimension. However, like a person with a conscience problem, I had this nagging feeling that something was not right. Although I witnessed what appeared to be slight changes from my normal present state of reality, I never became aware that I was not home. I had learned through other experiences that when one enters these other worlds of parallel dimensions, you actually create another awareness. The nagging feeling is your normal everyday consciousness but it has been replaced by a new consciousness. And your new consciousness becomes your new reality while the reality you just left now becomes your sub-consciousness. That is what is creating this nagging feeling. Deep within your conscious awareness you know something is different, but your new outer awareness provides the belief that everything is normal. Unless you personally experience this for yourself it is difficult for me to share some of these concepts.

There is so much about our consciousness and its many diverse worlds and parallel avenues that it becomes a twilight zone in theory to explain it. These things may seem strange to fleshly beings but to our real eternal divine selves, these are normal occurrences that we are very aware of from another realm or state of consciousness. These other dimensions can appear as real as ours here and now, but in truth until we unmask our higher selves it is all a virtual reality. You can become so enmeshed within a few minutes after entering this other world that you will begin to forget where you came from. That is why it is important to learn to control your consciousness, and OBEs are a strong benefit in allowing humans to learn these concepts. When I entered another dimension it took about 10 minutes to conclude that this was my world. I must accept it as it is, even though there was this nagging feeling. However that feeling began to subside as my new reality became the strong force of my new awareness. If I had not returned automatically then I would have never realized I had left in the first place.

Some may wonder why a loving Father would allow us to get lost in these dimensions of the mind. First of all, to our Father we are never lost, we are always eternally connected to him. If we weren't none of us would exist. Our Father is well aware of all things in all dimensions and universes. It is the desire orchestrated by divine law that we learn internally for our eternal awareness. And secondly by divine law you reap what you sow. I have had many experiences within the last few years that I never had before, nor did I even realize these things existed or were possible.

LAWS OF KARMA REAP BLESSINGS ALSO!

The laws of divine karma works both ways. They will help you advance as you walk the right path or set you back as you fail to proceed. Again, Jesus called this, "One who is rewarded according to their works." You will be blessed as you proceed in the right direction or cursed if you recede in the wrong direction. Yet it is all you, you are the one that brings all these things into fruition. As you begin to walk the correct path then the aspects of divinity begin to reveal themselves in your life. If you continue to walk the same path that everyone else takes, and reap further karma of debts to be repaid, then you will continue in these cycles over and over again. It is your choice! Not only do you reap evil by what you sow but also spiritual blessings by what you sow. The more these mysteries reveal themselves unto you internally then you will have more ability to tap into the "I AM" presence; it is automatic, guaranteed!

Jesus said, "Greater works will you do than I." Each and every one of us has these abilities lying dormant within us. No one can lay claim to greatness in the sense of being better than someone else. All have the divine power within them. We are all equals, but each discovers the mystical secrets in their own order of time. This is what separates people, not race, not creed, not color nor religion. It is your own divine awareness.

We of this earthly plane can assist others as divine helpers of the Father. If we witness another individual in trouble, even if it is by their own doing, we can help them using the divine love of our Father. We can show godly love one to another and help them out of a serious predicament, whether on this side of the veil or the other. We can help lost souls gain their awareness. At least help them understand they can enter the rest even if they're not ready to leave the cycles of illusion. There are many that operate on the other side who enter our lower realms and assist those out of their current situation, just as I spoke earlier about the angels that helped Lazarus into the light. The thief on the cross is another example, who by the word of Jesus was going to enter paradise because he believed in the work of Jesus. But the thief on the cross was not given a free pass key to leave the cycles. No not at all, he was given access to the light, or rest between lives, a type of paradise. Many on the other side have spoken of this place and it is like paradise, a wonderful beautiful place to exist. They are happy and filled with joy. Some are so enamored by this reality that they believe it is total heaven. But this is still not our destiny. We are still indicted to appear in another life to return to this prison to learn and attempt to gain greater awareness of what we are.

LOVE CAN COVER A MULTITUDE OF SHORTCOMINGS!

The Bible verifies that a multitude of sins can be forgiven by another's love. As people live their lives missing the mark, which is the true definition of sin, love can assist them towards a greater advantage in learning the truth. That is why Jesus said, "Love your enemies, do good to them which despitefully use you." Love is the power of forgiveness. Those that preach a doom and gloom God and teach that he is out to punish all those that break his laws have missed the most important point. If God is truly love then he will forgive. But notice what the Bible states, if you say you love God but do not love your neighbor then you are a liar. It reveals that if we hate our brother whom we can see, then how can we say we love God whom we can't see? Are you getting the vision of this great gnosis? Our love is the power to forgive, and we are co-creators with our Father and the divine Son, the Christ. We act in his stead as healers, forgiving and loving one another. If we can't do that, then don't expect God to do that, because he only does it through US!

OUR FATHER FORGIVES US THROUGH US!

Jesus went on to say, forgive your brother seventy times seven times. He taught, judge not that you be not judged! It becomes evident that we are responsible to act as our Father in the flesh or else it won't get done. Why, because the Father does his works through us, not without us. We are the co-creators with our Father, keep repeating this to yourself!

Too many times religion expresses the belief that God is a singular entity working only with a singular group of people. They are creating their own God, and they will by divine law create their own world after they pass over to the other side. Because as co-creators of the Father we are responsible for everything we create. A lack of internal knowledge creates eternal ignorance. Why do you think Jesus uttered the words, "Become you therefore perfect as your Father in heaven is perfect." Because we are his workmanship. We are the results of the Father's works through us. If people could only understand this simple point then religions would stop judging and begin teaching!

FEAR IS THE CENTRAL OPERATIONAL THEME THAT INCREASES MEMBERSHIP IN CHURCHES!

Most religion is built upon the precipice that God is an angry God ready to take vengeance on all that do him unjustly. Religion as we know it today could not survive under true Gnosticism. Religion and Government both function by using fear. If they did not use fear as their tactic to increase, they would become almost as though they were not there. Try taking your own personal polls and find out why people entered their religious structure in the first place. If you ask people why they chose to join this church or that, you will find that nearly 75% of them say because they were afraid of what was going to happen. Fear is the central operational code word and theme that increases membership in churches. It is not increased through love; but by spreading a damnable doctrine of fear of what God plans to do to you if you don't join. Think about that!

So the entire religious structure of our world is built upon fear, because the true Father is not the creator of religion. The Nephilm, the shadow Lords in their attempt to control used religion to keep the slaves in place! And if you are a dissident then they use Government to keep you in place, either way they got you! The only way to break away from these clutches is to enter the world of internal gnosis where fear is destroyed and love becomes the attribute to survive on!

Why is it that some are not assisted after death from the realm of mind illusion, while others are? Again it is karma, reaping what you sow. In this world today many have evil works. They are not using the power of their Father. They are using the power of their lower dimensional selves cut off from the Father by free will choice. They continue to use hatred, jealousy, lust, greed, envy, etc... They are using the faulty 'energy veil' to create their world. I repeat, the "EVIL" is the type of Acronym for Energy Veil of Illusion. Strangely enough many terms depicting realities are actually a type of acronym, such as GOD, Geometry of Divinity. Or God was also known as 'Good', the opposite of 'evil, energy veil!'

ENERGY VEIL = E-VIL

So as the energy veil or evil is used it creates a mind world that actually exists within the other realms. And the worlds you create are the world you by divine law must personally assimilate. Those who do not use their talents correctly in any given life must be accountable to what they have created. No one else is responsible for your creation but you! It is not wise to. continue to harm others and live your life without regard to those it may effect. Because when it all comes out in the wash you are only creating the world that you will have to abide in.

And those you harmed will no longer come under your energy veil as they did in this reality.

We are not to judge one another; this includes those that appear to be our enemies. For even Jesus while dying upon a cross uttered the words, "Forgive them Father, for they know not what they do."

UFOS, ARE THEY REAL?

There is another subject I feel needs to be addressed within the mystery of spirits. This subject is UFO, 'unidentified flying objects' and Alien life from other planets. I realize that what I am about to say will cause some ridicule. It has become almost a club initiation to ridicule or malign others' character for their belief in other realities. I felt I should hold off saying too much about this subject until the initial mysteries could be learned. If you have come this far into the book then it should come as no surprise where I am heading next. At least now you have been given some understanding of the mysteries, so it should not shock you as much as if I just blurted it out from the beginning. Although I have made references to alien life and other worlds I have not yet addressed this important topic.

Our solar system is represented by one single star called the SUN. Within this one single solar system we have a minimum of ten planets, that's right, *ten* that orbit around this one small star. This small solar system is only one of millions times millions of other solar systems, which inhabit the nucleus of a body, called a galaxy. Our Milky-way galaxy is 100,000 light years in diameter. Putting this in perspective our galaxy is approximately 100,000 times 6 trillion miles in distance from one end to the other. This should be enough to blow your mind away, but this is not nearly the vastness of what we call our universe. Our small spiral galaxy is one of billions of other galaxies throughout the cosmos. After you have contemplated this aspect then you need to realize that there are parallel universes, multi-dimensional levels throughout all universes. Then there are sub-divisions of the dimensions, with multiple dimensions within those dimensions. Then one needs to understand that we as spirit beings can live in many of these dimensions all at the same time. After you have brought your awareness up on these realities then you need to understand as spirit beings we are only located in a time spectrum while living in a veil of time and space. This is only one aspect of who we are. There are other aspects to our being that at present are not confined by our time restrictions, thereby making it possible to be past, present and future all at the exact same moment.

HYPER-DIMENSIONAL TIME SPACE ELEMENTAL QUANTUM PHYSICS!

I am using terms that can be learned through Hyperspace Geometry, Quantum Physics, etc... We are speaking of realities and dimensions that are vast and steadily growing at rates way beyond our comprehension. One would have to be a loony tune to believe that life as we know it only exists on this little piece of dust that floats in the darkness of space within the magnitude of this awesome universe of universes.

As our knowledge expands about the vastness of this magnificent realm it also helps magnify the vastness and awesome reality of the Father. If you continue to live in the dark ages where the belief was that the earth was the center of all there was, then you will remain in the dark ages concerning the great I AM presence.

Today we have many thoughts concerning this subject of alien life and other planets. It is in vogue to say that you believe that other life exists, but they could never come to our planet because of the vast distances. This is a way of protecting your image in a sense. It makes you appear intelligent without really having to admit there is alien life. But this is just another Dark Age theory being used for our generation to cover our own ignorance. Just because our scientists have not figured out how to curve the structure of time and space and use its own power as a sling shot to enter different realms and dimensions doesn't mean that life elsewhere has not figured this out.

WE ARE AT CLASS ZERO(0) IN OUR DEVELOPMENTAL STAGE!

On the totem pole of knowledge we are greatly behind in the school of gnosis concerning space-time travel. In fact certain scientists have rightly classified our race of people as a class 0 (zero). We are on the bottom rung of the ladder on this planet. It wasn't too long ago we did not even know that Pluto existed. But today we are able to pick up vibrations from another star that tells us that planets are orbiting nearby. We are able to tell the size of the body that orbits that star by how the star fluctuates. Yet this is children's stuff within the vast gnosis of the cosmos. It means absolutely nothing. We can now see stars forming and exploding or going Nova or Super-nova. We can detect what appear to be black holes that travel at speeds so fast they actually envelope light. We can see back into history millions upon millions of years, because we are receiving the light signal from far away galaxies and star systems.

Once upon a time in the not too distant past man believed the earth was flat. Today we know it is a spaceship traveling at awesome speeds throughout our solar system. How long will it take to comprehend that we are not alone in this megalithic domain? We have been and are being visited by travelers from other planets, galaxies, dimensions and yes, even time travelers.

WE HAVE HAD VISITORS FROM MANY DIMENSIONS!

Visitors have been coming to our small little home called earth since the beginning of the human race from both dimensional and inter-dimensional. The Bible reveals many space travelers and time travelers. Zachariah wrote about a flying machine that was setting between heaven and earth. Zachariah 5:1-11 He spoke of a woman coming out of it and defiling the world with false teachings. Other scriptures speak of the queen who comes from heaven, or the Queen of Heaven. Ezekiel describes flying objects from other worlds showing this was how the gods whom they worshipped traveled. Ezekiel 1:1-28 Our world has been inundated with visitors for as long as anyone has had written record. Every nation, every culture has written about aliens from other worlds and/or time that have visited this planet and made contact with us earthlings. All religions speak within their holy books about aliens from other worlds. When will people stop listening to those that keep ridiculing and debunking this truth?

Today most if not all of the Governments of this earth, including Vatican City and the POPE himself, know about aliens and alien worlds and civilizations. But the majorities have come to a consensus that this knowledge must not be revealed to the little person, meaning you and me! In the 60's there was a government research group that composed the Brooking's report. A little known paper that describes many attributes about what mankind can or can't handle. The belief was that the subject of alien life and their civilizations had to be kept away from the people for several reasons. It was believed religion cannot handle the truth, and that would cause the fabric of the societal Western peoples to collapse. But why won't religions accept the truth? They have lived this lie and they cannot allow themselves to be exposed as frauds. There is much more at stake finding out about alien life and civilizations than just whether it is true or not. There is a much greater reason, it will identify what and who we really are. That is the real fear! If you are spirit then how could anyone harm you?

AGAIN GOVERNMENT AND RELIGION TIE SUSPICIOUS UNIFIED KNOTS!

So as usual the Government has linked up with religion to keep the people in ignorance of these simple truths. When one realizes who they really are then they are freed from the shackles of bondage. And those in control cannot allow this. Once you realize you are a spirit being in disguise you can no longer be controlled by any flesh and blood mortals. They can take your physical life but they can't remove you. This Gnosis is the greatest fear for all religions and Government, because if their fear tactics no longer serve their purpose then they will lose their power over the people! Some may say we have to have physical governments or there would be chaos. This is another lie! Chaos is brought by those attempting to control. They create the chaos and then bring in the savior/order to reconcile your needs. The Latin term for this is Ordo Ab Chao! When the mystery of cause and effect is understood and everyone realizes their own responsibility in their lives then there will be peace. The Government wants you to believe they will take care of all your problems, and religion wants you to believe that God of whatever faith will take care of your problems. But none of them teach you are responsible for your own problems.

This is why there is chaos and always will be. This is the only true secret to controlling others. Once this attitude of oppression is lifted peace will then become a reality. When everyone lives within the law of cause and effect knowing full well each one is responsible for their own deeds whether now or another lifetime, then chaos will turn to order, and justice will become self-evident.

I wrote about near death experiences and the many millions who have witnessed these events in Mystery five. There is no difference with the UFO phenomenon. Millions upon millions have witnessed strange flying craft in our generation just like the ancients did. And they speak of what they have seen with their own eyes. But as usual they are mocked and ridiculed for believing in such things.

THE EVIDENCE IS OVERWHELMING, WE ARE OURSELVES ALIENS TO THIS PLANET!

What about UFOs and ALIEN life? What evidence do we really have? The evidence of life traveling throughout our universe has always been staring us right in our face. WE OURSELVES

ARE ALIENS FROM ANOTHER WORLD!!! We are the star travelers. We are the time travelers; we are the dimensional travelers. Each time we gaze upon another human we are witnessing a star being within another garment. We are the veiled beings of the stars. We are the Sons of God in flesh! Within the cycles many can incarnate within bodies into multiple dimensions.

TIME TRAVELERS!

Now let us go back in history and ask ourselves some very important questions. Let us peer into the prophets and the sages and wise men of the past. And yes, even angels; let's take a closer look at what these beings really were. If all life has free choice then that means everywhere life exists it was created by the life form? Each of us created our own lives by our own choices. We designed within our pattern our destiny as well as our past. Has it ever occurred to you how certain ones seem to know about events that have not taken place yet? Such as prophetic predictions, angelic protection etc... How do certain beings know when and where certain things are going to happen?

And furthermore what is prophecy? Is it a prediction or is it predestination? If it is a prediction then it is based on certain theories but with no absolutes. If it is predestination then how can it be changed? Predestination also implies no freedom of choice. So we have a paradox here! I am going to throw in another aspect to this equation. If angels or spirit guides are able to protect you from an incident that could harm you, then this implies changing a circumstance. But if everything is cause and effect, then what can possibly happen to you that is not already ordained by law? And if the law states that you are responsible for something, then how can angels interfere with that law?

What if I added another complexity to this issue? What if the angels and or spirit guides are actually YOU from the future? Now before you go bananas with this theory think about it very closely. How would an angel know what was about to happen to you before it actually occurred? If they are you it has already happened. And if that element occurred because of karmic debt being paid, then you, who are now the one that is in the future, had already paid it. However your present state of consciousness only allows you to perceive things from within the veil. So you visualize only three-dimensionally. You are now becoming aware that you are a multi-dimensional being. If you had already paid the debt, you at this level are unaware of this. Then by divine law you could come back in time and spare yourself having to pay that debt again, enabling you to gain a greater awareness of the here and now. As you continue to grow then you are given greater awareness to your other aspects including the angel who might very well be you from the future, that saved you in the past! Wow, I know this must sound very weird to many reading this.

Is this a hard concept to accept? It really shouldn't be if you understand the dynamics of your true divine self. As for prophecy, those that enter the spirit realm which I call the OBE state of consciousness are given access to records by time travelers, or you in the future, that warn of a certain event that will take place unless changes are made. There is no reason to undergo more destruction or loss of life once it has already been paid for. You can change the reality of your future by not doing the same things that were done before. So prophecies are warnings of futuristic events that have already taken place by virtue of the cycles and time and space. But because we have already gone through these cycles we are given the opportunity to make changes in the here and now which will also help ourselves in the future. Some believe we are aware of future events based only on possibilities because of how we have done things in the past. I do not accept this theory as an absolute. I can accept it partially. However I believe before we come here there are already records of what we will do, because it was passed down to the masters by time travelers.

I FEEL LIKE I HAVE DONE THIS BEFORE!

Have you ever had deja-vu? Have you ever felt you are doing the same thing over again? It might not be just a strange concept; you in reality may have walked this same path many times before. We are here to get it right. So don't be surprised if we are doing the same things over again. Except each time around as we grow we gain more assistance from the other side, or better stated from our futuristic selves. Now, what about Aliens from other planets? What is the possibility they are also us from another time and age? When you understand the mystical concepts I am relating, you then comprehend that we are manifesting in many ways. I know of several others who deeply believe that their spirit guides or angels whom they have met on the other side are actually their higher selves or a more evolved self. But how can you have a more evolved self, if you haven't evolved yet?

This is the question of the ages. It is simply because we are everything all at once until we become one with the whole again! We exist in historical times as well as futuristic times together with the present and the varied dimensions all at the same time. Why? Because there is no time until we come into time. Spirit beings have no timetable! If you died in the year 1999 you can't say it is 1999 where you will go, because it is not. It is only 1999 on one plane of awareness built around limitless dimensions and that is this earth and its rotation around the sun. That is the only place in the entire universe that it is 1999, for this example!

Each planet's rotation around their star gives that material planet its timetable. There is a myriad of timetables in our universe; they are all different and unique from one another. When you step outside of this time by death then you enter a plane of awareness that brings all time into one single category. Just like when I have slipped dimensions and saw my life being lived in another plane of awareness or another time period. That is still me no matter when or where it occurs. However I can only perceive the consciousness available in this present existence, as I can only perceive the consciousness awareness in other existences, as I AM there existing. As we enter time we have only available to us the conscious reality of one existence at a time, unless you enter the spirit world through OBE or NDE, or death. Then your consciousness expands to a greater awareness but only according to your evolved growth. You could die in one dimension and still be alive in another. It doesn't matter because it is all you existing at all time at the exact same time. This concept is hard to reconcile within the mind at present because it doesn't fit our illusion!

I often times use the analogy of electricity. As an example, you have a cord that operates three items: a computer, television and radio. Think of the energy or electricity as your real divine self. Think of the cord as the umbilical cord like the silver cord that attaches our real divine self to our lower aspects. Now see the computer, TV, and radio as your divine self living in three different awareness levels through the electricity that gives these objects the ability to function. Each object that the electricity flows through has a different use for its operation. It is the same exact electricity going through each object, but each object is for a different use. The computer has no awareness of the radio, neither does the radio have any awareness of the TV, but all three function according to the body that they have been given, and all three are using the same exact energy source to operate.

That is why it is possible to have multi-dimensional selves existing at the same time and yet having no awareness of those other existences. You can be in the future, and the past, and present all at the same time by the use of the energy that comes from your 'I AM' presence. Each aspect is gaining the needed awareness to exist in whatever plane you are in. As each aspect advances we can then help ourselves by reuniting with the lower aspects and sharing information that you have already learned. But having that information in the here and now may cause a greater awareness and growth for the entirety of you for the future you!

As we peer even deeper within this understanding it becomes vastly more important to ask who these alien Gods were that tried to kidnap us and use us a slaves. The sad fact is this, evolvement or evolution doesn't necessarily take the right turns. Sometimes we evolve into things we do not want or desire. Sometimes we become that which is not good. The Gods whom we served and made obeisance to may also be us! They are evolved individuals who have learned many of these concepts but for the wrong purposes of enlightenment. They are known as the Gods of both good and evil! Their entire purpose has become perverted into desiring the pleasures of the shadow rather than seeking the spirit. As far as I can tell there appears to be two groups from the future, one is called the black legions, the other is called the white brotherhood. Remember this is not race, but definition. Many have made acquaintances with the black legions over the millenniums. Today they are recognized at times as the 'Men in Black' whom I am sure you have heard about through Ufology. Others have made acquaintances with the White Brotherhood; these are beings that appear divine. People call them angels, spirit guides, helpers, guardians, masters etc... They are only concerned with our growth and have no desire to rule over us. Why should they, they know they are us! Do you see the beauty of this? Those that fail, fail unto themselves, and those that succeed, succeed unto themselves. You only can harm you! And you only can help you!

As I proceed through this mystery I thought it would be wise to speak about different beings from other dimensions and planets. You need to become aware of the possibility of what these beings might be. When you understand then you will realize that the shadow Lords who took us captive are by our own doing. We chose this fall into these realms, and the shadow Lords are the evolved result of our fall. *I repeat; the Shadow Lords are the evolved result of our FALL.* The mother Sophia may be our fauity decision and Ialdabaoth may be our creation of our dark side, created by our fall.

We in effect created our captors because of our fall. To reconcile them from the error of their ways, we must continue to come back and evolve righteously, time after time so that the shadow Lords and the shadow world which we created will forevermore be removed. Thus as we see both good and evil within us, we also see good and evil within them, because they are the results of US!

Everything in the shadow creations were created by our own doing. We must now clean up the mess we made for ourselves and return to the Father with a perfect identity. When we hear about the war in heaven and other planets that were destroyed, that was our doing. When you hear about ancient civilizations that were destroyed, again we caused it! The Father brings no responsibility upon any one that is innocent. We only pay for the crimes we committed. If we burned it down we will have to build it up. If we broke it we will have to fix it! If we killed we will have to give life. Can there be any fairer law than this?

THE MOVIE "GROUNDHOG DAY" REVEALS A TRUTHFUL PATTERN!

What is so ironic about the cycles is that eventually only good will come from them in the overall picture. It reminds me of the movie that Bill Murray starred in called "Groundhog Day." This movie depicted a guy who repeated one day in his life over and over again. As he struggled through sameness continuously he tried to devise ways to rob, cheat and steal. But after a while he began to see there was no hope in those things. He became so distraught he decided to kill himself. But because it was the same day repeated he would always wake up. Finally he decided to use that one day in building his talents. He used his time wisely and became proficient in many different tasks. He was able to use the monotony of repetition for his benefit and mostly the benefit of others. He used his time to help others and became happy with himself and his life. Then the monotony broke and he was able to advance to the next day. When we finally figure out that true happiness will only happen after we use our talents to benefit others, then we will finally advance to our next level of spiritual oneness with our Father.

ROBERT O. DEAN REVEALS HIDDEN MYSTERIES!

Returning to the UFO phenomenon, I have personally witnessed flying objects that are able to do things with Electro-magnetism and the gravitational field that our scientists have yet to discover, or at least haven't revealed they have discovered. My wife and I stared directly at an object no more than 75 feet away as it hovered over our moving vehicle. Within a fraction of a second this object was gone! So I have now become one of the many eyewitnesses to give a testimony to something that at least from our perspective has not yet been developed. It appears that we have had travelers from other planetary systems for quite some time. I watched a video called, "The Greatest Story Never Told," created by Retired Command Sergeant Major Robert O. Dean. At one time he worked for our Government in the 50's and early 60's, and was part of a strategic team in Europe classified under the name of "cosmic top secret." It was his job to investigate UFOs and the paranormal activity that came with such an investigation. What he uncovered revealed that we have been visited by at least 12-14 known species from different areas of our galaxy, as well as other galaxies. That figure now has been elevated to over 100 different races of aliens. Again most of this will not be revealed to the average person on the street. These things are revealed to those that thoroughly research. As Jesus once said, all that is in darkness will come to light. Those who seek shall find!

Robert Dean admitted he took an oath never to reveal this information. But he decided for the well being of humanity that it was pertinent on his part to break this oath of military secrecy. Along with possibly a couple of hundred military men and women that have been exposed to such information, so that the world could be forewarned on what has been taking place. What Robert O. Dean discovered in his findings was much more than UFOs or alien life. He discovered one of the hidden mysteries of what we really are. He learned by this research that we are all fellow brothers and sisters to these space travelers, and that we are divine beings. One of his most fascinating discoveries are paintings with drawings of spacecraft and/or aliens. It was amazing to see some of these paintings that went back to the 14th century AD where the clarity of the objects proved that what eyewitnesses are seeing today are the same craft that have been seen for ages.

Why have the citizens of Earth become so ignorant to eternal truths? Why are there fellow space travelers that appear to know many things while we seem to be on the bottom of the heap? It is because we have willingly taken of the waters of forgetfulness. We as a people have become brute beasts of the field. We still murder, rape and pillage our fellow man. Most of the space travelers want nothing to do with us because of our animalistic tendencies. These beings who travel from all over our universe with technologies that make us look like we are in 1st grade wear a myriad of biological garments. Some look exactly like we do but others have appearances that at first may seem very strange to us! Their technology would appear as a divine miracle. They can travel light years and cross between dimensions very quickly. Why are so many so arrogant, believing just because we can't do something, then no one else should be able to do it?

Many of these intergalactic beings realize they cannot interfere with our internal and eternal evolutionary growth. They can assist secretly; they can help individually. But it is not wise to make a grand entrance at this point, and say, "Here we are." We as earthlings sadly are not ready for such an entrance. We are still learning.

SUMERIANS REVEALED THE ALIENS 7000 YEARS AGO!

Zacharia Sitchin wrote at least 7 books dealing with a race of beings from other planets called the Nephilm. I have spoken of them a little throughout this book. His series of books began with, "The 12th Planet." These books go into detail about the Gods from other star systems that came to this earth and began interbreeding with the life forms. He details these findings from the interpretations of Cuneiform tablets of the Ancient Sumerians who existed circa 5000BC. The Sumerians lived in Sumer, the land in Mesopotamia where Abraham the Father to all Israel dwelt.

Some actual events, through destruction of certain historical evidence, became known as myths. Gods such as Zeus, Apollo, Hercules, etc. along with others claimed they were the divine lineage of the same gods such as, Alexander the Great, and Nimrod the great warrior. As I revealed earlier in this book the Bible plainly stated in Genesis 6 that these gods had sexual relations with the daughters of men and produced offspring that were biblically called Giants/Nephilm. The children of ANAK or Sumerian ANU of the ANNNAKI!

ALIENS NUKED SODOM AND GOMORRAH!

These beings had great technological advances; they even had atomic and nuclear power that we have just learned in this past century. There is mighty evidence that Sodom and Gomorrah was nuked. Evidence is strong that in the Middle East there were nuclear explosions. The Dead Sea itself is more than likely the result of this deadly technology.

Religion taught that an angry God who we are to worship destroyed Sodom and Gomorrah. And yet it is evident that these places were nuked by beings that had the force of the atom. You have to wonder why Jesus told the Pharisees that those of Sodom and Gomorrah had a greater chance of being in the Kingdom over them. And yet the Pharisees were strict followers of the God of the Old Testament, whereas those of Sodom were evil pagans and deserved to be destroyed. Why would Jesus make such comments about evil people? Because Jesus understood the mysteries, and he knew quite well that the gods of the Old Testament were not the Father, but instead alien travelers from other planets.

It must really be difficult to read these statements because the world has been taught the exact opposite. How can we humans be a slice of biological tampering when the Bible states that God created Adam and Eve? Because God did create Adam and Eve, except it was not the kind of God that many think they are worshipping. These beings called themselves God to enslave their creation. We are slaves in human form! That is what needs to unravel in your thinking. This place we call earth is not paradise, it is hell. We are in bondage inside biological vessels that were created by star travelers. And until you figure this out you will eternally remain in hell. People get upset with me when I state that earth is hell. They react by saying, "I love life." Well I love life also, but within the perimeters of life come freedom, truth and divine power. This is our inheritance! If you look at those that love this world, either they are well off, or they are so inundated within the philosophy of slavery that they don't have a clue where they are. Jesus said, "If you love this world then the love of the Father is not in you!" He also stated, "I am not of this world, neither are they who follow me." This world is like prison, yet you have been there so long it becomes your home. It is actually more frightening to a prisoner that has made those four walls his home for most of his life to leave and enter freedom than it is to stay right where he is.

We are all star children and are not from planet earth. We are stuck here in the loop of continuous cycles because these gods that people want to continue to worship have enslaved us. It was these gods who brought us religion of all the different faiths.

ALL RELIGIONS LED BY MEN AND WOMEN ARE CULTS.

Here is another mystery. Religion is a concept, an idea, and a belief that is brought down by others having certain mystical experiences. Religion is not evil but it can become evil. That is why followers of some cults have committed suicide directed by their leaders. Because they are obeying someone else's creed and ethic they have no Gnosis of inner awareness. And do not be deceived, all religions are cults. Just because the Catholic Church is humongous doesn't mean they are not a cult. A cult is any belief system that adheres to men and women's interpretation of the law. A real cult is simply anything that provides awareness from the exterior and not the interior. I have to cry sometimes when I see certain religious groups setting up cult awareness foundations when they themselves are a cult. Those that are trying to get you away from a cult are just as dangerous as the cult itself, because they want to indoctrinate you with their beliefs.

Truth is internal and eternal. You will find it within yourself. It exists nowhere else! I lived within external religion for more than 30 years. I can't even recall all the times that I made the statement, after hearing my church insist on this or that doctrine, that this doesn't make sense to me. They always said, in time it will. The problem is it never did make sense. I either accepted it because the church taught it or I became what they called a rebel because I didn't accept it. Where are the choices in this enigma? I find it strange how a church's door is wide open to get you to come in, but try to leave the same way you came in and watch what happens. You will be vilified, slandered, threatened, punished, spit on, gossiped about. And what is strange, it is by the same ones who were so nice when you first walked in. Why does this occur? Because religion is a placebo created by the false gods, it is not real. It is an illusion! Real true religion is internal awareness, and it belongs to each of us. It is a way of life, not someone else's idea of life. Jesus said, "True and undefiled religion is to help the Fatherless and the widow." It is not a place where people attend. It is an eternal identity through internal awareness. And it works by loving one another!

DO OUR DIVINE PARENTS SEEK OUR WORSHIP?
WOULD OUR HUMAN PARENTS?

All our life we have been exposed to theories brought by either religion or government that teach we are to worship something. The Father seeks worship from NO ONE! I repeat, the Father seeks worship from NO ONE! Why would a Father or Mother want their children to worship them? You can honor your parents, love your parents, but you don't worship your parents. That is an illusion brought down by false Gods who themselves seek worship. These are beings that have entered the darkness of the shadows and seek power unto themselves as their reality. Their love and compassion have been somewhat defiled, they insist on you kissing their rings. The Roman Emperors did it. The Babylonian Gods did it, and basically every kingdom on earth attempts to do it, yes, even religions.

MOSES COPIED FROM SUMERIAN LITERATURE!

Sitchin in his books shows incredible evidence that proves Moses didn't receive any divine utterance to write what has become known as the Torah, the 1st five books of the Bible. He shows that the Sumerians were handed the information that Moses copied. In fact what we have today in the 1st five books of the Bible is only a summary of the actual account. And through Sitchin's interpretations he found, by being proficient in ancient Hebrew customs and language, that the details Moses left out actually predate Moses! Later works such as the Book of Jasher, discovered in the 19th century, reveal a much different Moses and God than the King James Bible reveals. Therefore much of the information that was brought down to our time period is inaccurate. Much of the Old Testament had been copied from earlier accounts around the time Israel was taken captive into Babylon. The accuracy of such work would be a word of mouth report instead of actual historical data, thereby bringing the work into question. That is why these new documents that have surfaced are extremely important to weigh all information.

It is my belief that Moses was a powerful Pharaoh in Egypt and the truth be known, there is no such thing as a real Israelite. This was the name given to Jacob, the grandson of Abraham. These people that were wandering in Egypt were actually the ancestors of the Sumerians. Remember Abraham was born in UR of the Chaldees. This area was the land of SUMER, and Abraham along with his Father Terah, were Sumerians also known as Hebrews. The people of this tribe that went into Egypt were Jacob and his twelve sons. It was their children that went on to become the Israelites in bondage in Egypt. These people were following the God of Abraham, also known as the ONE GOD, some have called Aton. They had their own beliefs separated from the rest of the Egyptians, who were believers in the Pantheon of Gods or multiple gods. When Moses was sent out of Egypt he met a new God, one named Jehovah. He had not known this God; neither did any of the other Israelites know this God. It is my belief that this God was the Sumerian Enlil.

For the God of Abraham, Isaac and Jacob was different from the New God Moses met in the Wilderness. The Book of Jasher indicates that the Lord of the mountain, where the King James version says Moses met God/Jehovah, was not what people have always believed. Another error discovered from recovered historical data is that Moses was never at Mt. Sinai. In fact just as the Bible indicated he went to Mt. Horeb, which is a long ways from Sinai. Mt. Sinai only came into people's reality about a thousand years ago. Mt. Horeb was found outside Egypt. Much of this information was not released to the public for fear of panic caused by revealing that the main religions may be based in error.

There is ample proof within the scriptures themselves that the Sumerians were incredibly accurate discussing these star travelers and exposing the real truth of Genesis. It may make a little more sense on what the war in heaven was all about. It was even suggested that both Mars and Venus had structures and bases built on them for these battles. Some of the pictures that the Pathfinder brought back from Mars showed pyramids and even warlike implements. Later when new pictures were brought back from the Cydonia region of Mars it proved that this was home to an ancient civilization.

Sadly the media covered only what it was allowed to and so much was hidden from the people on earth of what was really discovered. I saw what appear to be building structures with very little room for doubt. And of course the mysterious "face on Mars" which was made into a joke when NASA downloaded faulty pictures. Later the real pictures were downloaded, but by then the media already had decided that the face was nothing more than rocks, which appeared under shadows and the trick of light as nothing more than a pile of natural debris.

WITHIN THE DESIGN OF A PYRAMID IS THE REVELATION OF MAN!

The Sumerian texts also reveal areas on this planet as well as nearby planets such as Mars, where there are landing strips for starships. Many ancient ruins such as the Great Pyramids of Egypt and the Nazca lines in Peru and elsewhere seem to be designed and patterned by the stars. There is a link between these ancient structures and star systems such as Orion, Pleadies etc...The pyramids may be more revealing than just their design. The four lower walls can very easily represent our four lower bodies: the memory body, the mental body, the emotional body and our physical body. The queen's chamber within might very well represent the divine Son. And from this chamber a small, very narrow entrance leads to the Kings chamber which in proper terms could be called the "I AM" presence- The Father.

Notice even Jesus stated, "Wide is the path everyone takes, but narrow is the road to righteousness." Through the Christ given to us by our immortal Mother, we can have access back to our divine I AM presence, the Father.

Did you recognize that the four walls of illusion cover the queen and kings chamber, and unless you go inside you cannot find them! I have not had the privilege of going to Egypt to visit these pyramids, but I have heard stories of many who stayed inside these chambers and had out of body experiences. Some have even disappeared in plain sight. I believe these pyramids are much more than they appear. I believe they may very well be some sort of time traveling device or even a dimensional star-gate. But without their capstones of pure gold they are not activated. Sitchin suggested that is why Egypt used to be a fertile land with beautiful landscape, because when the pyramids are activated life abounds around these areas. The position of the Pyramids on Earth and Mars linked with Orion are much more than an accident. These structures were built by some divine geometrically designed format.

PLANET X (NIBIRU) REVEALED BY SUMERIANS VERIFIED BY NASA & JPL

As stated earlier some of these ancient texts reveal another planet that until 1990 we had no proof existed. Some in NASA believed in the mid 70's there was another planet orbiting our sun by virtue of the drag and pull created on the planet Uranus, which appeared to be tilted. Sitchin called this new planet the 12th planet because the sun and the earth's moon were included in this count. NASA declared around 1990 that they had discovered planet 'X' which is the 10th planet by Roman Numeral. But soon afterwards nothing was ever stated about this find. One day while browsing on the internet I ran across something on the Jet Propulsion Laboratory's web sight that threw me for a loop. They showed our entire solar system with one added attraction. After Pluto and Neptune, one could immediately recognize another planet. J.P.L. did not keep that information up very long. But I was astounded at the clarity of what appeared to be a planet. Nothing more than a large asteroid, it is still much larger than planet earth. Could this be what the book of Jude and Enoch meant when it stated that these star beings lost their first estate? Did the great war in heaven cause the destruction of the 10th planet?

Also the Sumerians taught that Nibiru, the 10th planet, was much larger. I believe four times larger than Earth.

I believe these ancient travelers now exist on both sides of the fence. Some have incarnated and exist right along with us, and others are still in the astral plane creating havoc and controlling people from that side. Still others are time travelers that go back and forth. And there are still others that left here a long time ago and left information that they would return. I was able to meet Sitchin a couple years ago. He said that the sign posts of the Cuneiform tablets reveal that these travelers would return during Pisces. That means they have very little time, as we are now ending the Age of Pisces as we enter Aquarius.

TIAMET BECAME WITHOUT FORM (EARTH) AND MOVED INTO THE VOID (SPACE)

Other aspects that Sitchin brings forward from these records are that Planet Earth has not always been in the orbit it is now. The Sumerians called earth the water planet or Tiamet. They spoke of earth once upon a time located between Mars and Jupiter where the great asteroid belt is now located. They wrote about a Great War between the planets and how one planet was knocked out of its orbit and pushed into the void or empty space. A place where no other orbital track of planets came through. The asteroid belt is no doubt the remains of a shattered planet. In the book of Genesis it says god separated the firmament of the heavens from the water above and the waters below. The Sumerians show that all the planets were water planets at one time. And the separation of the firmament was actually speaking of Earth being placed into the orbit it is now. And the waters above are the planets from Jupiter to Nibiru, and the waters below are the planets Mars to Mercury towards our sun. The Bible actually uses the Hebrew term for firmament as the "hammered out one" or the "bracelet." Which is the same term used to describe the asteroid belt. Verse one in Genesis 1, describes, "In the beginning God created the heavens and the earth, and the earth became without form, and was placed in the void." This implies that something of great magnitude occurred that caused Earth to be relocated. Was this the war in heaven? If these things are correct by the Sumerian documents then it would be better if the first verse in Genesis said, "In the beginning the gods caused the heaven and the earth to become without form and moved it into the void of space."

It was understood that Nibiru, later to be called Maldek by the Babylonians, had come into a collision course with Tiamet where one of its moons actually struck Taimet, leaving it helpless and battered. The moon that struck Tiamet was destroyed into millions of pieces leaving an orbit of huge chunks of debris riddled throughout our solar system. Even today there are meteors and asteroids and comets that make their appearance time and again as a testimony to a great collision in outer space. Could this be the catastrophic event that eliminated the dinosaurs instantly? Can you imagine the turmoil that was created in our solar system when two bodies collided?

Is this what it meant when the scriptures teach that Lucifer caused the worlds to tremble? It was stated in Sumerian tablets that Marduk the son of Enki was a great warrior. The planet Mars was named after Marduk. He created most of the trouble in the great rebellion. It is possible that the name Lucifer, as I illustrated earlier, could refer to many possibilities, one of which could be the god Marduk. This is also how Nibiru the 12th planet was called Maldek, named after Marduk the Babylonian god. Also it could be a dual reference that Marduk tried to usurp his authority over Anu revealing the attempted overthrow of the Father of the Annunaki.

I believe before our incarnation on this planet we existed on many different planets, maybe even other galaxies. We were part of the war in heaven. We may have witnessed our world destroyed time and time again. I have had vivid dreams of living on a planet and watching our sun burn out in front of my eyes. I felt how the cold gripped our planet instantly and we just froze into oblivion. Was this dream revealing a past life? I believe it could have been, it was so very real to me. Memories of the event were so vivid and yet the sheer terror of this catastrophe was beyond anything most could imagine.

It becomes imperative that one understand the Garden of Eden, although a physical creation by the Nephilm, was set into a time sequence of events. It was to teach us of ancient mysteries as well as revealing that civilizations existed well before the Biblical Garden of Eden. Also that there were world and planetary civilizations that still do exist all through the cosmos.

THE GREAT BIBLICAL FLOOD MAY HAVE WIPED OUT ATLANTIS!

The Sumerians were the first civilization to appear on the scene after the great catastrophic events of Atlantis and Lemuria. Even the story of Noah was told in detail by the Sumerians long before the Biblical Noah came on the scene. Was the great flood an allegory? I believe all the stories in the Bible were allegorical. But these events also happened to real people, and most likely we were many of the ones it happened to. There have been many floods, many earth changes, and many civilizations. It is all part of the cycles of this thing called the shadow world. It appears that the final destruction of Atlantis may have been the result of the last great flood that the Bible describes. It occurred 12000-13000 years ago. Even the ancient "books of seventy" the original Hebrew Bible, seems to more accurately date this flood than our Bible does. It placed the great flood circa 11000BC. Many tribal Indian cultures speak of a great flood also, but again their dating places it long before the dating in the Bible.

THE DIVINE TWIN FLAME!

I also want to address more thoroughly our relation to our Father/Mother parents in retrospect to our own analogous lives in the present awareness. I briefly touched upon the reality of how each of us are a twin flame like our Father/Mother parents. When we were created we were given both aspects of our divine ancestors. When we exist on this earth in the three-dimensional plane we see ourselves as separate to one another by virtue of our biological garments. It must have been quite strange for the people living during the days of the Apostle Paul to hear him speak of marriage in the flesh in very mystical terms. He stated that when a male and female come together the two become one! This of course can only be ascertained through the mystery. I am not even sure Paul deeply understood this, but he realized it was a mystical affirmation of what we will become again.

Adam was told that it was not good for man to be alone, therefore Eve the woman was created for him. One of the most difficult aspects of being a human being is searching for love from that special counterpart. More money is spent every year on this aspect than anything else. Everyone wants to find Mr. or Mrs. Right. Love in the physical plane can sometimes become a cruel trick. So many want that special relationship. We may look high and low for that special partner to fill deep needs within ourselves. But it appears that most find a rabbit in a hat rather than this utopian idea.

Why is it so deep within each of us to look for that special mate? What are many really looking for? And why don't we usually find it? It becomes even harder to understand when people lose a loved one either by divorce, illness, or death.

The answer lies within our spiritual genes. We are a multi-dimensional being that was given the opposite end of the polarity at our creation. We were created "twin flames just as the great spirit divine is both the Father and the Mother." It is difficult enough to ascertain our very own multi-dimensional selves but now we realize we are also a twin of another half of the Father/Mother flame. When Paul stated the two become one flesh it was an analogy of our twin flame. The marriage in the flesh is not necessarily our twin flame. That is why death separates the two. We live in virtual realities trying to ascertain the real us! That deep hidden drive for the opposite sex is our hidden drive for our true divine reality. We are searching for our other half. Some may wonder about Homosexuals? Why do they desire the same sex? The truth is they don't really desire the same sex. In most of their relationships one usually characterizes the male and the other the female. This can easily occur to anyone if they are incarnated into the flesh as the opposite of their original polarity. There are masculine homosexuals and there are feminine homosexuals. These people are human beings and need to be treated as such. We are not to condemn or judge them.

However they have entered this incarnation in another sex because of karmic law. They may still have the pulls toward the opposite sex they had when they were here before, but now they are that same sex with different desires. Some may wonder why this happens? All I can say is, be careful not to judge! Now understand this mystery, we are neither male nor female. We are a single being that has within itself both attributes. Our other half is just like us but has the attributes fitting for that half. To become a complete spirit you must have both halves. As we are separated from our Father in these shadow worlds we will remain separated from our other divine half. When we return to the Father/Mother divine we will also reunite with our other half, and the two of us will become one again! When you hear that it is not good for man to be alone that is an understatement. Each of us is literally half of a whole, which is why we seek so diligently for the other half, but usually cannot find what we are really looking for.

This all may sound very strange to you, but enter into your heart and ask why we seek so diligently that other half. It is more than sex, I assure you! Sex can be fun, it can be rewarding but in the overall picture if that half is not there then you will always search for the part of you that seems impossible to find. Why do you think divorce is so prevalent?

Can you find the other half, and if so what happens? It is a rare thing in my belief that one finds their other half in the shadows. Even if you do, we live in a society that creates so many problems that it is possible to actually reject the other half based primarily on lack of understanding. It is very easy to cross paths with soul mates. These are dear close friends that you have known over many lifetimes. Finding a soul mate can become quite easy. Sometimes just searching for them can be rewarding, because you both probably planned your meeting from the other side before you came into this incarnation, but the twin flame is another story. Finding the twin flame would be shocking and quite frightening to most. The shock may be so strong that it actually deters you away from that person because of the fear of what has taken place. Whereas with soul mates there is more of a desire to be around each other in the sense of strong friendship. Soul mates create links to one another from previous lives.

WERE ADAM AND EVE TWIN FLAMES?

I believe Adam and Eve were twin flames. There is a strong theory that Jesus was Adam, and Mary, who became his mother in his last incarnation, was Eve. Who can know for sure, yet it could very well be true. The Bible does speak of Jesus being the second Adam. It calls the first Adam physical and the second Adam spiritual. Does this reveal the transition from the Old man into the New man?

When we entered the lower aspects of male and female our masculine and feminine aspects were also divided. This is what was really meant when it said, "It is not good that man (the masculine aspect of this dual polarity) be alone," separated from his feminine aspect of the dual polarity. We have been given the opportunity as a twin flame of our Father/Mother divine to become internally aware from both aspects of our divine being but from separate states of awareness. It teaches us that our Father (Pater) is where the spiritual idea originates, and our Mother (Mater) is the idea in matter form. So we have spirit as our Father, and Matter as our Mother. This teaches us to become co-creators, as above so below. As the Father's mind enters into our realm then we can bring into existence in the matter world what he thinks in spirit. Thereby the twin flame comes together as one creator.

Both Eve and Mary represent birth from the idea of the PATER in the MATER. Eve represents giving birth to biological entities to become vessels for the spirit children of the Father. Mary represents giving birth of this vessel for the divine Son of the Mother. When these two unite the marriage of the Lamb, which Paul spoke of, comes into congruence. Adam and Eve then became the symbolic twin flame of all spirit divine entities that had been divided by biological matter. And although men and women play different roles in these biological vessels, both are an integral part of the whole. Each gains its traits for the benefit of the whole spirit divine. Each of us male and female are equal before our Father because we truly are one divine being.

WHAT ARE THE STRANGE ENTITIES THAT WALK IN OUR PRESENCE FROM TIME TO TIME?

As I now conclude this 6th mystery I want to add one more aspect to this puzzle. I want to address the strange unexplained entities or spirits. There have been weird unexplained incidences of freaks of nature as well as spirits that exude evil beyond imagination. Strange phenomenon such as shadowy looking beings and monsters have been seen throughout the ages. And of course everyone has heard of "big foot" the "Sasquatch;" the "abominable snow man." And of course the "sea serpent" in Scotland and the tales surrounding him. Where do these creatures come from?

Are these biological experiments gone awry by our government? Are these spirit controlled animals from the other side? Or could it be these strange creatures are really from another dimension? Just what are these creatures? Each of these answers can be correct. But before I discuss this I want to address some ancient customs that may answer some of these questions.

CASTING EVIL SPELLS MAY BE MORE OF A REALITY THAN FIRST BELIEVED!

In times past we have read about the power of witches and warlocks and even Gypsies. They had the uncanny ability to cast evil spells using black magic against their perceived enemy. Most of you have heard the story about "Beauty and the Beast." This story relayed the account of a Prince that failed to show honor and love to others. By the casting of a spell by a witch he became this hideous looking monster until the day he could fall in love and learn what true love toward one another really is.

NEBUCHADNEZZAR WAS THE BEAST!

I know some may be thinking these are only dumb stories without any validity to them. Well, think again. These stories are not as farfetched as one would have you to believe. Imaginative stories like mythologies are based on something that really happened. One case in the Bible has truer context then one would ever realize. About 600BC a man named Nebuchadnezzar became King of Great Babylon. During his reign it was stated that the Elohim placed a curse on him and turned him into an animal for seven years until he could learn there was one greater than he. Nebuchadnezzar actually grew feathers and claws just like a beast. This is where the term beast was used in the Bible as an analogy for ruling evil empires. Daniel 4:31-33

There is much more to these stories than meets the eye. Gypsies over the years gained insight and talent to use a power that reigns in all of us. Yet they used it many times as a curse upon their enemies. Where do these strange powers come from that bring our deepest fears into reality? The victim generates the reality of a curse. Your belief in the curse gives it power to manifest into reality. You will learn within the last mystery that belief plays a major role in what occurs in one's life both good and evil.

YOUR THOUGHTS CAN BE USED TO CREATE!

Belief is the energy of thought brought together into one frame of reference. Our thoughts can create by the use of this energy. What you think in your mind and heart can be brought into reality even from another dimension. Some have gained the ability to bring their thoughts into reality in the fourth dimensional realm and slowing the vibration enough to bring them into this third dimensional realm.

Images of ghosts, goblins, goatsuckers (Chupacabras) and deformed looking insects have been brought into our three-dimensional plane of awareness by this power. It is this use of misqualified energy that can bring evil things of the mind into our world. Now don't get me wrong, these things can also occur by genetic experiments gone haywire or evolutionary changes from our past, but for this illustration I want to explain the spiritual possibilities.

Behind each of our thoughts are manifestations waiting to be fulfilled in the creation process. Each and every thought we think undergoes an alchemical change in another dimension. Why, because we as spirits exist in both planes simultaneously. When I went out of body I realized that my thoughts are instantly recognized. All you have to do is think the thought and it occurs. While we are in this flesh and blood vessel, that ability remains with us, but it is much slower in this vibrational reality. You, however, are the same, and while you think the thought it already manifests in the other dimension.

Our ability to create is forever with us! When we think the thought its matrix begins to outline the reality of that thought instantly in the next dimension. If we dwell on that thought, then the matrix solidifies with substance of molecules and atoms. As our divine self places the light of our higher self into this matrix we form that thought into a reality in another dimension. Once you become proficient in this process you can use the light to lower the vibration and bring the thought into your material world, thus creating! Voila!

The problem is the use of this power for wrong reasons. We as co-creators of the Father are to use this power to heal and to bring into existence that which benefits others. If you use this power as a curse then the Karmic law will seek your compliance in your accountability. Now maybe you can understand why Jesus spoke of controlling your thoughts. If you use evil with your thoughts like some Gypsies and witches have done in times past then you will reap your own creation after death. However if your creation is pleasing to your Father then you will reap the reward as treasures added to your higher being! If the use of this power is not done in the light then it will become darkness and add to your negative karma.

YOUR THOUGHTS CAN BECOME A DANGEROUS WEAPON!

People get carried away, thinking their thoughts are harmless. They construct all manner of evil within their minds figuring, who cares? No one can know what's in your mind, right? Wrong! The Bible spoke of not allowing the sun to go down upon your anger. There was a mystical reason for this.

If you go to bed with evil in your heart and thoughts, you then take this evil with you into the astral dimensions where your thoughts instantly obey. Your physical aspect of your lower dimensional body is now sleeping, but you the spiritual entity are in another dimension and most likely are not conscious of this fact. You are unaware that you are sleeping or dreaming or even OBE. If you take into your sleep thought forms created by the energy veil/evil then those thoughts begin to realign into a matrix and the energy programs its destiny to where that thought is applied.

This may seem quite innocent while you are sound asleep, but what takes place is far from innocent, and you will reap what you sow. Under karmic law your thoughts will bring swift accountability. If you play with matches you will be burned. Granted the debt will not be as large as one who actuates this formula for the wrong of another. Your ignorance covers most of your wrongdoing, but in time it can become a huge debt. That is why it is important to learn to love even your enemies. You don't want hatred to remain in your heart for any length of time!

Have you ever felt guilty about hearing that someone was in an accident, or even killed right after you had been thinking bad thoughts about that person? Some feel that is justification, and the person deserved what happened. Others even believe God killed that person because they may have done them wrong. Don't believe that for a second. Don't blame our Father for your evil thoughts. The Father's thoughts are always love and peace projected.

It is time we all take heed to that thing we call mind, because what orchestrates the power of that mind is the power of universes. People have become trained enough to use this power to bend spoons. Some have appeared in two places at the same time. And some have used this ability as Jesus did to actually create something out of their mind and bring it into this lower reality. Jesus learned the power to turn water into wine, heal the sick, cast out wicked spirits, raise the dead, and control the weather. He even had the power to rise up from his own death, giving him the power over the grave.

WE CREATE OUR OWN REALITIES EVEN THOUGH IT MIGHT NOT APPEAR THAT WAY AT ALL!

We create our worlds! We have at our fingertips the power of the kingdom of our Father. Our minds can access the supernatural within us because we are supernatural. The ability to move objects through the air as the study of kinetics is directly related to our mind. But our human brain can't do that; it is the spirit dwelling within all of us. Movies are showing more of these powers, but most believe it is either science fiction or demonic intrusion. Yes, wrong spirited activity is a demonic power. It means the power is coming from darkness and not the light. Jesus stated, "The kingdom of Heaven is taken by violence." This simply reinforces the fact that both good and evil can use the power of the kingdom. It reminds me when Moses came before the Pharaoh and tossed the rod of Aaron before him and it turned into a snake. Then Pharaoh summoned his magicians and they did the same thing. However in this story Moses' snake devoured the Pharaoh's snakes. This story reveals a mystery. Each tapped into the same power but one had greater power than the other, because light overcomes darkness.

Anyone who is trained can use this power. It just depends what you want to use it for. These abilities belong to the kingdom of righteousness, but because of our failure to comprehend the eternal LAW of ONE we have perverted use of this power for our own glory and not the glory of others. Everything is free choice!

We have been living in the density of maya and illusion for a very long time. The sad fact is we continue to boast on our own achievements and understanding of time and space, when in reality scientists know so very little. However, there are a few scientists that are beginning to comprehend the gnosis of hyper-dimensional space and the geometrical design of all life. And hopefully before too long some of the very things that I am bringing to your attention will become more common knowledge. Once we stretch our horizons of thought we will understand that our universe is teeming with life. There are many planets and systems of worlds that exist in the great beyond. We have brothers and sisters of the great I AM strung out all over this universe and other universes.

Some of these travelers are still as blinded as we are, but they have accessed the gnosis of the powers I have mentioned. In our recent history we have been given technology by these space travelers. Certain alien cultures have been coming here and giving us access to technologies. And we have rocketed in technological advances far beyond where we should be at present. This is not new however, this same story is revealed in ancient literature. That alien races came and brought our awareness to new levels, just as I pointed out about the Sumerians.

THE EARTH IS UNDERGOING A GREAT CHANGE BUT LIFE WILL ALWAYS CONTINUE! WHETHER HERE OR ON ANOTHER PLANET!

We are at a time when major earth changes will take place again. And weather systems will become so deadly that our earth will undergo a great transformation. Already we are beginning to see this around the world. Earthquakes, Volcanoes, Tsunamis, Hurricanes, Tornadoes, Blizzards, Cyclones, etc... These are increasing at a great speed across this planet. The Ring of Fire where volcanoes are becoming active again is frightening certain geologists.

I do not want to express a doom and gloom ideology here. I just want to make people aware of the changes and the turmoil that exist on this and other planets when this occurs. As I have also stated there are beings, space travelers, time travelers that are here for our good. They monitor our progress slowly, and they stand in careful guard for our defense. We are not alone trying to fight these supernatural or planetary shifting battles. We have with us the power of the universe. Those that are still covered by the veil need extra help from without, thereby the need for protectors, guides and angels. It is their desire that we evolve in righteousness of truth, and as stated before many of these protectors are actually us in the future. So be prepared earthlings, as you are about to enter the realm of what many call "first contact." As we get closer and closer to the end of this age more UFO activity and contact will be made because major changes both physically and spiritually will begin!

THE BLUE TAIL STAR!

In conclusion I wanted to address ever-prevailing meteors and asteroids that are flying through our space. These comets in times past have impacted planets and created unbelievable destruction. Even an asteroid no bigger than one mile in radius has the ability to wipe out all life. An asteroid this large impacting the earth would be tantamount to a Hiroshima explosion once every second for thirteen years. If that doesn't wake you up then nothing will. We live on a very dangerous planet, which orbits in a dangerous solar system.

Just what are these comets, asteroids and meteors? As stated briefly they are pieces of planets that have been destroyed. They are also signs in the heavens. These huge rocks and ice balls that orbit in their prescribed space return over and over in the cycles as a testimony to all our known history.

SIGNS IN OUR HEAVENS!

As of this writing the comet Hale/Bopp has come and gone. We witnessed this awesome object glide through our night's skies leaving a tremendous blue tail behind. This beautiful sight may in actuality be a sign of things that are about to occur on this planet. There are many, including Indian tribes such as the Hopi, that believe we are entering a cleansing period and these comets represent times of cyclical changes that have occurred throughout the ages. Since this mysterious comet made its appearance we are already seeing strange weather patterns, such as El Niño. This is a force which I firmly believe is created by oceanic volcanoes. It elevates the temperature of a large mass of water. I assure you this did not occur because of wind change. No winds could create that kind of temperature rise. For this amount of water to raise even a few degrees in temperature over a rather short period of time would take a major geological event. El Niño resulted in temperatures rising nearly 12 degrees or higher in some spots.

What occurred in the United States from this system has only yet to be unveiled. Weather changes have occurred to the point where in the winter places that were usually cold were warmer, and the summer is now proving to be a hot bed of activity of floods and dangerous storms. Other areas are heating up and leaving crops to wither and die. Fires are breaking out rapidly due to drought plagued areas. And now we have already entered into what is called La Niña, the opposite of El Niño, where the ocean water temperatures are dropping rapidly.

More and more volcanoes are becoming active and erupting. Earthquakes are jarring this earth as never before in our recent history. What can one really make of all this other than to conclude we are entering a NEW AGE! Great Prophets, Sages and Tribesmen have spoke of these times because they have been made aware of the cyclical history of our world. These comets define when our earth enters these changes because they are in a cyclical pattern that was created by the first catastrophe of the wars in heaven. And every time they make their entrance it should be a reminder to all those that remember their history, to prepare for the onslaught of new major earth changes.

Within some of the Hopi Indians' ancient prophecies they expected the blue tail star to return. Was that Hale/Bopp? If these Hopi elders are correct in their history then another comet is to follow that will bring the sign of great destruction to this earth, and it will have a red tail.

We are living in very exciting and frightening times, depending upon your outlook. Because with the apparent lifting of the light of Christ within us, a cleansing will first occur. Jesus spoke of times like this. We are not only entering an earth shift but a paradigm shift as well. And these events will hopefully wake people so they do not have to keep starting all over again, still not knowing who they are or where they came from. Earth citizens are about to experience major changes in global proportions. For those who have Internet access it will become imperative to keep up with these changes as they occur. Just click on this URL and bookmark this sight. http://www.earthchangestv.com

The handwriting is on the wall just as it was made plain to Nebuchadnezzar's Son in Babylon the night he would be put to death. He saw a strange inscription written by a hand that appeared out of nowhere that summed up in very simple terms the end of Balshazzar's days as king over Babylon! On that very night Darius the Mede, with troops provided by Cyrus the Great of Persia, conquered Babylon and killed its king. We as children of the light must stop our irreverence of this planet and our fellow brothers and sisters. There have been numerous signs since Haley's comet returned in '85 and especially since around 1990 when crop circles became prevalent. And now with the blue tail comet we have witnessed geographical and geological changes happen nearly over night. We are entering a new age, the Age of Aquarius.

If we cannot love one another as brothers and sisters without our petty hatreds over race, creed and religion, then we will nationally and globally reap what we sow. Karma, which is an individual reaping, would then become Dharma, which is a national or global reaping. We as a human family have come to an end of an age like so many times in the past. Again many have spent their inheritance on non-profiting trivial pursuits. We are failing in our service one to another and we are failing our heritage. Many will die the death of mortality again just to find that false logic and awareness compromised their life. We will see that our material lusts and our seeking the elements of the shadow have corrupted us again. Many will have to agonize again for not seeking that which is real and divine, and will have to return to the cycles of hell again and again!

When the day comes, and it most certainly will, people will recognize that everything we think or do will be brought under the law of cause and effect, reaping what we sow. Once this occurs great changes can be made in people's lives. The next time someone even contemplates committing a serious crime they will most assuredly have to think twice because they will be well aware of the consequences. No one ever gets away with crime. All things come back around. Maybe we can understand a little better why certain good people have bad things happen

311

to them. No one suffers unjustly; everyone pays something back to cause and effect. That is the law, and that is the beauty of the law. It reveals total fairness even though it may seem unfair that someone suffers unjustly. I assure you no one suffers unjustly.

Why did Jesus have to suffer? He was innocent of sin in his last incarnation. Jesus said he learned obedience by those things which he suffered. But why did Jesus need to learn obedience? If He were perfect and the only divine Son, then what obedience would he ever need to learn? How could he have ever lacked anything as the divine Son of God?

The answer is self-evident! Jesus was just like us, a man tempted in all points as we are. A man who had to incarnate like we do. He is our brother! If Jesus was truly tempted in all points as we are then he had to experience temptations that only come from sinning. In his past lives he had to suffer from the result of breaking laws. If he didn't then it would mean he never had to learn about the struggles of the cycles, and that is our greatest temptation. There were many things Jesus could have never experienced as a temptation in one lifetime. There had to be many lifetimes to experience all that we have to experience. We have temptation today that is surrounded around technology, and how we have to live and cope in this type of society. Jesus' world was a much different world than we live in at present. So how could he even come close to understanding what we suffer unless he had past lives and suffered the same things? As stated earlier, ancient Sumeria revealed that the gods gave great technology to us from the stars. Stories of Atlantis reveal this also!

Each of our hopes whether in the flesh or spirit are based on a perfect geometric design. So if Jesus, who was tempted in all points as we, could overcome this world and unite with the divine SON, then so can we.

It then takes true, real faith that will engender personal knowing. This is the same faith of energy that Jesus used to perform great miraculous works.

With the simple faith of a mustard seed you can truly move mountains, wherever you are in body or out of body. There is energy, a power through the flame of our true identity that can be used by each of us. To create within us our very own divine identities so we may evolve to the true Flame of our Father/Mother divine reality.

As we enter the seventh & final mystery of this book we can begin to envision our true potential from within, which is our very own use of the mystical law of faith.

MYSTERY SEVEN
The Mystery of Faith

Have you ever wondered what the Apostle Paul really meant when he said, "Foolish ones, what you sow is not made alive until it dies?" Paul is my favorite author of the New Testament primarily because he had an uncanny approach to the mysteries without really revealing them to those who were not ready. Even today many still read Paul's writings and come up with interpretations only in the letter. They do not understand that behind the written letter was a gnosis that could only be discerned by the initiated. The enlightened ones could grasp the inner meaning, while those that were not aware could grasp a more literal meaning, and the peace would remain. The early Gnostics were well aware of Paul's ability to create this dual effect using mystical references he was taught in trances and OBE's by Jesus Christ. Paul stated often, "When in Rome do as the Romans do." He knew how to blend in!

At times it appears almost as if he would contradict himself in one area or just create enough question to confuse others in another area. But when you understand the gnosis of mystery, Paul was able to relate, just as Jesus was, in dual form. Jesus taught this method because he knew many were not prepared for the inner wisdom of truth. Only those, as he stated in John 6:44, which the Father would call unto him, would he be able to teach the mysteries. Jesus understood that the Father had to open up within an individual before they could ever comprehend these mysteries. That is what is meant when it says, "No man can come to me except the Father draw him."

This is an extremely mystical revelation. If the Father is not activated within the individual soul matrix by the light of the divine Son, then a person could not understand the mystical gnosis.

EVERYTHING THAT NEEDS TO BE ACCESSED COMES FROM WITHIN

One of the important aspects to these mysteries is that all truth from heaven above and earth beneath dwells within the individual. If the person cannot already visualize the delicate components to a mystery, then they will not perceive what is being said, thereby creating a danger for them. Why would this create a problem? Because if a person is not properly prepared from within to receive this gnosis, then they could reject outright truths that will set them free from the veil. They will have to return to the cycles, but this time they will have produced a negative Karma for denying certain truths that were always within them. They would have crucified the Son of Man again, afresh as the scriptures speak. And it becomes nearly impossible to enlighten one, in that same lifetime, once they have tasted the powers of the kingdom and rejected it.

REJECTING GNOSIS IS LIKE REJECTING THE DIVINE SON!

Rejecting gnosis is tantamount to rejecting the divine Son, the Logos, the Christ, because gnosis can only come from within. Paul and Jesus describe this in the Bible by stating that the meat of the word is for the fully mature, but the babe in Christ must still be fed with milk. Paul goes on to say that the meat is for the discerning, who can grasp the realities of the truth from within, but the milk is the literal interpretation where one needs someone to teach them. The meat therefore represents the internal truth and the milk represents the external word. As stated in Jeremiah, in the future there would come a time when one would no longer need the word written down as it was given to Ancient Israel, carved into the stone. Jeremiah revealed that the WORD would be written in your heart. It was confirmed in 8th chapter of Hebrews, that no one will teach his neighbor nor their brothers, "Saying, Know the Lord." For all shall know him and none would have to be taught. This is what internal Gnosis is; everyone will know the truth from within their own heart, meaning within their truer SELF. No one will have to teach this, nor can anyone possibly reveal these truths, because it must come from within you to become part of you. Thereby decreeing, No man can come unto me except the Father draw him...

Paul taught that most in the church in his day were only babes in Christ; they still needed someone to teach them. This frustrated Paul because he knew he couldn't come right out with the mysteries. He understood that every individual had to learn them according to grace afforded within their divine higher self. The people in Paul's day just like today do not want to wean off the milk. They are fearful to let go of the easy road that teaches everything will be given them as a free gift, so they are not responsible. They have failed to understand the free gift is their divine inheritance, and of course that is free, but it can't be given to anyone from an external source.

PAUL TAUGHT MANY OF THESE SAME MYSTERIES!

Paul attempted to teach reincarnation, the cycles, the veil, the true Christ within, the "I AM," the mystery of death, spirits, and faith. He exposed these truths at every crossroad he could find, but the people failed to look at the truer source for this gnosis. Paul even elaborated that, he did not receive the mysteries from any human. It was Christ that revealed them unto him, the divine Son. It was his hope that others would realize this is how all truth is revealed. But most just took his comments as referring to himself and that these words did not belong to each of us.

How was Paul going to tell the people of his day that each would be revealed the mysteries of the Kingdom in their own way? They would have surely laughed this off as many still do today.

Once again we are coming to an end of an age, and great changes will begin to take place. Religion as we know it today will be replaced by another awareness in the next millennium. There has been a tremendous growth within millions who are now becoming aware of the internal truths. However this is only a small piece of the pie. The next millennium will show great paradigm shifts as well as higher consciousness shifts where the awareness of the Divine Son will become manifest. Those that fail to learn the higher truths will be taken away from this realm and will have to enter another, because Earth is going to become a training ground for the higher evolved individual.

ERRONEOUS TEACHING NOW UNVEILED!

I want to take a closer look at what occurred in the last 2000 years that has created the erroneous teaching we find plastered all over peoples' ideologies. One of the great influences to come out of the 1st and 2nd centuries is that people were searching high and low for a Second Coming of the Messiah. Remember as I stated earlier most of the Israelite persuasion never really believed the Messiah ever came, because Israel was still dominated by a Gentile empire and no KING had been set up to rule Israel again. As the years went forward it must have been a very confusing time. Not only did they not receive the Messiah to protect Israel, but Israel itself was completely destroyed by the Roman Empire around 68-70AD.

What could have possibly gone wrong? Where was the Messiah? Why was Israel destroyed? Many, as you can quite well imagine, probably had the greatest test of faith, and that would have been, "Is there really a GOD?" Most of Israel scattered into the mountains seeking personal safety. Their Great Tribulation had occurred just as predicted. The prophecies were all too real for these people. Their end had surely come in their minds. Many were slain; others like the sect of Jews at Masada committed suicide before the attack of Romans could occur. For a people who were anxiously awaiting their Messiah to give them back their homeland and place a king to rule over them, they were instead greeted with chaos and turmoil.

You would have to place yourself within the hell that these people suffered, believing in faith things would be much different. You would have to ask yourself, what would you do if everything you believed in came to nothing almost overnight? Not only was a religious perspective nearly crushed in millions of people's minds, but also an entire religious paradigm had to be created because the old one had failed. Very few came out of the first three centuries holding onto the mysteries that were taught by Jesus and some of the Apostles. Sad to say, most could not comprehend what was being taught. They kept following the letter, which kills, and forsook the spirit that would have given life. These people's foundations of faith were crushed because what they believed in was only the milk of the word not the meat. I repeat as Paul stated, that the "*reading of the Old Testament scriptures will never take away the veil which covers the Divine Son.*" Of course during Paul's day the New Testament did not exist yet. So I will go on to say that reading the Bible in its letter, taking it literally will never take away the veil that blinds everyone to the truth, which lies within the walls of our hearts.

There were a few Gnostics that came out of the first century that held onto the sacred spirit of the word. They understood the metaphor in scripture. Groups such as the Essenes, which predated Jesus going back thousands of years kept the mysteries alive. They realized that the Messiah was within the person. They understood that the great King the Divine Son reigned from within our hearts. They comprehended that neither Israel nor any other aspect of planet earth was the Kingdom. The Disciples asked Jesus before he ascended, Would God restore Israel as the Kingdom? At this point in time the early Apostles did not comprehend the gnosis of mystery either. That is why Jesus said, "The Kingdom of God is within you...it comes not by observation..." The Kingdom of God is not a physical ruling empire, it is a spiritual realm. And flesh and blood cannot partake in this kingdom. What good would it do for the Father to bring the kingdom upon a material earth when humans could not take part in it? They couldn't even see it based on the vibration rate of our material biological bodies. However when one understands the mysteries, one can realize that Earth will begin to change in its paradigm view. A new consciousness will unveil itself and many will be able to ascertain the secrets of the Kingdom of God while still being human.

IF YOU CANNOT GRASP THE MYSTICAL FRAGMENT OF ANALOGY BEYOND THE WORD OR WRITTEN LETTER, THEN YOU ARE DOOMED FOR DISAPPOINTMENT.

It was dangerous for the early church to interpret the scriptures literally. *Many today as we enter the next millennium are going to be disappointed when their prophetic views are not fulfilled. And they will also begin to wonder is there a god, and have we been deceived? Some in the Christian world as well as other beliefs are so set on their ideas that they actually want destruction to take place so that they can feel right.* And this is what the Gnostics understood. However from within the Roman Empire came a Church that would continue to grow to nearly one-billion as it is today. Three major groups of thought came out of the confusion of the 1st century. The Jews, Christians and Gnostics! Only one would survive as a power. When the people saw what had occurred within their cherished beliefs many became agnostic, and were looking for support elsewhere that would help them deal with the confusion and turmoil. Out of the Church that was set up as a result of Jesus' teachings came the Gnostics and the Agnostics. The first group realized that all truth came from within. The second group doubted everything and sought for another viable avenue that would enable them to rectify their own personal confusion.

319

The truth that Jesus brought with him, that the Christ is the Divine Son of each of Our Father, and that all truth would come through Christ, turned into a new gospel about the man Jesus and very little about what he taught. For the New Church decided that to quell the divisions and controversies and confusions, they needed to make Jesus the Messiah. And began teaching he is the Christ, the One and Only! This created the virgin birth, which espoused the theory that the Father impregnated Mary with his own divine seed, creating a special child that would in fact be God's only Son. The Church out of Rome made Icons out of Jesus and Mary so the people would see with their own eyes, a Messiah, a protector.

THE CHURCH DECLARED WAR AGAINST THE GNOSTICS!

The Church created a religion for man, but the Gnostics remained faithful in the belief that religion was for God and that we were all a part of the Divine light. The Church was angered by this philosophy because they would lose control of the people if they accepted this doctrine. It was then that the Church declared war on the Gnostics. And by the 4th Century Constantine the Great established a council meeting that would once and for all lay the foundation and set the rules for all of Christianity. Most of the Gnostics were murdered, and those that fled with their lives had to go underground for many centuries. The Christian Church under the auspices of Constantine set up what we today call Christianity. Later other councils would occur and new teachings and doctrines would be added or taken away as the church saw fit.

Then when Justinian the Great, of the Eastern Roman Empire came on the scene around the 6th century he lowered the mystical tradition another notch. This would continue all the way until the reformation by Martin Luther, which began the first great breakaway from the Mother Church starting a Protest movement called the Protestants, called by the name Lutherans. Yet they still held on to the letter of the law and not the spirit. Then other movements such as the Baptists,

Methodists, Seventh day Adventists etc... began to splinter away creating their factions, yet all of them denied the mysteries.

Finally King James came on the scene around the 16th &17th century protecting the Church of England and its ideology and bringing in once and for all the doctrines that were to be taught as the so-called true source of religion. Those few groups that tried to fight against James' authority were also murdered and removed. Just prior to this time men such as John Calvin began a movement against the king and the overpowering Church of England and created what was called the Geneva Bible. It revealed that certain people were not about to be followers of the King. They believed he was making changes in the word to suit his power. James, of course, outlawed the Geneva Bible. Anyone found reading it was severely punished. Also Tynsdale, the author of the Living Bible, interpreted the words more literally in a more up to date language, but again the mysteries were hidden.

Gnostics appeared throughout the ages in smaller less known groups such as the Bogomils and Waldensians and some of the Paulicians. But most were still branded heretics and constantly had to flee for their lives as the now two main powers, Catholic and Protestant, dominated by the Church of England, demanded obedience to their ideas.

What was first brought by Jesus, teaching us to follow the inner Father, was turned into following the outer man. And today Christianity has become a worship of men and women, such as the man Jesus and his Mother Mary, and not a worship of the true divine Son and our Father. The problem for some of these historical revisionists is that certain scriptures in the manuscripts, scrolls and documents that came down through the ages had apparent discrepancies with the new thought paradigm. This of itself was a great concern for Constantine. It wasn't that Constantine was an avid and faithful follower of Christianity or the Christ principle, because he was not. He was a follower of ancient mystical practices before the time of Jesus, later to be called pagan by the Catholic Church. Constantine was a ruler and with any ruler he wanted power over the people. But this Christ principle was really bugging him. He witnessed people by the masses turning to this idea all the way into the 4th century. As the old story goes, if you can't fight them, then you might as well join them. And that is what Constantine did. He so-called converted over to Christianity, not so much as one who became a believer, but one who could control this new uprising and gain fame and power.

COUNCIL OF NICEA SET UP IN 325AD CREATED NEW DOGMA FOR CHRISTIANITY.

So the Council of Nicea was formed by the order of Constantine in 325AD establishing a religious council that would begin the decline of knowledge of the true mysteries. Constantine was more of an observer than an actual participant. He really didn't care what they concluded between the Bishops and the Priests, his only concern was that something would be established. And he could then enforce those decrees by his power, winning both the supports of his followers in Eastern Rome as well as Western Rome. Thus a Roman Emperor of the East was able to set himself up over both State and religion. He was quite content with the doctrinal decisions that were made this day 325AD.

However the problem still arose that there were scriptures that seemed to espouse the Gnostic logic rather than the new Church doctrine. Therefore changes were made again within the scriptures itself, through much editing, and a snip here and a cut there. A book added there and a book deleted here. Thus a new book arose that combined many manuscripts and scrolls thereby making what we have today called the Bible, the literal meaning: a Book of Books! What began as an inner truth manifesting from deep within each of us as supplied by our Father, turned into a worship of a written letter that many deem sacred and impenetrable. It never really occurs to most people that the Bible is a mixture of many writings that have been edited from different languages, ideas and thoughts. People have asked me if I believe the great God could inspire this book to be put together exactly the way it was supposed to be. And to disbelieve this book shows lacking in Divine faith? I say, of course, the great divine Father could have done it. That is not even an issue, but there was no reason to do it. It was already declared in mystical form by Jeremiah and later by Jesus. That it would no longer be written in stone, the metaphor meaning no longer written in material form. It would be written within you the individual. So of course, the Father could do that, but that is not how Gnosis is gained. It comes from within not from without. It comes by experience not through reading.

IF YOU ARE NOT BEING ENLIGHTENED TO THIS ALREADY, MY WORDS WILL MEAN NOTHING AND YOU WILL REJECT THEM.

There is nothing in this book I can help you comprehend that is not already within you. The Bible can be a great help to uncover the hidden gnosis, but it can't give it to you unless you have the keys to break its code. If you do not have those keys then you will become like everyone in the past, your faith will fail you and you will become discouraged. This is what Jesus was trying to teach. We are to have faith in Christ within, where nothing can penetrate no matter what occurs. If your faith is on hay and stubble, meaning materialistic things, wherewith the Bible would be included, then your faith will collapse under the weight of an attack. The floodwaters would surely crush the material building that you have laid for your foundation. If your faith is built upon materialistic things, even if it's the Bible, then when the first flood comes that does not correspond with your interpretation, you will lose everything. If your faith is built upon an internal awareness that you know to be true, not that you believe is true, then there is nothing in heaven or on earth that could destroy that faith. It becomes a fortified wall impenetrable by any offences that may come your way.

It was exactly this reason why the truth that Jesus brought was undercut by a new paradigm of thought. Because people could not comprehend the mystery from within, and the only way to gain anything else was to look to the external. And this is exactly what I want to address. How scriptures lost their meaning because they were being mistranslated by using external thought paradigms instead of internal thought processes. When the metaphor in scripture was eliminated so was the intent.

THERE SEEMS TO BE A DICHOTOMY HERE.

There were certain aspects in the letters to the Church at Thessalonica that make one believe that the mysteries I have so diligently laid out for you are invalidated, such as the so-called rapture that many believe in today. These verses indicate a rising up in the clouds to meet the Lord upon his return. There seems to be a dichotomy here that reflects a contradiction of Christ coming to the earth to meet his people, versus the one that indicates we are to meet Christ in the heavens. So which one is it? Are we supposed to meet the Lord on Earth or in heaven? Some might say, well that is easy; we will first meet the Lord in Heaven and then come back to the Earth! Is that the answer here?

There are also scriptures that say that those who have died in Christ will remain in their graves until the blowing of a trumpet, signifying the calling out of their graves as the resurrection. It states the dead will rise and meet the Lord. First I want to reiterate, that which is dead and buried is only the vessel, the human carcass. So what is it that rises from the ground and meets the Lord? If one were to take this literally then I would wonder what happens if someone was cremated and their ashes scattered everywhere? What grave is this person going to rise from? Too often we interpret things literally but we don't want to follow through with our own literal interpretation. Paul states in I Corinthians 15 that when one resurrects they will be given new bodies, a spiritual body. If this be the case, then what need is there for your human form or body? Notice that in Ecclesiastes it addresses the subject of death.

Ecclesiastes 12:6-7 "Or ever the *silver cord* be loosed, or the golden bowl be broken, or the pitcher be broken at the fountain, or the wheel broken at the cistern, then shall the dust return unto the earth, and the spirit shall return unto God who gave it."

This is very precise and clear language. It is speaking of what occurs when one dies. It states whenever the silver cord be broken. Those who have become aware of the mysteries know about the silver cord that connects our projected soul spirit to the "I AM" presence of our Father. Some have witnessed this cord through OBE. When a person dies, the only thing that really dies is the biological garment we have been wearing. Notice the term above calls it dust. The real US, the spirit Projected soul goes back to where it came from, the dimension that is congruent for our new body and awareness. For as the Elohim said, "For dust thou art and dust shalt thou be again." They were speaking of only the biological body, not the spirit within!

That which operates this body, the spirit of man, goes back to where it came from, to the realm of the spirit. Notice in the previous verse how it also states whenever the wheel be broken at the cistern. It was understood by the ancients that what we call cycles today they called the wheel. It was the same principle and means the same thing. We are in the cycles or the wheel of life. When you die in the flesh, that wheel is broken at the cistern because you leave this presence and return to the spirit until you have to return to the cycles. But until you return, your wheel of life is temporarily broken.

Biological beings come into the cycles of the wheel through the birth and death process. And one thing that is immutable and undeniable is that humans don't just exist, they are born. It is a metamorphosis if you wish? It is not spiritually proper to bring a vessel back to life that has been dissolved into the earth just to send the spirit of your projection back into that same vessel. There were examples of physical resurrections in the early Church, of people that were brought out of their graves and lived again, but these were only examples of teaching physically minded people spiritual mystical truths.

Those that were brought back to life were never dead long enough for their bodies to become dissolved or extinct. They were all recent deaths. Even the scriptures of the dead rising from their graves when Jesus was crucified showed that these were people who had recently died. And they came back to rejoin their families and speak of the wonderful occurrence. It was to teach of a spiritual resurrection of one coming back from the dead, which I will explain very shortly. You never read about people that were 500 years old walking around the streets of Jerusalem after these resurrections. These were people that were well known by their community.

PHYSICAL RESURRECTION WAS SIMPLY A HEALING!

What occurred here was a healing from illness, not a resurrection, as one might perceive. There are people even today that have been diagnosed as clinically dead who have returned to the living. Even Jesus was not dead long enough for his body to have decayed; it was only about 3 days. When Jesus raised Lazarus from the dead it was only about four days, where the Bible stated his body began to stink. Again not long enough for the body to become entirely extinct. Even when the Disciples saw Jesus after the resurrection he still had the wounds and tears in his skin as he had during the torment. All of these things were to prove a mystery. Jesus didn't need that body after it had died. He was only using it to prove a very important aspect to the mystery of death and the resurrection. Jesus was already masking a spiritual garment that he could change and appear and disappear in front of people. The physical body could not do that without knowing the mystical relation of changing vibrations!

BEING SAVED, BEING HEALED, ONE IN THE SAME!

Some may ask, do I believe God could resurrect a person after their body has become extinct? Of course I do, and so could you if you knew how to tap into the power internally. However, there is no logical reason to disturb this law until the time is right. When the Bible tells of the physical resurrection from the graves as mentioned above it is referring to a healing of the flesh. The word for "saved" comes from the Greek word, "SOZO." It means to heal one from sickness, to deliver and protect, to make one whole again. When early Christians were healed from illness, this is the word that was used. Yet it is the same exact word that many Christians today use as their reference to being "saved from eternal damnation."

The commonality of this word used in both sequences actually refers to one being physically healed and proved that one needed to be spiritually healed. Thereby using the same word to describe two apparently different things. You never read anywhere in your Bible that Jesus raised someone from the dead who was centuries old. There was no reason to. He obeyed the law of karma! Most people were reincarnating from the past anyway. The physical resurrection of one who died within a recent set of perimeters was designed to teach a healing that needed to be understood spiritually. It was another mystical reference to our internal selves.

Jesus never raised a prophet from ancient times to be a witness to the people. The only prophet that was ever mentioned that returned during the time of Jesus was Elijah, who was John the Baptist, the BORN son of Elizabeth and Zachariah.

As an interesting tidbit about Elijah's death, it was never really verified in the Bible when he died. He was actually transported away so the people would give their allegiance to Elisha the second in command. It was described as a whirlwind, which transported Elijah into the clouds. I guess the people in those days would have described a UFO in this same manner.

Something similar happened to Enoch in the Old Testament. Hebrews 11:15 states, "By Faith Enoch was translated that he should not see death." Enoch actually left his body in an OBE and never returned, thereby he never saw a physical death in that lifetime. This is most definitely what Jesus was referring to when he alluded to not having to see death. When one was ready they could just leave the body from a waking consciousness without the body ever dying. Of course, after you exit the body it would surely cease to exist. You would never have to experience death or the sensation of death while inhabiting the body.

SAUL LOCKED HORNS WITH SAMUEL AFTER HE DIED!

Samuel is another case that produces Biblical evidence of an immediate afterlife. Saul the King of Israel had become paranoid and disillusioned. He started to rebel against the Elohim. He began experiencing severe emotional problems and needed advice on what to do. He knew Samuel was one of the prophets chosen by the Elohim, but he had already died.

It was Saul that made a proclamation that anyone practicing the art of divining that dealt with familiar spirits was to be put to death. However Saul had a paradox. He needed this service to answer questions that no one else could answer. The only one he knew to call on was Samuel, because it was Samuel who told Saul what would befall him for his disobedience to the Elohim. He was told that he was going to lose his Kingdom. But to be able to speak with Samuel he would need to go to one that had the ability to talk to the spirits who had passed onto the other side.

Saul decided to disguise himself and came to the woman of Endor who had the ability to contact the dead. When Saul approached this woman to ask for assistance, she was oblivious of the fact that she was speaking to the great King of Israel, the very one who declared death to anyone that practiced these arts. Had she known who Saul was, she would have never assisted him. But Saul was frightened and needed help, so he disguised himself. Here is what occurred:

I Samuel 28:11-20 "Then said the woman, who is it that you want me to bring unto you? And Saul said, bring me up Samuel! And when the woman saw Samuel she cried with a loud voice; and the woman spoke to Saul saying, why have you deceived me, for you are SAUL? And the King said unto her, be not afraid; tell me what you saw? And the woman said unto Saul, I saw GODS ascending out of the earth. And Saul wondered what did Samuel look like? And she said an Old man...and he is covered with a mantle. And Saul knew it was Samuel... And Samuel said to Saul, "Why has thou disquieted me to bring me up?"

If the prophet Samuel had been dead as most perceive death, then how was he summoned to appear after he died? Again these were hidden mysteries that the Elohim did not want us to know. In those days the people were not evolved enough to handle these mysteries. It would be like me going back in time to ancient Israel and describing our technology to them. It would appear to them as evil spirits and they would probably desire to put me to death. There are those in the Christian world, because of their lack of Gnosis, who say Saul was conversing with a demon and not really Samuel.

This is absolutely ludicrous! If Samuel was a demon what purpose would he have in supporting God? Samuel told Saul that God's word is firm and he will not change. And he stated he had already warned him about these things and there was nothing Samuel could do to change it. Samuel even after death was entirely obedient to the will of the Elohim. So much so that it appears his belief system followed him to the other side where he was working with the gods/Elohim. The woman of Endor saw Samuel amongst all the Gods who were coming to and from the earth.

When you understand the Biblical usage for the resurrection, then the mysteries will begin to unfold from within you. The resurrection is not about the flesh and blood coming back to life. It is your awareness of your true identity, your true salvation and healing.

WE HAVE A PHYSICAL AND A SPIRITUAL GENETIC DNA CODE!

Our vessels have within them the soul-projected spirit of each one's "I AM" presence, a genetic code of physical matter relating to the life forms on this plane of awareness. It was brought into existence by the male spermatozoa and the female egg of your biological parents. Once this vessel perishes then the genetic carryover will follow through the offspring of this same biological pattern. The real you after death leaves the decaying corpse to enter another reality, until it is time for you to advance or return to another biological family. You will enter another genetically coded vessel and the new vessel will be given to new progenitors that will become your material biological parents.

Just as we are genetically connected in the physical form through our DNA, we also have spiritual DNA from our true parents of the universe. Our spiritual Father/Mother Divine. We are their children!

Paul teaches this in I Corinthians 15:44 that each of us has two bodies: the physical body and the spiritual body. He also states that the flesh and blood cannot inherit the kingdom. It is because we must have the genetic equivalent of our spiritual parents to inherit what rightfully belongs to us. The physical biological body only has the genes from the Elohim and it can inherit nothing but death. Only the spiritual DNA has eternal life abiding within it. So why would the Father raise physical beings from the grave when you must have a spiritual DNA to inherit the kingdom?

Phillippians 3:21 "Who shall change our vile body, that it may be fashioned like unto his (Christ) glorious body?"

I John 3:2 "Beloved, Now are we already the sons of God, and it does not yet appear what we shall be, but we know when we shall appear we shall be like him. (Christ)"

John is speaking of the mystical revelation of our Christ, the divine Son from within. When he is revealed within us then we will recognize what has always been there, our true divine DNA. Paul shows that our vile corruptible bodies had to change (DIE) to put on the new glorious body like Christ.

Romans 8:18 "For I reckon that the sufferings of this present time are not worthy to be compared to the glory which shall be revealed IN US!"

THE GLORY IS ALREADY WITHIN US!

Jesus asked his Father in prayer to give him back the glory he had before the world was. We must now all realize that we all have that same glory in us. The glory shall be revealed IN US, it is not given to us. IT is already in us but needs to be revealed.

The body that was given for our inheritance was already prepared for our taking. Our flesh and blood bodies cannot inherit that which does not belong to them. Only our true divine spiritual self will inherit what is already rightfully ours. We are already Sons of God meaning the Father, and children of the Most High. Revelation 17:8 asks how many will wonder whose names were written in the book of life from before the foundation of this world? And Ephesians 1:4 declares that we were chosen in Christ from before the foundation of this world. My question is this, how can you have been written in the book of life and chosen from before the foundation of this world if you had not yet existed? The answer is simple and not complicated at all. YOU COULDN'T HAVE!

Can it be any clearer? We are the Royal children of a powerful consciousness and have a cosmic connection with the great divine, which we call the Father/Mother divine. Peter even states in his letter that we who are the initiated, meaning those that have come to understand this, are now the Royal Priesthood. As I described earlier, back in ancient Israel there arose a Priesthood designed by the shadow Lords, to become a copy of the true divine Priesthood. Aaron the brother to Moses was chosen as head over this Priesthood. Aaron and his children were the only ones who could walk into the Holy of Holies in the physical temple.

Later the Book of Hebrews taught how the Christ through Jesus became the High Priest after the order of Melchizedek. The name Melchizedek means Son of righteousness. The Dead Sea Scrolls relate to them as the Sons of Zadok or the Sons of Righteousness. The Essenes carried this gnosis with them from the past. They spoke often of the Sons of Zadok in the Dead Sea Scrolls. When we unite with the divine Son then that same Christ that was in Jesus is also in us. We then become once again the High Priesthood after an order that goes back before the foundations of this world. An order called the Sons of Majesty in Righteousness. Some have called it the Great White Brotherhood, not referring to race, but to light versus darkness. The veil of our flesh separates us from accessing the Holy of Holies within us, just as the shadow portrayed to Israel that only the Levitical Priesthood could enter this realm. The veil also separated that part of the inner temple from the outer temple. Are you starting to understand the comparison now? If we are the temples of God and there is an outer and an inner temple, then it becomes clear why Jesus said the Kingdom would come from within you. We access the inner temple of the Holy of Holies by going within. It is metaphoric language for comprehending that our true spirit resides within the body of flesh or entering within this veil. When Jesus died on the cross, the scriptures taught that the veil that separated the inner temple from the outer temple in Jerusalem was actually torn in two. The veil was rent! But there was a much greater divine purpose for this. It showed that the veil that separates us from our divinity had also rent in twain. All of us were given access to the inner temple, but so very few walked that inner road. And till this day most are still separated by the veil, because they do not realize it has been removed.

HEIRS OF GLORY!

Once we qualify to regain the inheritance that is prepared for each of us we will then rejoin the Father, which is in all of us. And then all will be in the Father, and the Father will be all in all. We are now co-heirs with Christ the divine Son and heirs of the very realm of the FATHER, the eternal one.

I Peter 1:4 "...to an inheritance, and undefiled, that fades not away, reserved in heaven for you!"

II Peter 1:4 "Whereby are given unto us exceeding great and precious promises; that by these, you might be partakers of the divine nature, having escaped the corruption that is in this world through lust."

Do you recognize how Peter is describing our treasures in heaven in the first verse? Our inheritance is the result and byproduct of a treasure that is building and evolving around an incorruptible realm reserved for each of us. Peter then goes on to reveal that it is our destiny to partake of the divine nature, which in Greek means the very Godhead. We will once again gain entrance to the Royal family of our inheritance by returning home which we left a very long time ago.

WHO WAS THIS MAN CALLED PAUL?

I want to center your attention now on the Apostle Paul to learn more about the man and what he stood for. Paul was a learned and educated man who sat with the upper echelon of the Pharisees. He was taught personally by one of the most respected men of his day, a man named Gamaliel. Paul wasn't some novice who just walked off the street so-to-speak. He knew his business and I assure you he knew and understood Old Testament law probably better than anyone alive today! He was a zealot and extremely devout in his beliefs. Even to the point where he personally saw to it that detractors of his beliefs were put to death, as in the case of Stephen, one of the first deacons in the New Testament Church. Some today deny this ever occurred. All I can say is that I am relaying what was written to bring out a point.

When it came to Saul, whose name was later changed to Paul, he played no games when it came to religious doctrine and ideology. But something very traumatic occurred in Paul's life that made him change many of his beliefs. Paul entered the world of the metaphysical, which was once denounced as being evil by the Elohim, and later called pagan by the Church. Paul began walking the road into spiritualism. He began to have trances and OBEs that took him to the spirit world where he could communicate with beings; namely Jesus.

Paul was a young man when he was struck down with blindness as he entered the world of the paranormal. This enabled Paul to understand the great gnosis from within. If Paul were alive today to express how he learned the inner truths of the Father he would be laughed out of mainstream Christianity and labeled demonic.

Through these personal experiences Paul was able to see how to use the two-edged sword. He learned how to address nearly every spiritual subject in such a way that both the unenlightened and the enlightened could ascertain whatever they needed from it. He could fuse the two ideas together so that those that were babes in Christ could only grasp the letter. But those that were spiritually minded could grasp the inner wisdom. The churches in the centuries that followed Paul were also at a loss to understand the hidden wisdom within the written letter.

Paul was like a modern day Nostradamus. He could bring two ideas and blend them together through various writings and languages. And keep the true meaning away from the wrong people, while at the same time divulging the truth to the learned individual that had an eye to see and an ear to hear!

He understood many of the mysteries as much as he could at his level of evolvement or spiritual development. That is why he could say, "Foolish ones, know you not that whatsoever is to live must first die." He understood that for one to be cognizant of their inner true reality through the spirit the veil of maya and illusion must be removed.

He also understood the mystery of sleep and death. He, unlike what many understand, was able to speak to the living but address them as if they were dead. Why is this, because the mystery of life and death were his approach to this wonderful gnosis.

Ephesians 5:14 "Awake you who sleep, Arise from the dead, and Christ will give you light."

TO BE ASLEEP IS TO BE DEAD!

Time after time the New Testament authors would use the terminology of sleep and death as meaning the same thing. And this is exactly how Paul used this in his letters to the churches. To be asleep was only meant to describe our condition while living under the illusion of the veil. It was this same illusion of maya that brought about our death from paradise, locking us into the cycles of the shadow world. As the scripture above plainly reveals, Paul was speaking to the living when he said they were dead. Jesus also used this same terminology when he taught. While he was seeking followers, one man had a controversy. He told Jesus his Father had just died and he needed to bury him. Jesus said, "Let the dead bury the dead." This was a very strange statement for the people of his day. How could Jesus be so uncaring? Jesus was teaching that until the inner light is turned on, we are all dead, and are no different than those who physically die.

AN AMAZING EVENT REVEALS THE FIRE BAPTISM AND THE RESURRECTION!

The term "to be asleep" was in direct reference to our ignorance of the divine truths and our awareness of who we really and truly are. In John Chapter 11 an event occurred that began to reveal these truths. Jesus was called to aid a friend named Lazarus. Jesus was told that Lazarus was very ill and had died. When he heard this report from a distant city, he said, "Our friend Lazarus sleeps, but I go that I may wake him." This was a very unusual response to the news that a friend had passed on. However as this story unfolded, those that had the inner awareness would ascertain the secret behind Jesus own words.

There are two words that come from the Greek interpretation of the word sleep as used in the New Testament. The first word is "exupnizo." It implies to be awakened from a sleep. And this was the word Jesus used when he said he would awaken his friend Lazarus who had actually died.

The disciples were quite confused when he used the term "sleep" for Lazarus' death. They felt that Jesus literally meant Lazarus was sleeping, as one would do if they went to bed. Jesus had to reiterate his statement, and this time he said, "Lazarus is dead."

Why did Jesus use the term sleep, if Lazarus was really dead? Obviously the disciples would not understand what Jesus was teaching from a literal point of view. Because in their language Jesus said Lazarus was sleeping, and then turned around and said he was dead. Jesus was using another instance to teach a mystery embedded within a literal meaning! When he described Lazarus as being deceased he used the same phrase that would continue throughout the New Testament, that death is sleep when understood mystically. Lazarus was truly dead by all Biblical accounts, but Jesus used this event to unveil a powerful mystery.

The true meaning of the Baptism and resurrection was about to be revealed, yet throughout the last two millenium most have never comprehended this truth. Lazarus' death was the revelation of the Baptism by fire.

Baptism was taught by Jesus to instruct on the mystical revelation of the death of the OLD MAN. When one is illuminated they can rise from this death a NEW MAN. When we are mystically asleep we are living as the OLD MAN buried within the veil of forgetfulness. When one is being raised from this death, which was represented by the ritual of coming out of the water, they are to become enlightened of their pre-mortal past and therefore arise from death. This is why Thomas made the strange comment in John 11:16 that he wanted to die with Lazarus.

Why would Thomas utter such words? Why would he want to die with Lazarus? Some of the disciples were beginning to comprehend that Jesus was teaching another mystery. They began to comprehend what was meant when Jesus spoke of the Baptism by fire. They had already been instructed about the water baptism, but Jesus spoke of a greater Baptism, one that John the Baptist never introduced. Lazarus was not only being awakened from the dead, he was being initiated by the fire baptism. He was becoming united with the divine Son. Jesus was teaching the disciples that for us to return to our home in the spiritual paradise we had to be awakened from our death of illusion. The churches never understood this reality.

WILL HE RISE THE LAST DAY?

When Jesus finally entered the town where Lazarus had already been placed into the tomb, Jesus came to Martha, a sister of Lazarus, and said, "Your brother will rise again." Martha's response was not shocking considering the beliefs of the day. She said, "I know he will rise the last day." This is the thinking that continues among Bible believing Christians. Many are waiting a time that the Old Testament revealed through the Holy Day that ended the feast of Tabernacles. They believe there will be one set time that the Bible speaks of called the resurrection. This is what Martha believed in and this is what she was telling Jesus.

What they did not understand, nor do many today understand, is that the resurrection was not supposed to be a physical return unto this life within the same body. Those of that generation and through all the generations to follow have perceived only the literal meaning of this gnosis. They have failed to understand this was a representation of our awakening from spiritual sleep, not physical death. Martha did understand the physical aspect of the letter of the law, but now Jesus was about to teach the spiritual meaning to the ancient wisdom.

"I AM" THE RESURRECTION AND THE LIFE!

Jesus had selected this event to reveal a new mystery that if understood would create a dynamic paradigm shift in materialistic thinking people. The Mystery was simply this, "I AM the resurrection and the life, whosoever believes in me shall never die."

He was revealing that the last great day of the Feast of Tabernacles was to teach that one is raised from the maya of illusion back unto their true divine heritage of their I AM presence and the divine Son within. The last great day is when you are awakened, and this is not at some futuristic time period that all will be awakened at the same time. No not at all! That is why it states in 1st Corinthians 15 "That every man in his own order..." Each resurrection or salvation of eternal awareness is given unto each individual upon their own personal growth and evolvement. Just as it states in this same chapter "the glory of the stars all differ from one another, so also is the resurrection." The resurrection will differ in everyone's individual case.

338

Lazarus was being initiated into this light by the mystical fire baptism while using his physical death to reveal this mystery. This is why Thomas decreed that he wanted to die with Lazarus. They understood that Lazarus was being initiated into a higher awareness of self-internal revelation. Lazarus was one if not the very first follower of Jesus to be awakened unto his eternal blueprint that was set before the foundation of the world. He also became aware of living outside the body while his physical body had perished. You can only imagine the stories he brought back with him when he discussed his near-death experience and going out of body.

When Lazarus died in the flesh he was still very much alive in the spirit. It was then that he could attest to the mysteries of going out of body. He became proof for the other disciples of what Jesus was trying to teach them. That you really don't die, you just change consciousness and wear another garment in another reality. He also became living proof to Martha that the last day Martha was seeking was being revealed within Lazarus at that very moment, "You shall never die." What Martha understood to be a literal interpretation of the Old scriptures, she now was made aware of the spiritual interpretation of the divine!

John and Mark appear to be the most enlightened of the original Apostles when it came to understanding the mysteries. It was later discovered that Mark had written a special book that described the mysteries that Jesus taught them. But in this book it was revealed that Jesus told Mark to only give these words unto them that were ready, and to write a second book that would be given to all. The Nag Hammadi library speaks of this book as well. Throughout the ages following the first century there have been no actual recovery of this entire book except for bits and pieces that are held in England. This book has come down through history to be known as the "Secret Gospel of Mark."

As stated before, Paul was also instructed through trances and going out of body. These are the same in the sense that both bring an internal awareness to the spirit plane, but they are separated by different elements of consciousness. A trance can be very similar to an OBE even to the point one might not be able to tell the difference. When Paul spoke of how he was being instructed, he wasn't sure whether it was by trance or out of body. Paul had many trances that the Bible speaks of. It appears those that tried to eliminate all the spiritualism out of the Bible couldn't get everything out.

PAUL WAS BEING PREPARED TO SET UP THE TRUE REVELATION OF FAITH!

Paul was being awakened to the mystical law of the resurrection from our death in which we enter the maya of illusion. He was being prepared to set up the spiritual revelation of true FAITH! I think it can now be better understood what Paul meant when he said, "Even when we are dead in trespasses, made us alive together with Christ, (by grace you are saved). And raised us up together in heavenly places in Christ Jesus." The death we died was in the metaphorical Garden of Eden, not the physical Garden of Eden, which was only the shadow of the true. This brought about a false sense to what we really are.

Paul then goes on to repeat this affirmation to the Church at Colossi. Colossians 4:1 "If you then are risen with Christ, then seek those things that are above, where Christ is sitting at the right hand of God."

Are you beginning to recognize some of the same terminology that was used when Paul wrote to the Church at Thessalonica about our rising up and meeting the Lord in the air? As you can plainly see this was only meant to be a metaphor to teach a spiritual awareness. Paul was speaking to human beings that were still in the veil when he stated, "If you are then risen with Christ..." What could he have meant? It is quite simple. To rise and meet the Lord means to be spiritually united from within your heart and mind and soul, not a physical resurrection, but a spiritual one. **Mystically we are already with Christ Jesus in heaven when we follow the same path he followed. So does this mean the resurrection in Thessalonians is just a metaphor? Of course it does, whether anything was added to it or not.**

The death of the physical body means absolutely nothing. It is the illusion that we live under that is the true death. The only reason the scriptures seem to indicate a physical rising from the grave is because it was a way to bring forth the mysteries in esoteric form, keeping the unenlightened away from this truth until they are ready to evolve. Some may feel this is cruel and unfair, but even Jesus taught in Mark Chapter 4 that the mysteries are only given to the initiated, not to those that are without.

Physical baptism of water, was revealed by John the Baptist as only a continuation of the shadow, that revealed partial truth to those that were beginning their initiation. But to enter the realm of the true baptism you must be baptized by fire. And that takes internal gnosis. You must be prepared. When Jesus used the Lazarus story to illuminate the truth on the mystery of the fire baptism as well as the resurrection, it was to reveal each one's personal source to their own Godly divinity.

ERROR IN PERCEPTION OF THE RAPTURE OR RESURRECTION!

I have attempted to lay a foundation for this final mystery called the mystery of faith. Paul stated that if Jesus did not rise from his grave then we would all be dead in our sins and have no future hope. He went on to say our faith would then be in vain. I want to conclude this mystery by addressing one of the most difficult aspects to perceive by modern day Christians. This is the subject of either the rapture or the resurrection, depending on your particular faith! I am not writing this book to denounce your life long faith. I am expounding on the glory, which can become your faith, once you understand.

Faith must be built upon truth, not error or preconceived notions. We must understand that faith is not a concept, where one believes this or that thing. Faith is another of the mystical teachings of the divine Son. Faith is a cosmic LAW!

FAITH CAN BE CUT OFF LIKE AN ELECTRICAL CORD!

There is a formula that anyone can use to access the fruit of true faith. You can, as Jesus did, do great miracles. Within the law of faith there is a spiritual genetic structured code that must be adhered too, or else it will come to nothing and fail. Within faith there is a cut off point or a barrier of resistance that will disconnect the energy.

It is like plugging in an electrical appliance. If you cut the cord, the appliance would then cease to function. Faith is a law of electrical, or better-stated, spiritual power. But as with electricity, you can cut off the power! Before I write about this in more detail I first want to address a few scriptures that will enlighten one about what I have been trying to reveal!

II Corinthians 4:6 "For God who commanded the light to shine out of darkness, hath shined in our hearts, to give the light of the knowledge of the glory in the face of Jesus Christ."

This light that shines within us is the light of the divine Son, and it shines in the darkness of the veil. That same light was also in Jesus from our Father of all glory.

II Corinthians 4:7 "But we have this treasure in earthen vessels..."

The treasure is each of our inheritance of the divine Son's awareness. The light shines within this body of flesh. This is our personal treasure in our earthen vessel. How can this be?

II Corinthians 4:10 "Always bearing about in the body the dying of the Lord Jesus, THAT THE LIFE ALSO OF JESUS MIGHT ALSO BE MANIFEST IN OUR BODY."

If we continue to follow these verses, Paul is describing that the same power that was in Jesus is also in each of us, and Jesus was not a one and only. The glory he had we have also. That which was revealed by his death and resurrection is also in our mortal vessel.

II Corinthians 4:11 "For we which live are always delivered unto death for Jesus sake, THAT THE LIFE ALSO OF JESUS MIGHT BE MADE MANIFEST WITHIN OUR MORTAL FLESH!"

The flesh, which we all have, is meaningless in this first principle. It is the power that is within us that remains the key to all eternity. The Life that was in Jesus was his Father through the divine Son, the Christ, thereby making Jesus the Christ. That very same life and attribute is within each of us. So when the scripture points out in verse 14 that the same power that raised Jesus from the dead reigns also within us, we then can understand that we have the same pattern as our beloved brother Jesus, and like him can do the same things.

Verse 16 then sums up this entire thesis by indicating our flesh is not what is at stake here, but the being or the spirit soul within the flesh that has this inheritance and power.

Verse 16 "For which cause we faint not, BUT THOUGH OUR OUTWARD MAN PERISH, YET THE INWARD MAN IS RENEWED DAY BY DAY...For we look not at the thing which is seen, but the thing which is unseen. For that which is seen is temporal, AND THAT WHICH ARE UNSEEN ARE ETERNAL."

If our vessel that contains or houses our soul spirit were to die, we will just exit this mortal and be clothed with true spiritual vitality. We will continue being renewed day by day, in spiritual vessel that comprehends the vibration rate of the new dimension we will enter after death. That which is seen is our physical bodies, that which is unseen and eternal is our projected soul spirit consciousness.

Then in chapter 5 of this same book Paul blows the lid completely off a physical resurrection. II Corinthians 5:1 "For we know that if our earthly house of this tabernacle were dissolved, we have a building of God, a house not made with hands, eternal in the heavens."

This is a parallel description given also in the book of Hebrews where it states that God dwells not in temples made with hands. And also where Paul decrees to the Corinthians that the spirit dwells within this mortal flesh. All these verses placed together reveal an eternal reality. A component that belongs to our God, which in fact dwells within our flesh. What Paul was describing in beautiful metaphor by the previous verse states unequivocally that when our earthly house, our flesh and blood dies and is dissolved, we still have a building of God, our true divine projected soul spirit that goes beyond this veil into the realm of the spirit Biblically called heaven or paradise. It enters a realm not made with hands, meaning our true bodies are not biological creations by the shadow Lords as our Physical bodies are. But are creations of the divine immortal Father/Mother in a realm of the spiritual.

II Corinthians 5:4 "For we that are in this Tabernacle do groan, being burdened, not for that we should be unclothed, but clothed upon, that mortality might be swallowed up by life."

Oh, if only the children of the light would awaken from their death of sleep and comprehend the beauty of the words from within. We are beings living in vessels. The flesh and blood bodies are nothing more than a vehicle of awareness for the conscious illusion of our four lower bodies. We have entered this realm in hopes of learning lessons that will eventually restore us from death in illusion back unto eternal life by internal awareness.

344

ETERNAL LIFE WAS TRULY A FREE GIFT! SALVATION IS OUR AWARENESS! AND OUR REWARD IS OUR ILLUMINED EVOLVED GROWTH.

Reincarnation is our grace bestowed upon us to afford us more time to make these spiritual changes, and to accomplish what would otherwise be impossible.

OUR DIVINE GOAL IS TO ASCEND BACK TO THE FATHER!

As we advance to higher and higher levels it is the ultimate design that we unite with our Father and become one with him. This is known Biblically as the ascension. None of us know the time of this grand event, which will occur at different intervals with all mankind. Not even Jesus can know the exact time of each of our own ascension back to the heart flame of our great Father-Mother divine.

Why is it that all these Tele-evangelists continue to bombard the airwaves teaching of a second return of Jesus where the good will be saved and the evil will be destroyed? It seems that prophecies in many people's minds are given to prepare us all for this suspicious event. I could give you a myriad of reasons why they believe this. Much of the reasons I have already addressed in this book are due to misunderstanding the mysteries. But I don't think it is prudent to discuss this. If you need to know just turn on your television and find out for yourself.

But one must wonder why the whole religious world seems to believe we are at this fateful day. Jesus said no one can know the day or hour, only the Father knows. It is not according to one specific time-period. There is no time and space in the eternal heavens. If an individual took one hundred lifetimes to succeed while another took a thousand it would not matter in the spiritual plane of things. It would appear that both

345

accomplish this great feat at the exact same time from a spiritual perspective. But from our perspective there is no way we can know this time period.

If our Father set a time-table limiting humans to a prescribed set date while at the same time allowing most of the world to remain ignorant of this date and what is expected of them, then we are all in a lot of trouble. Those that fail are in trouble, and those that succeed are in trouble, because you will have to spend your eternity with this same God.

Prophecy was not given to usher in a date of the ascension or the resurrection. Prophecy is given to remind humanity that we are not alone and this materialistic world is only one small vehicle of awareness. It teaches that there is a multitude of greater awareness and consciousness that exists around and through our time. It shows that time travelers can enter the future to become aware of what has already taken place. It teaches us a myriad of Lessons. That our Father is greater than all we can see or understand in this limited potential. It also reveals that within the cycles are operational events that occur over and over again, and that there is a higher consciousness attempting to make us aware of these events. And no, it is not a loving Father destroying his evil children.

If people are aware of predicted events that occur within the cycles then they can prepare themselves for these changes. And if there are aspects to our character that are invalid, then these events can help us reorient ourselves to change in the right direction before it is too late. Also one aspect to the cycles is that prophecy can fail as spoken in the Old Testament. Nothing is ever absolute when dealing with the cycles, because changes can be made that can stop an event from occurring. Dimensions can change and our reality can shift. The problem with most so-called prophets in our day and age is that they are looking for a following, because they feel they have an inside with God and people should bow before them. Everyone has this ability but few know how to use it. You should never give allegiance to anyone who claims to know this or that about our future. Your future is what you make of it and you can change it. However a prophet's warning should never be ignored either. The problem is that too many of these so-called prophets seem to almost want these events to occur so they don't look like idiots. But that is a tragedy. These events do not have to occur and we shouldn't be hoping they would.

If prophecy is only given to a few enlightened ones as some claim then what good is prophecy? If people do not recognize these events then what good is prophecy? How can they change? And if you are already enlightened what purpose would there be for you to have this prophecy, except to warn others? Around and around the merry-go-round goes. Cycle after cycle, it just keeps occurring generation after generation. These ideas keep crossing our paths without any true enlightenment of what it is really all about. For millenium after millenium man keeps grasping for the wind to comprehend a spiritual truth. You can continue to hold on to these ideas in the hopes that they are correct. Or you can finally stop where you are and ask the simple question. Why do these disastrous events always occur and yet nothing ever seems to change? I can only give you one simple answer. The shadow lands are always in a state of decay. All matter in the universe is in a state of constant change. As we continue to remain within these cycles we will continue to enter these changes that for centuries have been viewed as a God punishing his people.

ARE COSMIC CHANGES AN ANGRY GOD TAKING OUT HIS VENGEANCE?

The truth is we need to move away from the cycles and return to the world of peace and love, not chaos and confusion. All prophetic events are recurring events that come about through the cycles. Earthquakes, volcanoes, earth shifts, Novas, Super Nova's, are all events that exist within a matter universe trying to reflect a perfect spiritual light. As a human being we all need to realize that we live in a very dangerous earth and universe.

347

We are but a speck of dust on a moving machine that carouses throughout the solar system without regard to what we are.

Even Daniel was given prophetic instructions about the forthcoming events that would end the age he lived in. Daniel's prophetic warnings all came to pass from his time period to the beginning of the age of Pisces, where all the prophecies were fulfilled.

Daniel was told to seal up the book so this gnosis would not be comprehended until the end of his age, which came to pass about 483 years later about the time when the temple of Jerusalem was finally destroyed in 69AD. Yet a few years after this event another man named John, the beloved of Jesus, spoke of almost identical prophetic events that were already fulfilled by the word of Daniel. It never seems to dawn on mankind that these events are in cycles, they keep reoccurring.

2000 years have now passed and we have seen event after event take place over these last two-millennia that reveal prophetic events constantly reoccurring. From earthquakes to volcanoes, floods to pestilences. These events continue to occur. Our loving Father is not punishing us. He wants us to awaken to come out of this cycle of hell.

Even Peter spoke of the events that Joel described where the sun turned to black and the moon turned blood red. This is an event that has occurred many times. A volcano can create this same effect, when the ash plumes into the air and blocks out the sun it will appear as if it were nighttime during the day. And the Moon would appear blood red because we would only see it through the ash. Peter stated that these prophetic events were fulfilled during his time 31AD. And yet John later circa 96AD described similar events from the Isle of Patmos. Do you see the pattern? These are not periods of proclaimed punishment by a great God. Neither are prophecies given to warn us of a punishment of a great God.

Our Father is a loving Father, not some trick artist trying to fool the masses into obeying him out of fear for their lives. Our misunderstandings are not our Father's fault, they are ours.

FALSE KINGDOMS ARE SET UP BECAUSE OF A LACK OF GNOSIS!

I believe if the Christian world is not careful they are going to be seduced into believing that a kingdom of God will reign on the planet earth for a thousand years. And it will begin about 2000AD. All because too many are looking to the Bible as a literal document and not a spiritual enlightenment tool. I am afraid people may be lured into worshipping a type of antichrist theology, which is the denying of the true Christ from within. And seek to worship one who will claim he is the Christ and is here to set up a physical one world Government order designed to force everyone to obey this ruler. Sadly, as before when people begin to realize their beliefs are shattering because they are only following the letter, there will be more chaos instead of enlightenment.

This is one of the very reasons I am writing this book and sharing my personal experiences with you, because I know that after the year 2000 there is going to be millions of disappointed people. People who have been relying on the written letter being deceived by men and women they thought were god fearing Christians. And I AM trying to help so the transformation and paradigm change is not too difficult.

Why do you think the Holy Roman Empire was a kingdom made up of Emperors and Popes? These were physical attempts to make it look like the kingdom of God was a humanistic kingdom and not spiritual. Later others also tried to prescribe to this same notion. If you continue to follow the literal letter of this book called the Bible you can rest assured that you will be easy pickings for a mighty con job that the world's governments and religions could bring together because of their faulty reasoning.

349

This entire deception that there would be a physical kingdom that Jesus would rule, only began to make real head roads during 18th century Europe. Even with the deception of Christianity it was unheard of to believe in a physical ruling kingdom of God. The closest this idea came to fruition was the church being the kingdom on earth. Today almost all professing Christian church leaders teach this erroneous concept, and I am afraid it will destroy many people and karma will be increased.

Again, Jesus is a spirit being who lives in another dimension. The Bible makes it so clear that flesh and blood cannot enter into the kingdom, nor can it see the kingdom. So why would the great Father come into the fleshly world from a spiritual divine Kingdom that is vibrating at an entirely different rate, to rule over flesh and blood humans who can't be in that kingdom in the first place? It makes absolutely no sense.

Matter and spirit are separated by vibrational rates. This entire thesis of God coming back to this earth and pouncing down on this wicked creation called man, just to show force of authority and power, comes directly from the spirit of good and evil. The Father's very nature, his make-up is absolute pure undefiled love. He does not judge his child, neither does Jesus. Jesus didn't tell us not to judge one another so that he and his Father could do all the judging. One is not to judge by the command of the great law of the infinite cosmos. We judge ourselves by the divine light of the Only Begotten Son. It doesn't matter whether you are awakened to this light or not, the law of cycles will take care of that lack and will continue to work. Each will still be accountable to every broken aspect of the law. This is the Judgement!

NATURAL LAWS ARE SET IN MOTION TO BE FOLLOWED!

We understand that there is a law called gravity. Just jump off a building and watch how fast you fall to the earth. If we were to die because we contravened this law and came crashing down to the ground, you can assure yourself that neither Father nor Jesus had anything to do with it. There wasn't a being sitting upon his throne saying, "Off with his head! He broke my law of gravity." No, to the contrary, our Father is saddened when we feel pain that we bring on ourself, because we are a part of this great divine. A loving parent can tell their child not to play in the street. But I assure you that if a car strikes that child and he or she is killed, the parent is not standing there condeming, "Well, I warned you kid. You broke my law, now you're dead." The parent would be saddened for their loss and heartsickened.

The great divine set in motion various laws of perfection and truth long before this earth came on the scene. These laws were designed to keep order and peace and perfect functionality. They were not designed to punish anyone! But the truth is, if these laws are broken then they will break you, you will reap what you sow. The Father desires not to judge anyone of his children. That is why in John 5:22 it states, "The Father judges no one, for he has committed all judgement unto the Son."

There are those that live in this world that would dearly love you to misunderstand these verses so you will obey them in fear of God's wrath. Many of these so-called leaders of the people claim they get their authority from Jesus, Buddha, Abraham, Matreiya, Mohammed etc... We must finally understand once and for all, no matter what takes place in our immediate future, and no matter what anyone tries to scare you into believing, the Father/Mother divine love all their children, because they are Love. It is because of this great consciousness love that they will not interfere in the laws of cycles, because they know the perfect creation that was designed will ultimately win out and bring the children out of the darkness. We are the Father's expansive creative character. We are the progeny of this great cosmic force. We are the Father in a microscopic sense. We are the lower design of the higher design. We are the workmanship of this great power. For this authority to have condemned anyone of us would be

351

tantamount to condemning himself. Yes, there is wickedness all around us. When women are raped and children are violated and molested, you can believe this is evil to the core through and through. But understand, nothing just happens. We bring all things upon ourselves by virtue of reaping what we sow. No one gets away with anything. This is what needs to be addressed. Not that there is an avenging angel ready to destroy, but that everything that is thought or done brings with it blessings or cursing. Make no mistake about this.

We are all as close to the Father/Mother divine as to repeat the very words, "I AM." Each of us has this higher counterpart working in our lives and watching over everything we do. Not as a judge, but as a very part of us! Even loved ones who have passed onto the other side are seen helping those that remain, as the law permits.

FAITH BECOMES REAL!

Faith actually becomes a working piece of machinery instead of an ideological concept. Faith becomes a formula, not wonderment. Faith becomes real! As James said, "Faith without works is dead..." Faith is an electrical energy that can be tapped into like plugging an appliance into the wall and turning it on. When you plug an appliance in the wall you are not sitting there hoping and believing it will turn on, you know it will.

The electrical power of faith is our belief and hope. Hebrews 11:1 states, "Faith is the substance of things hoped for and the evidence of things not seen." However, this power will disconnect if doubt or unbelief enters, it is automatic. You turn it on it will work, you disconnect it and it will fail. Faith is an operation of a law! Paul spoke of this often; it can't fail if it is applied using the correct formula. If one fails to realize their true divine origin then faith will become fleeting and subsequently pass away. You do not realize the power you are accessing is a power that comes from within you, as Jesus often times spoke, "Your faith has made you whole." It is possible to gain this power from another depending on your

352

faith in that person, but it will only drain the supply of the one giving, and eventually they will not have enough for themselves. Read the parable of the 10 virgins in Matthew 25!

Most have been instructed in the false concept of faith and they rely on everyone else including Jesus to fulfill their needs, instead of their Father. Out of mercy, Jesus along with many in the kingdom, will do all they can to help. Yet in the long run it will not help the individual. Until they realize the inner truth, these acts of mercy usually become no more than religious sign posts with no true value. Notice the single great command Jesus gave to the people. He said, "Love God with all your heart, mind and soul, and love your neighbor as yourself." Now let's break this formula down. The Bible teaches, how can you say you love God but hate your neighbor? If you hate your neighbor whom you can see, then how can you love God whom you can't see? And then it states to love your neighbor as yourself!

TO LOVE GOD IS LOVING YOURSELF AS LOVING YOUR NEIGHBOR!

Let this mystery begin to evolve within you because the clearer you are on this, the greater your ability to use faith will become. This simply means we are to first love ourselves, then we can love our neighbor as ourselves, and then we can love God. Why, **because all three are one!**

Formula number one is to love God with your entire heart, mind and soul. Formula number two is to love yourself and your neighbor alike. To love God is to love your higher self. Thereby making number two, not a separate formula, but equal to number one! Remember the Father works the great works through you. You are his workmanship, because we are this great divine consciousness at another level. To love your Heavenly Father is to love yourself, and to love your neighbor is to love your Heavenly Father.

Thereby Jesus made the statement, "YOUR FAITH HAS MADE YOU WHOLE." Our belief can access the power within. Jesus was the instrument to bring about this awareness. It is likened unto a child as they are growing up. They depend fully upon their higher selves, meaning their progenitors until a time when they can depend upon their true higher selves, their Father/Mother divine.

Parents do not help their children in life because they want the child to continue to trust in them for all their needs for the rest of their life. No not at all, they help them until the child has matured so they can fend for themselves. Jesus was the same, he came to help and assist until we became fully mature to go on without assistance, because we would realize where Jesus received his power and we could do the same.

When we awaken and recognize that within us is the light of the Father's consciousness, or the Christ, the divine Son and creator of all, then we will realize that we are the creators of the universe. Once an individual recognizes this power from within, all they have to do is use the formula to access this wonderful grace. Faith then loses its capacity in being a concept. It becomes a reality of knowing, not an instrument of hoping. When Jesus recognized within himself that, "I AM the resurrection and the life," he was tapping into the formula for faith just by repeating that decree.

FOUNDATION FOR FAITH HAS NOW BEEN LAID!

It has taken quite some time to lay the foundation for this final mystery. So just what is the formula for Faith? How can we use it? Jesus said, we can all use it if we doubt not! Here is the formula!

1. **LOVE GOD WITH ALL YOUR HEART, MIND AND SOUL.**
2. **LOVE YOUR NEIGHBOR AS YOURSELF!**
3. **KNOW THE "I AM" AND USE ITS POWER AND DOUBT NOT.**

The above formula is the correct formula for faith. Now look below and you will recognize the accepted formula for faith that seldom ever produces any real fruit. This is the formula that most have accepted as being the true formula.

1. **Love God and man by ritualistic living!**
2. **Seek God's will because he may not want you to have your desire!**
3. **Believe on an external power and if it doesn't work then it probably wasn't supposed to!**

Do you recognize the formula for the more accepted thesis of our religious culture? All three points produce one important belief, and that is *you can't be sure of anything*. This produces doubt, the very element that cuts off true faith. The true formula teaches us to love God with no ritualistic additives. You will love God with your best ability to know love. But how can you do this? By first loving yourself, and then loving your fellow man. These are the keys to teach us how to love our Father in heaven. It is simply defined in the golden rule, "Do unto others as you would have them do unto you!" Whatever you send out will return. If you can love yourself and your neighbor whom you can see, then you already love your Father whom you can't see.

YOU ALREADY KNOW THE FATHER'S WILL, JUST USE IT!

The true formula teaches you to bring the power of the "I AM" within your use as being co-creators with the divine Son. Some will no doubt use the scripture that teaches, you must seek God's will. I would simply reply, go back to the true formula #1, and you will have the Father's will.

Jesus said that greater works would we do than he did. Yet 2000 years have gone by and these miracles don't appear to be duplicated by anyone else, at least in the open. Why, is it because everyone has been using the wrong formula?

Faith is not an emotion, it is a power! By faith you can create. By faith you can heal! By faith you can die yet never taste death. Faith is the tapping of the power within us. If you doubt at all in anything that you desire you have already instantly cut the cord that produces the results. To regain your desire you must send your request back out in the form of prayer, decree, or thought to reformat the matrix in your dimension.

If you want to make life changes for the better then pray for it, decree it, believe it and then know it. Praying is only acknowledging what your Heavenly Father has already placed within you. It states that your Father already knows what you need before you even ask. Of course he does, you are the Father's lower consciousness that produces his works in the flesh. You don't pray to your Father trying to entice him to act for you. You are praying because it is your Father speaking through you. You just believe it! You are the co-creator of his thoughts. So make sure you create righteous thoughts. If a child asked his father for a fish, will he give him a serpent? If he asked for bread, will he give a rock instead? Believe your Father is greater than your human family and just KNOW. This is how true faith works!

Once you finally comprehend that your heavenly Father is the great spark which produced your I AM presence, which is in all, then how can you doubt your own "I AM?"

Your life will begin to change towards the manifested decree that you sought from within yourself. However if you doubt for any reason this process will falter and cease to function. You will then have to reconnect and begin the process over. You can send forth the alchemy of change wherever you desire, but be careful. If it is fruitless desire you will add more karma to your soul. Once you understand this fundamental law of faith, you will know it has to work as much as you know that an appliance will turn on when you plug it in!

All power on heaven and earth is ours for the use, but we must learn how to use it. If in the process of using this formula for faith things do not materialize as quickly as you would like, do not doubt or lose heart. You have stifled this power for many ages and it might not be that easy to regain the necessary components. You will fight against doubt left and right before things begin to click into gear. It is like having to turn on an old appliance that hasn't been operational for years. You might have to clean the cobwebs and other stuff out before it will work again. Rest assured it will work, because it is a law.

The mystery of Faith teaches us we have access to the realm of our Father and Mother as their Son and Daughter. We are the children of the HIGHEST spirit divine that exists eternally and internally ever present. Our success is already written in the book of life! Now we must use the power of this great gift called faith to finish our walk in this lower dimension.

FROM YOUR BROTHER "I AM" OF THE ANTIQUITY

MAY THE FATHER BLESS YOU ALL AND THE SON ENLIGHTEN YOU!

SINCERELY, *John V. Panella*

ABOUT THE AUTHOR

John V. Panella's understanding and grasp of theology and Biblical truths is quite remarkable considering the trials he had to endure during the first months of his life. He was born with cerebral brain damage and was given up on by the doctors. He often had convulsions, and for 18 months he was a living vegetable unable to do anything. During that time his parents were looking into religious beliefs, and found a church that believed in Faith healing. They were not particularly religious but thought they had nothing to lose, because John was either going to die or spend the rest of his life in the vegetative condition. One of the ministers of this church did a laying on of hands, and he was healed instantly.

As John grew he spent 30 years in various Christian organizations, including some theological training in College. He was searching for something that made sense, because he had not found the answers within orthodox religion. He began to develop his own gnosis. Part of it was that the Bible along with other great works of literature were created to expose a secret mystery using analogies, types, and metaphors. These things were not meant to be taken literally, but figuratively and mystically.

John had personally been experiencing what would be defined as paranormal activities that had existed in his life from a youth, never really understanding the purpose for these strange occurrences because he wasn't able to place these activities in the world of religion in which he was raised. In time he realized that these happenings were teaching him a greater reality about God versus the limited reality of religion. After the death of his parents John began to take this new gnosis seriously.

It took a great deal of belief and faith to hold on to his unorthodox beliefs, because around 1986 he became very ill with liver and heart damage. He believes this was caused in part by inner turmoil. He had been battling over religious differences in his church, and the persecution of others who could not understand. This caused him to drink heavily for 6 years as he tried to escape the turmoil he was being put through. In 1986 he sensibly realized that alcohol was not the answer and quit drinking totally, but extreme damage had already been done. For two years he was on his death bed with no strength to fight the circumstances. He attributes his recovery to his faith and the will of God and his indestructible spirit. When he realized what was happening he left the church that had been a major part of his life, and entered the world of metaphysical teachings. From that point his health improved, and his knowledge of the mysteries began.

To contact John V. Panella, please write him at:

John V. Panella
Box 712
Springdale, UT 84767

and enclose a self-addressed, stamped envelope.

www.thegnosticpapers.org